The Making of
Modern Social Psychology

The hidden story of how an international
social science was created

Serge Moscovici and
Ivana Marková

polity

Copyright © Serge Moscovici and Ivana Marková 2006

The right of Serge Moscovici and Ivana Marková to be identified as
Author of this Work has been asserted in accordance with the UK
Copyright, Designs and Patents Act 1988.

First published in 2006 by Polity Press

Polity Press
65 Bridge Street
Cambridge CB2 1UR, UK

Polity Press
350 Main Street
Malden, MA 02148, USA

ISBN-10: 0-7456-2965-2
ISBN-13: 978-0-7456-2965-2
ISBN-10: 0-7456-2966-0 (pb)
ISBN-13: 978-0-7456-2966-0 (pb)

A catalogue record for this book is available from the British Library.

Typeset in 11 on 13 pt Berling
by SNP Best-set Typesetter Ltd, Hong Kong
Printed and bound in India by Replika Press

The publisher has used its best endeavours to ensure that the URLs
for external websites referred to in this book are correct and active
at the time of going to press. However, the publisher has no
responsibility for the websites and can make no guarantee that a site
will remain live or that the content is or will remain appropriate.

Every effort has been made to trace all copyright holders, but if any
have been inadvertently overlooked the publishers will be pleased to
include any necessary credits in any subsequent reprint or edition.

For further information on Polity, visit our website: www.polity.co.uk

To

Leon Festinger

and

John Lanzetta

Contents

List of Figures and Tables

Figures

Tables

Preface

There is more than one way in which the history of modern social psychology, just like the history of any science, can be told. There are today several full-scale exposés treating the history of social psychology as a succession of theories and of empirical discoveries. They serve as necessary intellectual guides for textbooks and courses, showing admirably how and why the scientific reputation of social psychology largely depends on the achievements of its practitioners.

The history that we shall unfold in this book goes back forty years and the events and accomplishments presented here are probably being told to the public for the first time. Our account will show the broader social and cultural perspectives in which modern social psychology has established itself, politically and historically, as well as scientifically and institutionally, in different parts of the world. It will focus on an international group of pioneers who significantly contributed to the field and devoted their energies to creating a large space for this new science. During these endeavours, they had to face situations in which the 'little history' of our science clashed, over time, with 'big history'. More often than not, indeed routinely, these pioneers related their practical concerns to scientific goals. Pursuing these over the years, their work reflects the problems and features of modern social psychology in general. It is to be hoped that the history of this international group will attract readers from a wider audience interested in seeing how they tried to shape a science rather than a particular scientific programme; and that it was a labour of history rather than a planning of events by man.

The chapters in this book tell the story of the Committee on Transnational Social Psychology. The question as to whether this Committee may be singled out as an exemplary group – and we believe as a unique one – is already clearly answered by its name: it was an international committee and its single task was *science building*. Of course, with the passage of time new layers of emergent realities came into view, each calling for a deeper and more comprehensive revision of the previous view of social psychology. In facing such cultural challenges, the Transnational Committee surreptitiously yet genuinely transformed the scene. It is this that makes its history fascinating and well worth knowing. What is more, if we pay attention to the larger context, the following three issues become apparent as the prime movers of this history.

– With the benefit of hindsight we can see that the first issue refers to the circumstances that resulted in the flourishing of social and human sciences after the Second World War. At the beginning of the twentieth century, Ebbinghaus wrote that psychology 'has a long past, but short history'. What he meant was that whereas psychological knowledge has had a long existence as recorded thought, only twenty years had elapsed since the pioneer scientific group appeared and created psychology as an independent discipline. It has occurred to us that a social psychologist could have said the same thing in the middle of the twentieth century. Having been for a long time a subject of philosophical inquiry about human nature and a branch of moral and human sciences, social psychology has become a unified and independent field during and since the Second World War. It has become so in the strict sense of the word, created concretely and purposefully by its practitioners.

The two decades following the Second World War were characterized by an unprecedented expansion in the human and social sciences. This was due to the general belief that they could alleviate the suffering that befell so many nations and facilitate the development of solutions to the new political and economic problems. In addition, they would enable cooperation and exchanges in a divided world, regenerate the intellectual and scientific communities that totalitarian regimes had devastated and in general would energize a new democratic life. We can recall here the beautiful writing of Kurt Lewin on the democratization of Germany and the role of social science after the war.

Despite, or rather because of, the rapid expansion and significant advances in the knowledge of social behaviour in economy, psychology and various related social phenomena in the United States, it was natural that the United States was expected to take a lead in the general reconstruction effort, particularly in Europe. Yet taking on such leadership was not an easy task without appearing alternately imperialistic and inadequate. Moreover, and without attempting to offer more detail here (but see chapter 1), this role of leadership was not unrelated to the explosive political events into which humanity was thrown in the aftermath of the war, and specifically, into the clash between the United States and the Soviet Union, resulting in the infamous Cold War.

The flux of American social scientists and scholars in humanities orientated itself towards Europe where, despite all the deprivation and destruction caused by the war, there were still thriving and spirited scientific traditions and universities. For some scholars it was a return to the *alma mater* and most of them could say, like Job, 'I have heard of thee by the hearing of the ear: but now mine eye seeth thee' (42:5).

— But while the first set of circumstances was *political and historical*, let us turn to the second set of circumstances. These involved *intellectual and scientific* issues which changed the course of social psychology. In the gallery of figures who have been involved in the genesis of our new science, Kurt Lewin is perhaps the most visible and exciting (see chapter 2). He created a school, an orientation that attracted very bright students. On the more popular level, his group dynamics revealed a new practice and introduced a new vocabulary of social psychology that soon became conventional. But the new is rarely born without something else being discarded or destroyed. What was discarded then was methodological pluralism which, to some extent, represented the empiricist view of traditional science.

The essential feature of social psychology became experiment (cf. Lanzetta's story in chapter 3). Indeed, the strong emphasis on experiment symbolized the contrast between the new and the old social psychological currents. It became an essential characteristic that distinguished social psychology from all other human sciences. The exclusive and undivided monopoly of the experimental method over field studies went uncontested – or at least it was not strongly contested – by other research trends. This monopoly unified the new social psychology to the extent that it has given it definition: *experimental social psychology*. For most practical purposes, the training and diffusion of social psychology entailed being trained in and deploying this method, as well as basing theories on it.

To be scientific means to search for generalities. In this respect social psychologists were not the first to have good reason to travel and look for colleagues who could help to generalize knowledge. However, what made this peculiar was that, to start with, a large part of their activity was dedicated to the replication of studies and the comparison of results obtained in different countries. Most importantly, they applied the dictum that for anyone wanting recognition, the way forward was to promote his or her own theory as a model of good science and good social psychology. Its features will then become a textbook paradigm.

If one wanted to summarize how social psychology is defined by textbooks and certain specialists, it would be sufficient to read the chapter by Edward Jones (1985, p. 47) about the major developments of social psychology in the second half of the twentieth century. His chapter concentrates 'on American social psychology with occasional references to European developments. Although European social psychology (at least quite recently) has been largely derived from American models and methods . . . it should be noted that many outstanding contributors to the field were European refugees.'

In other words, when defining modern social psychology, one can say that it is national, that it spread from the United States to other countries and that it uses a prescriptive model of what science should be.

— The third circumstance rests on an *institutional* issue. A handful of American social psychologists, involved with comparative studies in the 1950s and with disseminating social psychological knowledge, drew conclusions from their experience. In 1962 they came up with an idea. Although circumstances were not in their favour, these psychologists succeeded in convincing the Social Science Research Council in New York to sponsor a committee in order to further the cooperation and training of social psychologists from different countries and cultures.

Their attempts to establish the committee were guided by ideas opposing the point of view that studies, originally conducted in the United States, could be reproduced in different cultures, even translated into different languages and hence provide 'comparisons' between very different parts of the world. One might expect that studies repeated in different countries, out of context, are likely to produce ambiguous results that are difficult to interpret. Indeed, this is a recognized limitation which will occupy a part of this book. Moreover, even if this constraint is allowed for by the scientist or would-be scientist, these researchers will find themselves stripped of their creative impulse, of the feeling of being useful and having a voice of their own.

The awareness that merely exporting the American model of social psychology could become an obstacle to the development of social psychology in the United States and elsewhere appears to be the underlying reason for the emergence of the Transnational Committee. Certainly, it was Leon Festinger who had a major influence in the formation of the Transnational Committee on Social Psychology, as it was baptized. Its purpose was – or became – to foster interactions among social psychologists internationally in order to postulate hypotheses about and propose convincing explanations of meaningful social phenomena. Stimulating interactions would lead to the development of theories that could answer questions specific to a variety of cultures and relevant to different places and countries. Knowledge so obtained would produce alternative modes of thinking and combine ideas originating from diverse local and intellectual settings. The proper meaning of 'translating' procedures from one culture to another would not be based on imitation. Instead, it would involve 'the recognition' of that culture rather than 'a comparison'. At some point in this research, Festinger delivered a telling proposal: 'From a purely United States social psychology to a social psychology of human beings.' This extraordinary phrase expresses the following idea: it would be irresponsible, even unrealistic, to justify the belief that Americanization is a substitute for the universality of our, or any, science. His quest was for an international social psychology. It informed the evolution of the Transnational Committee and its journey to redesign the map of social psychology in several parts of the world.

The other major influence was John Lanzetta, at that crucial time an officer at the Office of Naval Research stationed in London. He had a clear view of scientific communities in Europe and Latin America. He visited many countries on both continents to seek and establish contacts with social psychologists.

Festinger and Lanzetta did not stand alone. There was a whole company of established and 'maverick' social psychologists at their side who believed in, were capable of and were willing to pursue an experiment that turned out to be stranger and more intricate than had appeared at first sight. But in the end they altered the modern visage and dimensions of the short history of our scientific discipline.

Wisely, no doubt, the Transnational Committee was not deterred by the obstacles that accumulated rather than decreased as time went on. Some of them were intellectual or institutional, others political, as for example, the Soviet invasion of Czechoslovakia or the military putsches in Chile or Argentina. The increased commitment of the Committee, reflected in its perseverance and conscientiousness, succeeded in gathering social psychologists and building continental associations on a model of science rooted in local research or teaching communities, and better suited to the realities of these communities and cultures. During the ten years of the Committee's work, this map, having extended to Western Europe, then embraced Eastern Europe and Latin America and started spreading further afield. It is beyond any doubt that this was a significant result. At that time few disciplines had tried to bring into being a voluntary project for creating a scientific community. It is true that the magnificent mission to create an international field of social psychology was only a means to an end. And it is the end which made this project original, if not unique.

It is probably no less true today than when Hegel stated it that ideas create institutions and that institutions kill ideas. A historical account is not an account of the history of an idea, nor of an institution or a scientific community, but of what Fleck (1935) called a 'collective of thought'. According to him a collective of thought signified a group of individuals having intellectual contact with one another, exchanging ideas, mutually influencing each other in the pursuit of the same goal. In writing a short history of the Transnational Committee, we are not attempting a rational reconstruction of past events in which judgements and explanations provide a coherent and justified logic for the development of scientific associations, and thus for the theories that are in play. The present account is different. That is to say, it attempts to reconstruct the genesis of the relations between the protagonists, the dialectic of their actions and their common improvisations and strategies, in short, their work across continents. In this account we do not attempt to select or rectify the events in which they took part or to infer intentions that were not necessarily present. This is particularly important in order to avoid slipping from a history to a linear story, a myth that would misrepresent the singularity of the protagonists and the relatively discreet ways in which all those events took place. It would also misconstrue the ways, comparatively discontinuous in time, in which the members of the Transnational Committee identified their common goals. All this has some overtones of Marx's dictum that humans make history, but that they do not always know the history they make. Even in science, as it will appear, history is made, not planned.

This historical account is almost entirely based on archival documents of committee meetings, memoranda, letters and reports that were meticulously kept. Although we have appealed for the oral testimony of witnesses, we have kept this to a minimum in order to limit reconstruction, liable to produce and perpetuate myths. We wish to thank the following for their help and advice:

Dr Darwin Stapleton and Dr Ken Rose of the Rockefeller Archives Center in New York; Mr A. S. Divack and Ms Idelle Nissila-Stone of the Ford Foundation; Professor J. Roegiers, Mr Mark Derez and Mr Guido Cloet of the Archives at the Catholic University in Louvain; Dr Brigitte Mazon of the Archives of the Maison des Sciences de l'Homme; the staff of The Michigan Historical Collections, Bentley Historical Library at the University of Michigan; and the staff of UNESCO in Paris.

Acknowledgements

The authors wish to thank the following for permission to refer to and reproduce materials from their archives: Rockefeller Archives Center in New York; The Ford Foundation in New York; The Michigan Historical Collections, Bentley Historical Library at the University of Michigan; The University Archives at the Catholic University in Louvain; The UNESCO Archives of the International Social Science Council in Paris. The authors thank Faber and Faber for permission to publish one line (on page 102) from 'Gerontion' by T. S. Eliot from *Collected Poems 1909–1962* and twelve words (on page 247) from *Endgame* by Samuel Beckett. Serge Moscovici wishes to express his thanks to the Balzan Foundation. Ivana Marková thanks the Carnegie Trust for the Universities in Scotland for their support.

Abbreviations

ALAPSO – Latin-American Association for Social Psychology (La Associación Latinoamericana de Psicología Social)

APA – American Psychological Association

CNRS – Centre national de la recherche scientifique (National Centre of Scientific Research)

EAESP – European Association of Experimental Social Psychology

EPHE – The Ecole Pratique des Hautes Etudes

FA – Ford Archives, New York

GDR – German Democratic Republic

IREX – International Research and Exchanges Board

ISSC – International Social Science Council

LEPS – Laboratoire Européen de Psychologie Sociale

MHC – The Michigan Historical Collections, Bentley Historical Library, University of Michigan

MSH – Maison des Sciences de l'Homme, Paris

NSF – National Science Foundation

ONR – The Office of Naval Research

P&P – Problems and Policy Committee of the Social Science Research Council, New York

RAC – Rockefeller Archive Center

SSRC – Social Science Research Council, New York

UAL – University Archives, Catholic University of Louvain, Belgium

UNESCO – United Nations Educational, Scientific and Cultural Organisation

I

The Quest for a Social Psychology of Human Beings

1

The Birth of a New Science

The USA and the Reconstruction of Science after the War

All beginnings are difficult and their outcomes often unpredictable. It is small wonder that the beginnings of the Committee on Transnational Social Psychology (Transnational Committee) were uncertain and very strenuous. The Transnational Committee had to travel a more difficult road than it had envisaged. And if we think what it means for a group of scientists to engage in the unique enterprise of creating and proclaiming a new scientific field, we can see that the Transnational Committee has made spectacular strides. The difficulties that it encountered on the road scarcely mattered, so long as its members believed that they were advancing towards their main goal: establishing international social psychology.

After the Second World War, Europe faced the reconstruction of its ruined towns and industry as well as the revitalization of its market economy and the rebuilding of its democratic institutions. It took even longer to revive universities and centres of research and to regenerate the tissue of intellectual and scientific life destroyed by the war. To be sure, many refugee scientists and scholars were returning home from the USA. Some of them took part in rebuilding pre-war institutions like the Institut für Soziale Forschung in Frankfurt in Germany. Others participated in the creation of new establishments like Section Six of L'Ecole Pratique des Hautes Etudes (EPHE) in France. The origins of the Tavistock Institute of Human Relations in London belong to the same period. From its establishment in 1946, the Tavistock Institute fulfilled a number of roles. It developed a programme for studying human relations under conditions of well-being, conflict and family breakdown in work groups and larger organizations. It soon took on a pioneering role in the post-war situation as it combined research in social and psychological sciences on the one hand and the development of professional practice on the other. Referring to psychological sciences in the post-war situation, the psychoanalyst Jacques Lacan (1947, p. 299, our translation) remarked that 'some disciplines which had hardly appeared on our horizon, including so-called *group psychology*, have attained in the Anglo-Saxon world a sufficient degree of elaboration that enabled them, in the work of Kurt Lewin, to express themselves at nothing lower than the mathematical level of vectorial analysis.'

The USA assumed a different role to Europe. The war had mobilized local talent as well as intellectuals among European refugees. As a result, after the war, the USA did not merely re-enter the scientific arena but began to assert its intellectual leadership. The resources for science and technology were plentiful, research flourished and new institutions boomed. American business and technology sought new markets for scientific and technological products. Offering help in the reconstruction of Europe through the Marshall Plan and challenging the threat of communism went hand in hand.

Social science in the USA followed this trend, exchanging ideas with Europe. Even during the war, social science had become more important than ever before. Lewin (1981a, p. 355) draws attention to the dramatic change in attitude towards social science that had taken place. He points out that, while before 1939 both the natural sciences and the general public had regarded social scientists as being interested only in an imaginary, unreal world, in analysing words rather than taking action, the war totally changed that view. The invention of the atom bomb and the devastation of Hiroshima and Nagasaki led to a radical transformation in the implications of physical and social phenomena, bringing them closer together. It made it obvious that social phenomena were just as real as physical phenomena and could be studied just as rigorously as physical events.

Social psychology was therefore born as a discipline in the USA during the war. This is not to say that prior to this there were not important social psychologists and books. We can recall the names of many famous social psychologists in the nineteenth and early twentieth centuries such as Tarde, Baldwin, Halbwachs, McDougall, Klineberg, Mead, Bartlett, Floyd Allport and Gordon Allport, among others. During the war, a period of extreme human catastrophe, social psychologists, along with other social scientists, 'proved their worth'. They were called on to provide social knowledge that could be applied to specific military problems. Wartime activities such as rebuilding civilian integrity and combating demoralization, involvement in military administration, studying domestic attitudes and providing strategic information, as well as developing international relations, all required refining as well as inventing new concepts and research tools (Cartwright, 1948). In particular, Lewin's (1939) research on group dynamics and studies of *The American Soldier* (Stouffer et al., 1949) were unprecedented in their practical impact. They significantly contributed to the recognition and esteem of the discipline.

When the war was over, as Cartwright (1948) points out, the field was incomparably different from what it had been only three or four years earlier. As a result, the prospects for social psychology were excellent and morale was high. In the post-war situation, social psychologists continued their involvement in important organizational, business and management problems. They also continued to develop new theoretical approaches in order to apply them to practical problems of the time.

Post-War Aid to European Social Sciences

The USA helped Europe in its effort to rebuild universities and academic institutions. In the 1920s, Americans instituted a tradition of philanthropic foundations, generously stimulating social sciences in Europe and financing new academic and educational establishments (Mazon, 1988; Gemelli and MacLeod, 2003). After the war, in addition, the American Social Science Research Council (SSRC) recognized the importance of its international involvement and affirmed its commitment in its *Annual Report of 1947–8* (pp. 24–6). The report stated that for some time 'the Council endeavoured to promote scientific communication and cooperation at the international level', in particular in Europe, and was gradually developing a general policy. For example, in 1948 it established several committees concerned with international policies such as international relations, international exchanges of individuals, international relations research, Slavic studies, social relations aspects of international tensions and social science periodicals in Europe. Moreover, the SSRC has participated, since 1948, in the Fulbright Exchange Programme and developed its own programme of international conference travel grants to assist American social scientists taking part in international meetings abroad. It has also made specific efforts to promote the research interests of UNESCO. The President of the SSRC stated that this quest was:

> to follow the study of any given phenomenon – urbanization, economic growth, political modernization, or any other – wherever it leads and to enlist competent research talent wherever it may be found. The analytical, empirical, comparative, if you will, broadly scientific pursuit of knowledge concerning human problems across national and cultural boundaries is the purpose, and international cooperation is a means. (Herring, 1964)

By 1949 the Cold War was at its height and became probably the most important determinant in the effort to develop cooperation among social sciences and to provide aid to Europe, which by then was divided between the Eastern Soviet bloc and Western capitalist countries. Part of the American effort involved reinforcing non-Marxist social science in Western Europe. Let us not forget that two countries, France and Italy, had very powerful communist parties and Marxist groups. Moreover, these countries also had intelligentsia which, while not being Marxist, sympathized with Marxism. Many of them thought that what was coming from America was politically dangerous and intellectually unoriginal. As a result, cooperation between Europeans and Americans was something of a delicate matter.

This political division posed a threat to the free world. Political interests related to the Cold War were orientated towards specific kinds of activities, both by government agencies in the USA and by philanthropic foundations. Documents of that period (Gemelli, 1995) clearly show that government agencies and foundations did not work independently of one another. Many people who led foundations became very important in government agencies, some of them as senior as Secretaries of State. In a way, the government agencies and foundations had a kind of division of labour. The federal government was responsible for ordinary exchanges of scholars while foundations tried to do something that was less conspicuous, taking responsibility for emergencies, exceptional cases or short-term needs. Some grants sponsored the independent research of individual scholars while others were awarded to academic institutions for pursuing specific projects. It was difficult, in the first decade of the Cold War, to separate political and scientific agendas. When we consider some important personalities at that time, for example Shepherd Stone at the Ford Foundation, it is hard to tell whether the international exchanges he organized were politically or scientifically motivated.

In the early 1950s, there was also a strong effort on the part of various international organizations, including UNESCO, to co-ordinate social science internationally and to create the International Social Science Council (ISSC). Such an international institution would advance social science throughout the world. It would facilitate the use of scientific knowledge, methods and skills in the study of major problems of the time (Young, 1952). UNESCO took decisive steps and in October 1952 the ISSC was set up. Its main tasks included the support of interdisciplinary and comparative research, the advancement of cooperative work and the provision of assistance in the solution to key world problems. It also took charge among other things of organizing symposia on innovative work (Friedman and Rokkan, 1979). Well-known social scientists of the era became associated with the new institution, for example, the French anthropologist Lévi-Strauss, who became its first Secretary General (1952–61).

Among many activities sponsored by UNESCO in the early 1950s was an exploration of the quality and quantity of social science teaching at higher education institutions in different parts of the world. This large and important study took place in 1951. Social psychology was included in this examination and grouped together with sociology and cultural anthropology. The study identified predominant methodological approaches, main research centres and ways in which researchers and teachers were educated. It took the form of international surveys and was published by UNESCO (de Bie et al., 1954) under the title *Les sciences sociales dans l'enseignement supérieur; sociologie, psychologie sociale et anthropologie culturelle*. The publication was co-authored by prominent social scientists such as de Bie for sociology, Lévi-Strauss for cultural anthropology and Nuttin and Jacobson for social psychology. It consisted of a general text and of specific reports. The general part of the book maintained that social psychology as a scientific discipline was less firmly established than sociology and cultural anthropology. A more specific report about social psychology, based on that survey, viewed the position of our subject as a particularly difficult one because it seemed to be attached partly to psychology and partly to sociology. Moreover, respondents to the survey found it hard to separate it from either cultural anthropology or sociology because of the considerable overlap of these social sciences. It was apparent that the question of where social psychology should be situated had already been raised at that time and the UNESCO study identified its ambiguous status.

While the international social science organizations and UNESCO placed it together with cultural anthropology and sociology, in higher education institutions social psychology was more often found in psychology departments. In the specific report mentioned above, Joseph Nuttin (1954) recommended that both at undergraduate and postgraduate level social psychology should be closely attached on the one hand to psychology and on the other to cultural anthropology and sociology. Both sociology and cultural anthropology benefit equally from social psychological knowledge in explaining the phenomena they study. Nuttin pointed to the danger that social psychology might be split between psychological and sociological social psychology. He suggested that it should develop as a single field rather than as two branches, that is, one psychological, based on controlled experiments and one sociological, based on field studies. Nuttin was aware that these two orientations existed and would no doubt persist. However, they should complement one another. Nuttin concluded: 'This is the obligation that [social] psychology must pay due to the complexity of its subject matter as well as to the fact that it is a young discipline' (p. 159). Nevertheless, the difficulty the survey detected with respect to the identity of social psychology has not been resolved and, as we shall see, persists today.

Despite the fact that American social psychology experienced an unparalleled period of expansion both intellectually and geographically, there were nevertheless, at that time, only a very few social psychologists in the USA. According to the above UNESCO study in the early 1950s, less than one per cent of chairs in social science were in social psychology (de Bie, 1954, p. 24). The study recommended that more chairs be established in order to bring about a balance within social science.

Further development of the discipline was shaped by a number of projects that involved exchanges between the USA and Europe. This bustling transatlantic traffic was initiated on both sides, each continent motivated by its specific goals.

European social psychologists were understandably attracted by the general activity in the USA. The journeying of scientists and artists to centres of excellence has a very long tradition. We can recall the nineteenth-century migration of scientists to Germany, which, at that period of time, had laboratories that provided the model for science. However, this is not the only case. There has been an even longer tradition of painters and sculptors travelling to Italy, both to admire and learn from classic and Renaissance art. Equally, artists travelled to Paris in the first half of the twentieth century to acquaint themselves with modern art. Migrating artists learned by imitating and copying the masters, subsequently creating their own original work. Not surprisingly, European social psychologists after the war wanted to learn in the USA in order to improve their discipline. They could do so largely thanks to American fellowships. For example, in the 1950s and 1960s, a number of European social psychologists travelled to the USA in order to learn in American laboratories. Thus, Jaap Rabbie from Holland, Henri Tajfel from the UK, Claude Faucheux and Robert Pagès from France, and Ragnar Rommetveit from Norway, among many others, went to the States to learn from and to collaborate with Americans. In addition to American fellowships, these exchanges were supported by other agencies: Faucheux, for example, went to Bethel in 1955 with a European group, which was sponsored by the European Agency for Productivity.

Europeans were welcomed by Americans as their collaborators. Europe had already given the USA some excellent social psychologists and social scientists before and during the war. Post-war, Europeans established traditions in the USA that strongly influenced the development of social psychology, for instance Lewin's group dynamics, Sherif's intergroup theory and Heider's attribution theory.

But the transatlantic movement was in both directions. Some American social psychologists, such as Leon Festinger and Stanley Schachter, travelled frequently to Europe. Festinger was a consultant for some projects at the Tavistock Institute in London. Schachter for a while held a university position in Amsterdam. In sum, by the late 1950s, links and strong relationships between social psychologists on both sides of the Atlantic were firmly forged.

A Miraculous Coincidence – Then a Few Hiccups

The American dilemma

Despite the fact that the post-war and Cold War years saw the foundation of close connections between European and American social psychologists, the Transnational Committee was not a child of that era. Indeed, it came about in a different fashion. By the 1960s, social psychology was established as a discipline in the USA and was getting under way in several European countries. Nevertheless, already by the early 1960s there was a noticeable undercurrent of urgency and uncertainty which eventually surfaced. Specifically, we can observe that Americans, who laid down the foundations of this new discipline, faced a dilemma as soon as it was established. By the early 1960s, the time had gone when they thought that they could build international social psychology through mutual exchanges and cooperation between psychologists in the USA and other countries which were, in one way or another, replicating each other's work. Or, at least, they became aware that social psychology could not become a scientific discipline if it continued its existing activities without considering the necessity for change.

In a nutshell, the discipline was new. If Americans wanted to establish social psychology as a recognizable discipline among other human and social sciences, they could not set it up in the USA alone as an American discipline to be exported. They realized that it had to become an active and diversified science in different parts of the world. However, to achieve this goal required more than intensified contacts and exchanges. As we shall see later that much was clear to John Lanzetta. Neither was it sufficient to replicate one's own experiments in other countries or, so to speak, to clone one's ideas elsewhere. Festinger (1980, p. 242) had observed this after the Second World War, 'the most seminal period in the history and development of social psychology'. It was necessary to do something else – but what? Other human sciences in the USA were already international due to their pre-war grounding. In contrast, social psychology was a new science. It had 'not yet come to the point where almost every department of psychology had to have a program in social psychology. There were still relatively few active research workers in the area, and all knew each other' (ibid., p. 245). Evidently, for Americans, it was during this time that the pressing question emerged: how was an international social psychology to be created? With hindsight, we can see that this explains why Americans took the initiative in the early years of the 1960s. And if our above analysis is correct, we can also understand that for them it was no longer possible to think about promoting internationally the kind of field that had succeeded in establishing itself in the USA.

Annus mirabilis of 1962

Social science research in the USA since 1923 had been coordinated and sponsored by the SSRC in New York which had played a central role in helping to launch new fields of inquiry. The overall guidance, the selection of research interests and the establishment of new committees had always been the task of the Committee on Problems and Policy (P&P) which made its recommendations to the Council's Board.

This is also where we must start in order to understand the paramount concern of American social psychology. If we examine the files of the SSRC in the Rockefeller archives, we find that two

American social psychologists, Lanzetta and Festinger, each put forward independent proposals on how to establish the field outside the USA. These two proposals, underlined by different visions, appeared on the table of the P&P on the very same days, 8–9 September 1962.[1]

Lanzetta's initiative to bring Europeans together

Lanzetta was Professor of Social Psychology at the University of Delaware, USA, and the Director of Delaware's Center for Research on Social Behavior. During 1962–3, Lanzetta was stationed in London as a representative of the Office of Naval Research (ONR). The ONR was the most important source of financing for Lewin's group dynamic research in the USA during and after the Second World War. In the early 1960s, another social psychologist, Petrullo, was the head of the ONR in Washington.

Lanzetta was an experimental social psychologist whose main interests were in the study of conflict, uncertainty, information and decision making. He liked Europe and during his stay in London he visited most West European countries. However, he did not travel just for pleasure. The purpose of these visits was above all to seek out and establish contacts with social psychologists. In almost every country he found knowledgeable and competent colleagues who had some contact with American social psychologists but who, he thought, had no interaction with other European social psychologists (Lanzetta, 1963).

The ONR had a reputation for funding non-military basic research. Yet Lanzetta needed an academic and non-governmental institution to approve and channel these funds. Universities in the USA and possibly in Europe might worry about being financed by a navy grant. Lanzetta thought that the SSRC could provide this needed mediation.

He therefore proposed that the SSRC hold a conference for European social psychologists in London in 1963, for which the ONR would offer $7,500 (in today's value approximately $45,000), a generous sum at that time. This conference would bring together social psychologists interested in theoretical and experimental research. Such a conference could be followed up by other conferences. This therefore was the proposal that was discussed at the P&P meeting on 8–9 September 1962. The Committee voted favourably for Lanzetta's proposal and recommended seeking solicitation by the President of the SSRC to authorize the funds from the ONR.[2]

Lanzetta proceeded carefully. He formed an international planning group to prepare the conference. This group included Mulder (Leyden Institute of Preventative Medicine, Utrecht), Pagès, (Director of the Laboratory of Social Psychology, Paris) and Tajfel (Department of Social and Administrative Studies, Oxford). Lanzetta's planning group represented those European countries which in the 1960s had relatively well-developed social psychology fields. By May 1963 Lanzetta had extended his group by another two members, Rommetveit from Norway and Thibaut from the USA. As Lanzetta (1963, p. 6) stated in his report, 'this committee itself was a case in point of one of the major premises motivating the conference: although active in research in their respective countries and frequent visitors to the USA, none of the European members had previously met.'

In the end, the venue for the proposed conference was changed from London to Sorrento, Italy, and we can read in the Council Minutes that 'Under a contract accepted by the Council, the US ONR will support a conference of about 25 European social psychologists at Sorrento, Italy, on December 10–17, for the purpose of developing closer research collaboration among them . . . The contract also provides support for a second conference, which might be held in Asia, at a later date.'[3] Lanzetta's group invited potential participants and stated the aims of the European Conference, which included:

- presenting a small group of European social psychologists with an opportunity to share their experiences and views on the use of experimental methods;
- providing for an exchange of information on experimental research and on facilities and personnel in different European centres engaged in experimental social psychological research;
- facilitating informal discussion of common problems and some measure of personal contact, both of which could facilitate the

establishment of a 'permanent' international committee to encourage and assist in the development of experimental social psychology (Lanzetta, 1963; Nuttin, 1990).

Military funds cannot be taken for granted

The preparation for the conference proceeded smoothly and progress was reported at the P&P.[4] However, in November 1963 the President of the SSRC, Herring, reported the first signs of uneasiness of the Executive Committee of the SSRC about ONR funding:

> P&P was asked to review a number of implicit policy questions, including the relations of the Council with ONR, since their con-tract provides for support of a second conference . . . In this case the Council had accepted funds from a governmental agency that combines a military mission with a genuine interest in basic research. The relationship was essentially a fiscal one but this might not be clear to social scientists in foreign countries and there might be some resulting disadvantage in future attempts to plan confer-ences. It would be possible to withdraw from the present contract, under which the Council had agreed to sponsor conferences planned and controlled by another agency. This situation was one it preferred to avoid, and if a second conference were held, the Council would insist upon taking a more active role.[5]

The ONR money created two problems. First, the SSRC Council wished to preserve its own initiatives on the matter of conferences and accepting military money could compromise its indepen-dence. Second, the Council considered it dangerous to involve the military institution in social scientific matters and the members were presumably worried about possible interference from the military establishment. In fact, the contract between the SSRC and ONR stated:

> The Contractor . . . shall conduct a series of foreign symposia of Navy-relevant group psychological topics to augment ONR research programs with inputs from research centers outside the United States and to catalyse such research programs in friendly countries. . . . In discussion, members of P&P with experience in foreign countries pointed out that although ONR is free of mili-

tary directives, this fact would not be understood in many countries outside Western Europe. The importance of maintaining the image of the Council as a civilian non-governmental organization was stressed, and caution was urged in considering Council support of a conference of non-European psychologists from ONR funds.[6]

In support of these views, one Committee member recommended that immediately after the conference 'proceedings be started to disengage the Council from the present contract' and 'to return the balance of funds' to the ONR. The only satisfactory arrangement would be for the Council to have 'total control of such conferences'. Members of the P&P agreed that it should not be concealed that the conference was to be funded by the ONR. Another member said that 'if ONR were willing to support a second conference of European psychologists, it would still seem desirable to move toward cancellation of the present contract'. It would be inappropriate for the Council 'to use the funds at the initiation of ONR'. The Council and not the ONR should make decisions and take responsibility for the second conference.

Clearly, the worries about being linked with the military establishment were quite extensive. Some members were willing to terminatè the present contract immediately after the first conference. Other members, however, were reluctant to invite an action that might be interpreted as a breach of faith. In the end, the motion that the Council withdraw from the commitment was not seconded. A compromise was reached: the Council would send an official representation to the Sorrento conference and no decision concerning the second conference would be taken until the P&P could review the results of the first one. The decision concerning the second conference of foreign social psychologists would be made on the merits of the proposal.[7]

Fear that the scientific community might misinterpret ONR involvement was at least partly justified. For example, Raven (1999, p. 111), in reflecting on his work at the Research Center for Group Dynamics after the war, pointed out that some of the newly appointed research assistants were shocked when they realized that their work was supported by research grants from the ONR. He himself asked: 'Why are we involved in military-supported research? Hadn't we finished the war and headed toward peace?' Raven recalled that they were told that it was necessary for a while to maintain the armed forces and it was important that the military understand social psychological issues such as the nature of leadership, effects of cohesiveness on performance of groups, communication processes and so on. Researchers were reassured that the results of their work would not be classified. Instead, it was recognized that research would be relevant to all social behaviour and not just to military concerns. Nevertheless,

> those who would take the trouble to review research from that era would be amazed at the amount of significant social psychological research that was in fact supported by military funds, particularly from the ONR, as well as the army and the air forces. . . . It took the Vietnam War, which many social psychologists actively opposed, finally to reduce that money to a mere trickle (ibid., pp. 117–18).

It was a result of such opposition to military funding after the war that other agencies, for example the National Science Foundation (NSF), the National Institute of Mental Health and later on, private foundations, such as Ford and Rockefeller, took on the support of basic research.

From a 'United States social psychology' to a 'social psychology of human beings'

The second proposal discussed by the P&P on 8–9 September 1962 was submitted by Leon Festinger, one of the leading, if not *the* leading, experimental social psychologists at the time. Festinger became interested in the problems of research on transcultural social perception and he enquired whether the SSRC Council would get involved in this question in some way. Reflecting on these problems, Festinger thought that science could not restrict its activities to America or to Europe or to this or that locality, and at the same time consider itself involved in a universal discourse. That would be absurd.

Such views seemed reasonable and the P&P approved that feasibility of planning some research on transcultural social perception should be explored. For a start, the Committee proposed a meeting between Festinger, the sociologist de Sola Pool and another social psychologist, Schachter, to discuss such possibilities further and to find other researchers interested in this area.[8]

In order to pursue this, two meetings took place, first in October 1962,[9] and subsequently in March 1963, covering a broader range of interests in transnational research on social perception. Participants included Aronson (University of Minnesota), Katz and Bradburn (University of Chicago), Osgood (University of Illinois), Kimbal Romney (Stanford University) and Thibaut (University of North Carolina). This meeting recommended that a committee to promote the development of such transnational research should be appointed. Festinger wrote a long and passionate letter to the SSRC, which the President summarized for the P&P. Festinger stated that:

> such a committee, in my view, would . . . encourage, facilitate and initiate active working interaction and cooperation among the experimental social psychologists in various . . . countries in order to hasten the change from a purely 'United States social psychology' to a 'social psychology of human beings'. I do not think that it will be fruitful to attempt to do this simply trying to get experiments replicated in different countries around the globe. This has been tried in the past, the most striking example being the simultaneous replication by seven European countries of experiments on deviation and rejection under the supervision of Schachter. While one learns something from such attempts, they do not ultimately lead to the goal that I think is the important one. . . . I think what is necessary is sufficient training of, interaction with, and opportunities for research for social psychologists in widely diverse places so that within each country there are indigenous research programs developed, sparked by the ideas which the local investigator has and nourished by theoretical interaction with psychologists in other countries. The international social psychology will gradually come about as a result of having to formulate theories and explanations of diverse data.[10]

Festinger said all that with ardour and conviction. He proposed crucial ideas that are central to this book. Let us first consider his idea of changing a purely 'United States social psychology' to a 'social psychology of human beings'. As we have already commented, after the war the USA experienced an unprecedented expansion of social science in general and of social psychology specifically. New theories about social behaviour and about attitudes were developed, experimental techniques became more sophisticated and data were analysed by multivariate statistics. Since, as Festinger[11] pointed out, 'the vast bulk (perhaps about 99%) of this research had been carried out in the USA, it was natural to question whether something was being learned about humans generally'. That massive amount of work could reflect nothing more than 'the particular brand of western culture that existed in this country'. Festinger was quite specific about his concerns. He critically analysed the simultaneous replication by seven European countries of the experiments that were designed in the USA under the supervision of Stanley Schachter.

Let us explain. In the early 1950s Schachter designed cross-cultural experiments on threat and rejection. This extensive study was carried out with a number of collaborators under the auspices of the Organization for Comparative Social Research. The aims of the organization were to encourage cooperation among social scientists of different countries. In addition, emphasis was put on the necessity to increase training in the newer techniques of research into human problems and to explore potentialities and difficulties of cross-cultural research within social psychology and sociology.

As the authors (Schachter et al., 1954) claimed in their paper, in most areas of social sciences it was impossible to separate universally and culturally determined phenomena and their relationships. Most studies explored specific characteristics of sub-groups in one culture; replications with different sub-groups within a culture, or in different cultures, were rare. It was 'difficult to distinguish the limits of generalizability of specific propositions or narrowly determined lawful relationships' (ibid., p. 404). The authors argued that their research was the first exploratory step towards a programme of replicated research in Western Europe. The unique and central problem of such research should be concerned with the following question: 'If there are differences in the results of several experiments, how are they to be explained?' Such differences could be attributed to many factors, including experimental artefacts, for example, a failure to produce independent variables, non-equivalence of techniques and poor translation of measuring instruments from one language into another. Alternatively, differences could imply a cultural variability. Methods, the authors argued, should be designed to provide comparative data which would allow choices among the possible interpretations of potential differences. Much more was desired than 'protective-evaluative measures'. Although it might be interesting to learn that differences between two experiments could be due to an experimental artefact, it is important to eliminate such explanations by standardizing those experiments. The researchers thought they should devote considerable attention to the methodological and interpretive details of the overall study.

Festinger was well aware of these problems. They were not new. As early as the 1940s and 1950s, American social psychologists were curious to know whether the results obtained in American laboratories were indeed 'culture bound'. This curiosity was stimulated in part by criticism from anthropologists and other social scientists sensitive to cultural differences and 'national character'. Festinger[12] referred to the many attempts to repeat in other countries studies that were originally designed in the USA. He did not find that very fruitful and questioned the value of such experiments: 'For example of what value is it to know that 80% of a sample of Norwegians as compared to 40% of one of Frenchmen conform in an Asch-type situation?'[13] Such repetitions were hardly more than playing with mirrors.

Festinger thought that the national character of social psychology in the USA hindered scientific advance in the field. The relative paucity of research in countries other than the USA was particularly limiting because of the intrinsic character of the subject matter. For example, imagine that a physiologist in a mid-Western university in the USA discovers that single cells in the lateral geniculate nucleus fire in response to certain patterns of visual stimulation. One can be reasonably certain that the work leading to this finding can be replicated as easily in Pakistan as in other parts of the USA. But in the social field this is not the case. One does not know to what extent a finding is 'universal' and to what extent it is 'culture bound'. Moreover,

> one cannot simply 'repeat' a procedure in another country with another language and a different culture. One has to 'translate' the

procedure. Then how does one know to what extent agreement or lack of agreement in the results of the studies is due to lack of cleverness or too much cleverness in the 'translation?' Many who were concerned with this problem came to believe that it was necessary to proceed differently. If there could be sufficient training of, interaction among, and opportunities for research for social psychologists in widely diverse places, then indigenous research programs would develop, sparked by the ideas of the local investigator.[14]

Since Festinger puts 'translation' into inverted commas, we can reasonably assume that he was not concerned with the literal translation of words from one language to another one, but with the translation of cultural and symbolic significances that are more than meanings of words. Festinger well recognized that in the culturally diverse world the assumption of homogeneity is an illusion. In each culture people live in a world of its own practices. Festinger had yet another concern. It was necessary to train indigenous social psychologists. But in what aspects of research should they be trained? This question Festinger never made clear. Since he did not explain what training would mean, we may assume that he meant training in methodological techniques as they were developed in the USA.

In any case, this point remains ambiguous.

Towards an international social psychology

It appears that at first Festinger was not quite sure about his intentions. It was after his involvement in transcultural social perception that he took an interest in the general problems of comparative social issues and in developing international social psychology as the 'psychology of human beings'. The problem was how to do it? Whilst he argued for a 'social psychology of human beings' and against the exportation of social psychology from the USA to other countries, he also believed that Americans were trained in both theory and method and, therefore, they could teach others. This was clearly expressed in his conviction that the time was ripe for well-founded transnational studies. Although ten years earlier he could hardly have considered such an option, in 1963 he thought it possible to find methodologically competent experimental social psychologists in various countries. Many of them had previously had an opportunity to learn in the USA as they had spent a year or so there. Others were in contact with Americans abroad and participated in research with them; and he added that 'sometimes, in a few spectacular cases', they learned almost entirely through their own self-development.[15] Moreover,

> most of these people are isolated in their own countries without good opportunity to interact with experimental social psychologists in other countries, without good opportunity to do research of their own choosing. I think the first steps of a committee set up by the Social Science Research Council ought to be to bring some of these more active and most promising people together in order to locate some areas of common theoretical interest from which indigenous research in each country could start. Great care must be taken to choose the right people from sufficiently diverse countries like Poland, Japan and India and try to get support for them so that a spark, so badly needed, is provided.

Festinger's goal was ambitious and, we could also say, unspecified. He insisted on collecting and explaining diverse data in other cultures using indigenous talent and on the formulation of appropriate theories grounded in those cultures. At the same time Festinger was preoccupied with the question of training and with the diffusion of existing methods and knowledge. His proposal was broadly conceived but it was ambiguous. It included two main concepts: the diffusion of knowledge along with the advancement of knowledge. However, he did not indicate how these two concepts could be brought under the same roof. Therefore, the question of how international social psychology should look still remained unanswered at that stage.

The complexity problem

Festinger thought that the SSRC should set up a Transnational Committee. The first step should be to bring together some of the more active social psychologists to locate some areas of common theoretical interest in which research in each country could start. But the Committee should also engage in some additional tasks. For example, it might prove valuable to collate and organize data from cross-national studies. Moreover, it could provide training opportunities for experimental psychologists in different countries to extend the potential for further research. It could also prove useful to coordinate these activities with 'facilities development' in different countries. Finally, there were demands from the profession that a committee could address. In sum, one needed a committee 'to help provide training, the opportunity for interaction, and the opportunity for independent indigenous research in social psychology'.[16]

Festinger's views did not find an immediately enthusiastic response from the SSRC. In discussing Festinger's concerns, some members of the P&P suggested that not only social psychologists but also some additional social scientists should be invited to bring their experience and contribute to the Council's programme in this area. The members of the P&P thought that it would be premature to appoint the full Transnational Committee. Moreover, they saw Lanzetta's and Festinger's proposals as having some similar concerns and that the two proposals 'might appropriately initiate the program of the proposed committee'.[17] In view of this, Festinger, Osgood, Pool, Schachter, Strodbeck, Stycos and Whiting were invited to consult on these issues with the SSRC Council. It was agreed that the matter of the proposed committee would be reviewed in September 1963.

Despite reservations about the full Transnational Committee, in June 1963 the P&P voted that Festinger, Osgood, de Sola Pool, Schachter, Swanson and Whiting be appointed at the discretion of the President as the nucleus of the committee, which would be further expanded in September. However, the meeting of this nucleus committee with the SSRC in July 1963 did not result in any concrete proposals. It was not agreed what tasks the committee should undertake and, in general, the purpose of the meeting was not accomplished. Festinger and the SSRC Staff Officer Willerman made only informal proposals. Interest in the kind of committee tentatively approved by the P&P therefore was not likely to be developed without undertaking further exploration and getting acquainted with a wider range of social psychologists in different countries who would be interested in collaborating in such an enterprise. It was agreed that 'no committee should be appointed at the present time and that the results of further exploration by the staff would be reported to the P&P at its next meeting'.[18]

The results of further investigation with Festinger were reported in November 1963,[19] describing what should be done to encourage experimental testing of similar hypotheses in dissimilar cultures. Festinger wanted to bring together a number of psychologists sharing similar theoretical and experimental interests, hoping to organize some collaborative projects in different countries, particularly in Asia. However he knew very few experimental psychologists outside Europe and the USA and was willing to devote two months to canvassing the situation in Asia. The P&P voted that funds should be made available for him to identify foreign social psychologists with strong theoretical and experimental interests.[20] In addition, the P&P thought that the representatives of dissimilar cultures could also be found in Europe and the USA, where scholars from different cultures were coming to study social psychology. If Festinger undertook such a search there, it would enhance the possibility of a future conference.

The meeting of the P&P in November endorsed the decision that had been made in September 1963: no single committee concerned with transnational research of different kinds should be appointed at present. Instead, the members of the P&P expressed their continuing interest in studying the possibilities of encouraging cross-cultural research of various kinds.[21]

Within a month, however, Festinger revised his proposal. It appeared that he would be able to spend only one month in Asia which would not give him sufficient time to identify talented social psychologists in that region. Moreover, when the SSRC Council attempted to identify individuals in Asia through correspondence, the search yielded only a few names. His decision was welcome because of another development at the same time. It was announced that the Division of Social Sciences in the NSF was interested in supporting collaborative research by American and foreign social psychologists. The Division hoped that the SSRC would help, possibly through the appointment of a committee to identify and bring together potential collaborators. This committee could consider proposals on how to advance research in social psychology in other countries through summer institutes, workshops or conferences or through assistance to persons wishing to organize such activities. Festinger agreed that these issues could form the programme of the Transnational Committee and expressed strong interest in participating. He agreed in consultations with Herring and Willerman that such a committee should consist of both American and foreign social psychologists.[22]

While this prospective development was acceptable in principle, the members of the P&P expressed further concerns. How could one appoint a committee in such a vaguely defined field? What indeed is social psychology? Shouldn't the SSRC appoint a committee more closely comparable with other Council committees that had collaborated with foreign scholars? The intention and purpose of the proposed Transnational Committee was not clear. Was the intention to foster comparative research, in which scholarly experience and data from several cultures would be brought together? Or was it primarily to bring social psychological research in Europe and elsewhere more into line with standards in the USA?

The situation was no clearer in January 1964. The P&P[23] still questioned the role of the proposed Transnational Committee. It was thought that, instead of the Transnational Committee, there should be a committee on comparative social psychology. The concerns of such a committee should not be restricted to Western Europe, although perhaps they might start there. Moreover, since social psychology was such an ill-defined field, the committee should not limit itself to social psychology or to specific approaches, for example, experimental or otherwise. Instead, the committee should be interdisciplinary. For instance, the relevance of cultural or environmental issues should be explored; it should be concerned with raising the level of research and the quality of personnel in other countries so that good research would ultimately benefit the development of theory in the USA.

In March 1964 the P&P[24] finally approved the initial membership of the new Transnational Committee: Festinger, (chairman), Ancona, Lanzetta, de Sola Pool, Rommetveit and Schachter.

The P&P pondered how rigid the definition of social psychology should be. Should sociologists engaged in applied research as well as experimental psychologists be included in the Transnational Committee's activities? It was agreed that the interests, activities and significance of research were more important than disciplinary boundaries. The Transnational Committee had confirmed its strong commitment to cross-national research in different parts of the world.

Solving the military and the complexity problem: a third way

Rockefeller SSRC archives tell us that the aim of establishing social psychology around the world was directed in two ways. Both approaches were orientated in the first instance towards Europe. Festinger and Lanzetta had respect for Europe and it stood high in their preferences for building international social psychology. Each of the two initiatives had advantages as well as drawbacks.

Lanzetta paid primary attention to the scientific community. His proposal had a visible horizon and a clear goal. He focused on Europe and on the idea of bringing together Europeans so that they could start talking to one another about experimental social psychology so as to initiate long-term collaboration. Reinforcing relations among Europeans would encourage them to develop their own research. In order to give legitimacy to social psychology in Europe, his planning committee constituted an international group and included both Americans and Europeans.

His problem was that he had military support. Academic institutions were cautious about getting involved with institutions that might interfere with their norms and independence. This is why Lanzetta's proposal encountered difficulties in the USA. But we shall see later that the history of the Transnational Committee is full of military concerns, some of them very ugly.

In contrast to Lanzetta, Festinger focused on the science itself. His aim of creating international social psychology around the world was not only grandiose but also much more difficult to achieve. He also had the difficult task of making himself understood by the SSRC because his proposal seemed vague. The P&P thought that Festinger's idea was premature and accepted it only slowly and gradually. Festinger's theoretical vision 'to hasten the change from a purely "United States social psychology" to a "social psychology of human beings"' in the text presented above is both very dense and tense. And yet somehow it structured the subsequent history because it became the compass direction of the Transnational Committee. It gave its members the understanding that it was their task, which they had to accomplish.

The person who played the key role in crystallizing ideas and bringing the two proposals together was Ben Willerman, a well-known social psychologist who, years ago, had carried out studies on food habits with Lewin. He was on leave from the University of Minnesota and had been the Council's Staff Officer since 1 October 1963 (*Items*, 1963, 3, p. 37). He was highly esteemed, devoted to the interests of the Council and to social psychology. All who knew him warmly appreciated his sensitive understanding, sympathy and thoughtfulness, and keen sense of humour. He worked for several committees of the SSRC, including the Transnational Committee (*Items*, 1965, 3, p. 43).

As an academic who was an officer of the SSRC dealing with the daily problems of the Transnational Committee, Willerman carried out conciliatory work and contributed enormously to bringing the Lanzetta and Festinger proposals together. He provided information, made suggestions, wrote letters and proposals, reported to the Executive Committee and looked after the interests of the SSRC. Like Mercury, he played the role of messenger between the SSRC and the two perspectives, working out solutions to the problem of military money and negotiating the controversial perspectives of both the SSRC and the Lanzetta and Festinger proposals. The archival documents show that the P&P always sent him as an observer, a temporizer of solutions, someone who could find answers to difficult problems. And he found a solution to the problem of bringing the two committees together.

The Transnational Committee finally in place

In September 1964 the P&P[25] reappointed the nucleus of the Transnational Committee. Moreover, two further members were appointed: Koekebakker from Amsterdam and Moscovici from Paris. At last the full Transnational Committee was in place. This fact was acknowledged in the SSRC bulletin *Items* in December 1964 under the heading 'Transnational Social Psychology', stating that the P&P had appointed the Transnational Committee.

Festinger remarked that it took one and a half years of organization and intermittent activity to arrive at the appointment of the Transnational Committee. The purpose in establishing this committee was to stimulate and promote communication and collaboration among social psychologists in different parts of the world. Festinger intended to appoint more members from countries outside the USA and, equally, to decrease the number of American members.

The President of the SSRC, Pendleton Herring, wondered how social psychology might look in five years' time as a result of the Committee's activities. He hoped for the development of international community and for a clearer concept of social psychology in different parts of the world, especially in less developed countries. Young scholars, particularly, would benefit from such developments.

The future now looked more promising. However, all had yet to be done.

2

Two Sources of Modern Social Psychology

Preamble

Today it might be said that the social psychologists who shaped their new science were born under a lucky star. They entered social psychology when it was *in statu nascenti*, when all the social sciences were pushed forward by the fresh winds of change and rising expectations. The usefulness of their contribution to the world's problems was taken for granted and so these pioneers looked towards open spaces of new universities under reconstruction – first in North America, then Western Europe, then Eastern Europe and lastly Latin America. In this endeavour, amateurs had the same opportunity of entering the new discipline as the few professionals in the field. It must not be forgotten that among these pioneers were many who had experienced a terrible war which had revealed unexpected and shocking aspects of human behaviour. Needless to say, this unique tragedy focused the attention of the new science on trying to unravel the roots of that malaise in order to avoid its repetition. Kurt Lewin's (1973) *Resolving Social Conflicts*, we believe, is the book that best portrays the *zeitgeist* of social psychology at the time.

But of course if a science is called into existence by new problems, it is also built on existing traditions. Perhaps it could be said that the authors of academic textbooks, just like the companions of Ulysses, always have a fear of navigating high seas. In other words, they are worried that they might suffer vertigo because of the elevation of their ideas. Social psychology has never really wished to take the risk of recognizing the real diversities in its past. Instead, it has tended to tone them down, to ease polarities or tensions inherent throughout its history – and throughout the history of science. The greatest danger, until now, to social psychology has not been the risk of getting lost in the turmoil of different kinds of discovery throughout five continents. Neither has social psychology seriously desired its presence in the whirlpool of world cultures. Instead, the danger has been that of locking itself up within its own horizon. And so, its history and consequent debate have been the history of, and the debate about, American social psychology.

But if we search for indicators of better definitions of the epoch, for the trends in the field and the inclinations of the members of the Transnational Committee, we find that two traditions[1] underlie modern social psychology and exert a living influence. And once we know what these traditions are, one older and one newer, we are also closer to better understanding the discipline's making.

The Indigenous-American Tradition and the Euro-American Tradition

Twice in the history of American social psychology, scientific traditions appeared and twice they were related to a world war. As suggested by one of the reviewers of this book, we shall call the first of these the Indigenous-American tradition.

The Indigenous-American tradition

One of the most popular symbols of the Indigenous-American tradition is exemplified by the Allports' perspective, although Floyd and Gordon Allport may not be even *the* most representative figures in that tradition. During the Second World War, this tradition focused on the study of the attitudes, thinking, motivation and social adjustment of the returning American soldier. The four volumes of the series *The American Soldier* are 'perhaps unparalleled in magnitude in the history of any single research enterprise in social psychology or sociology' (Stouffer et al., 1949, pp. 29–30), both as its monument and illustration.

The authoritative five volumes of *The Handbook of Social Psychology* (Lindzey and Aronson, 1954/1968) start with a historical

chapter on the background of modern social psychology by
Gordon Allport. There the author states: 'While the roots of social
psychology lie in the intellectual soil of the whole Western tradition, its present flowering is recognized to be characteristically an
American phenomenon' (Allport, 1954/1968, pp. 3–4).[2]

Reflecting on this quote, Farr (1996, p. 1) comments: 'this is
how Gordon Allport . . . introduced the discipline to a new generation of graduate students in America' soon after the Second
World War. The editors of *The Handbook*, Lindzey and Aronson,
considered Allport's historical chapter to be such an important
statement that they placed it on its own as an introduction. The
subsequent chapters in Volume I, as if they were to make a stamp
on Allport's statement, presented systematic positions on specific
issues. They are all written by American social psychologists.

According to Allport, 'social psychology began to flourish soon
after the First World War' (Allport, 1954/1968, p. 2). The war, he
argues, accelerated the development of all branches of the social
sciences. Among the events which stimulated this development
were the spread of communism, the depression in the 1930s, the
rise of Hitler, the genocide of the Jews and the Second World War.
In this context, Allport argues, a 'special challenge fell to social
psychology'. It was because of these gloomy events after the First
World War, he thought, that a fundamental question needed to be
addressed: 'How is it possible to preserve the values of freedom
and individual rights under conditions of mounting social strain
and regimentation?' An attempt to answer this question, in his
view, led to the creative study of a variety of issues such as leadership, public opinion, prejudice and attitude change. The early
work of Gordon and Floyd Allport also took place in the period
after the First World War. Gordon Allport's fundamental concern
to protect the individual from increasing 'social strain and regimentation' expressed itself in shaping American social psychology
as the psychology of the individual. Challenging the threat of
social regimentation, both Allports focused on the individual.
Floyd Allport entitled chapter 1 of his *Social Psychology* 'Social
psychology as a science of individual behavior and consciousness'.
In accordance with this title he maintained that 'there is no
psychology of groups which is not essentially and entirely a psychology of individuals . . . social psychology . . . *is a part of the
psychology of the individual*' (Allport, 1924, p. 4). For Floyd

Allport, consciousness belongs only to individuals as 'dependent upon the functioning of neural structure' (ibid., p. 5) and therefore, 'psychology in all its branches is a science of the individual' (ibid., p. 4). Gordon Allport corroborates Floyd's perspective. He declares that 'With few exceptions, social psychologists regard their discipline as an attempt to understand and explain how the thought, feeling, and behaviour of individuals are influenced by the actual, imagined, or implied presence of others' (Allport, 1954/1968, p. 5).

Apart from focusing on the individual, Allport introduces another important theoretical aspect: the positivism of Auguste Comte. He maintains that increased interest in social psychology after the First World War was due to two factors. The first was the already mentioned post-war sociopolitical scene. The second, 'a more formal way of viewing the recent upsurge of interest in social psychology', was Comte's positivism. Comte's theory of the three stages in science – theological, metaphysical and positivistic – has a specific significance in this context. Allport explains: 'While Comte himself endeavoured to inaugurate the third stage, it is clear that the fruit of his effort was delayed for nearly a century until the positivistic tools of experiment – statistics, survey methods, and like instruments – were more adequately developed' (ibid., p. 3). The time had now come and the Allports contributed to the acceleration that marked 'the delayed entrance of social science into the era of positivism' (ibid., p. 3).

Individualism and positivism, alongside mechanistic epistemology, had both theoretical and methodological implications. These factors were the background to Allport's compelling statement about 'the soil of social psychology' and the field's flowering after the First World War. The Allports established a tradition in American social psychology that seemed to capture, with plausible arguments, the theoretical, empirical and societal nature of the discipline.

However, when we open any journal or book on social psychology, we are bound to say that the Allport tableau is too coherent and too unilateral to be true. It gives the impression of being forcefully constructed. It eliminates too much of what is generally known about the history of social psychology and therefore does not leave us feeling at ease. We only need remind ourselves that, before and after the First World War, there were many social psychologists of very different orientations in the USA, the UK, Germany, France and elsewhere who shaped the history of our discipline. Some of them moved it towards positivism, others very far away from it.

The Second World War and European refugees

We pointed out earlier that social psychology emerged as an autonomous science during the Second World War. This is endorsed by Dorwin Cartwright (1948, 1979), among others. In contrast to Gordon Allport, he claims that 'the most important single influence on the development of social psychology' was 'the Second World War and the political upheaval in Europe that preceded it' (Cartwright, 1979, p. 84). And if he were required 'to name the one person who has had the greatest impact upon the field, it would have to be Hitler'.

The rise of Nazism had two fundamental influences. First, when Nazism came to power, social psychology was ready for accelerated development. Nazism speeded up this process by bringing into focus the humanitarian crisis it created. The second influence was of a different, though related, kind. Cartwright emphasizes the importance of the migration of European scientists and scholars, among them social psychologists, to America:

> Although this massive displacement of intellectual talent had important effects upon all branches of science and culture, it was especially critical for social psychology. One can hardly imagine what the field would be like today if such people as Lewin, Heider, Koehler, Wertheimer, Katona, Lazarsfeld, and the Brunswiks had not come to the United States when they did. They not only brought to American social psychology a fresh and stimulating point of view at a time when it too was to embark upon a period of unprecedented growth, but they also exerted a direct personal influence upon many of the individuals who were to come to play a leading role in the subsequent development of the field, and through them, an indirect effect upon the training of the present generation of social psychologists. (Cartwright, 1979, p. 85)

Of the immigrant scholars, the most influential was Lewin. His novel viewpoint was inspired by Gestalt psychology and by the neo-Kantian philosophy of Cassirer. Hence we have here a psychology opposed to behaviourism and a philosophy opposed to positivism. Lewin and his students were interested in dynamic interaction rather than in social behaviour or in the differences between individuals.

Allport and Cartwright are both correct: the history of social psychology is related to the most devastating wars of our time. However, can we say that wars are the breeders of theories or of their origins? Can we say that wars are the mothers of invention of social psychology? Do they really explain its history – or any history of science in general? This is doubtful. Cartwright's brilliant and rich narrative describes the rise of a new tradition which constitutes a turning point in the history of social psychology. This new perspective altered the course of our discipline just as the introduction of statistics by Maxwell and Boltzmann changed the course of physics.

The second tradition, which we shall call the Euro-American, emerged at the beginning of the Second World War. From that time on, one can regard the history of social psychology in terms of a tension between the two traditions. We do not mean to say that the second tradition is European in the sense that it was carried over from Europe and adapted to the USA. Rather, it is a genuinely American tradition, just as some Italian-American or Afro-American customs or music are genuinely American. The Euro-American tradition started with the European refugee, Kurt Lewin. Theoretically, this tradition was based on orientation and attention to the reference group and to group dynamics. After the war, this tradition inspired important centres of research. Wherever such centres were created, they attracted talented students, both in the USA and in Europe. In France this tradition appealed to philosophers like Merleau-Ponty and Sartre. It also attracted psychoanalysts like Lagache, who created the first laboratory of social psychology at the Sorbonne in Paris. Lewinian concepts and practices penetrated the world of management, as for example, at the Tavistock Institute in London and similar institutes in Holland, Germany and France.

Most of the membership of the Transnational Committee belonged to the Lewinian school. Was this fact quite clear to the SSRC Council? Probably.[3] It was perhaps the Lewinian attitude of the Committee that facilitated its contacts with European social psychology. Lewinian ideas penetrated the milieu not in the sense that their effect was unique but, rather, that they had the most distinct and significant influence on the Transnational Committee. In 1978 there was a reunion at Columbia University of almost all the surviving members of the Research Center for Group Dynamics. That reunion included four members of the Transnational Committee: Morton Deutsch, Leon Festinger, Stanley Schachter and Harold Kelley. Deutsch remembers: 'At the reunion the participants were asked to indicate Lewin's effect on their work. From the discussion, it was evident that all of us had been very much influenced by Lewin's way of thinking about science and by his general orientation to psychology' (Deutsch, 1999, p. 10). This included, above all, the importance of theory, the usefulness of theory for practice and the interrelatedness between the person and the environment. In a different context, writing about science- and knowledge-building, Lewin (1981b, p. 73) emphasized that it must not lead *zur Angst vor der Theorie* (to fear of theory) but must involve the study of concepts.

Some Precision Related to the Two Traditions

The two names that we have proposed for the two traditions, the Indigenous-American and the Euro-American, certainly do not explain the issues they encompass, any more than they can give us clues concerning the contents to which they apply. We must therefore say a little more about them in order to pin down the main ideas of the two traditions and to clarify the differences between them. What systematically separates these two traditions are their different epistemological positions. As Einstein put it: 'The reciprocal relationship of epistemology and science is of noteworthy kind. They are dependent upon each other. Epistemology without contact with science becomes an empty scheme. Science without epistemology is – insofar as it is thinkable at all – primitive and muddled' (1949, pp. 683–4).

   Just as epistemologies become habits in thinking and communicating, traditions become habits underpinning science. This is why neither epistemologies nor traditions are of a fleeting nature: they are durable habits of the mind.

Our account of the two traditions of course can be no more than schematic. Yet at the same time, it seems to us that the diverse epistemological positions between them are so striking, so black and white, or positive and negative, that even schematic distinctions between such contrasts can sharply reveal their differences. In order to clarify the meaning of each tradition, such schematization is not only important but inevitable. Moreover, there are other reasons why we cannot disregard these contrasts between the two traditions; they express certain choices which were previously formulated by other scholars. Despite that, we consider it important to reaffirm and reinterpret them in order to throw into doubt the current tendency of presenting history without paying any attention to these two traditions and their inherent tensions. The issue is the same as if, for example, someone tried to present the history of optics without reference to the two opposing tendencies, the wave and the corpuscular, when discussing the nature of light.

In writing a history, one has a number of choices. It has become routine, whether in articles, textbooks or monographs, to present accounts of the history of social psychology as a succession of topics and their more or less minimalist theories, usually those developed in the USA. If we take some recent examples of social psychological historical accounts, like the excellent paper by Greenwood (2004), 'What Happened to the "Social" in Social Psychology?', we find that he critically analyses one theory after another and documents factors that provide historical explanation of the phenomenon in question. Similarly Danziger (2000), in his thought-provoking paper on the history of experimental social psychology, presents one 'programmatic' account after another in historical sequence.

We are adopting a different strategy. Our account of the two traditions is not based on the idea of one tradition succeeding or alternating with the other. What we suggest is the following. We shall give an account of the two traditions and the topics of their exploration, focusing on the main epistemological points of their contrasts. But these contrasts do not peacefully embrace one another but are sources of conflicts, misunderstandings – indeed of strife. This will not only provide a more lively historical account but also an account that will more closely correspond to the reality of the history of social psychology. Specifically, we shall characterize these contrasts between the two traditions in terms of four fundamental points.

The door and the bridge

The history of scientific disciplines follows a well-known pattern. Originally, human knowledge was integrated within global fields like philosophy or the natural sciences. From the seventeenth century onwards, specialized disciplines started emerging one by one, slicing the contents of the original global fields into specific sciences like biology, chemistry or psychology. This division became the basis of scholarship and specialization so that social psychology was defined as a speciality of psychology, alongside physiological and developmental psychology for example. However, as Chomsky (1995, p. 15) wrote, '[s]pecialisation is no proof of progress; it has often meant displacement of penetrating insights in favor of technical manipulations of little interest. That remains practically true today.'

As a speciality of general psychology, social psychology is conceived as a door through which social phenomena pass in order to fit the rules and principles of general psychology. This means that they are decomposed into simple elements adapted to causal explanations and so forth. The metaphor of the door is pertinent here. A door can open or close itself to other disciplines. As a speciality, social psychology is open to general psychology but closes the door to other disciplines.

The Indigenous-American tradition was firmly placed in general psychology. Allport (1968, p. 4) states: 'Social psychology is above all else a branch of general psychology.' This is so because the focus of general and social psychology is the same. In both cases, the centre of emphasis is, specifically, 'human nature as localised in the person' (ibid., p. 4). He elaborates on this point by showing that social and general psychology overlap but are not identical with one another. Allport differentiates this approach from others, like cultural anthropology, political science and sociology, which start from the social systems in which the individual lives. Allport explains his perspective: some people argue that it is 'others' who always influence personal and mental life and that, therefore, all psychology must be social. He himself disputes this point of view and draws attention to the fact that there are many problems of human nature that need to be solved separately, like 'problems of psychophysics, sensory processes, emotional functions, memory span, the nature of personality integration' (ibid., p. 4).

Allport's list seems to imply the independence of each of the above psychological processes from one another, like parts of a mechanism. It considers emotions, memory and the nature of personality integration as being processes of the individual (Graumann, 1986; Farr, 1996). If one studies the individual as an isolated, and, indeed, as a mechanistically conceived psychological unit, then, as Berkowitz (1999, p. 161) observes, 'Social psychologists are psychologists first and members of social science fraternity second.' In passing, we note that this observation might be interpreted in two different ways. First, it could be assumed that social phenomena are reducible, and hence explainable, by physiological or neural processes. Indeed, Floyd Allport explains his position as follows: 'Psychologists agree in regarding consciousness as dependent upon the functioning of neural structure. Nervous systems are possessed by individuals; but there is no nervous system of the crowd' (Allport, 1924, pp. 4–5). Second, it could be implied that social psychologists are above all 'neuro-disciplinary', closing the door to sociological or anthropological theories. The latter interpretation has the following consequence. Since social psychologists are trained first of all in 'scientific' general psychology and since social psychology is placed within the realm of general psychology, its reference to 'social' does not involve 'social scientific' knowledge established within social sciences such as cultural anthropology or sociology. Due to lack of training in social sciences, social psychologists use only a common-sense understanding of social phenomena. As a result, it seems that social psychological knowledge combines the 'scientific' understanding of psychical aspects, statistics and measurements on the one hand, and what one could call a common-sense 'sociological' knowledge of the phenomenon in question on the other. Let us take an example to clarify the meaning of 'common-sense "sociological" knowledge'. Anybody can find a number of proverbs in different languages of the world that refer to common-sense meanings of the concept of, say, 'competition'. Competition takes place at any time when people are together at play, engaged in cooperative tasks or simply when someone observes another person during some kind of activity. For instance, proverbs like 'men surpass one another while they are working together' or 'no one is another's brother in play', or 'a potter envies a potter' are some examples that contain the common-sense meaning of 'competition' and one finds it in various versions in different languages and cultures.

This common-sense notion of competition entered 'scientific' social psychology towards the end of the nineteenth century. Textbooks often quote that it was the American psychologist Triplett (1898) who performed the first experiment in social psychology and that he conducted the first empirical test of psychological hypothesis. He had read that bicycle racers reach higher speeds when paced by others and he thought that it might generally be true that an individual's performance is affected by the presence of others. Yet as Zajonc (1966, p. 3) points out, the knowledge and technique that was necessary for Triplett's experiment had existed for at least 4,000 years. It is a kind of common-sense knowledge about the regulation of social behaviour that was required during the building of the pyramids and which was also embodied in ancient law like Hammurabi's Code and the Old Testament. Triplett brought this common-sense knowledge into social psychological experiments when he found that children winding fishing reels would do so faster in competition with each other than alone. As Allport stated, Triplett's social psychological experimental problem, 'indeed the only problem studied in the first three decades of experimental research', was formulated as follows: *What change in an individual's normal solitary performance occurs when other people are present?* (Allport, 1954/1968, p. 64).

This topic became well known through the work of Floyd Allport under the label of social facilitation and the influence of group on individual behaviour. Although he thought that the presence of others had a perceptual (visual, hearing) and a rivalry component, he considered them both as individual characteristics. Specifically, rivalry was to be explained physiologically and emotionally: 'The visceral reaction in rivalry as in other emotions probably liberates internal secretions, and involves other responses characteristic of the sympathetic system' (Allport, 1924, p. 283).

In contrast to the Indigenous-American tradition, in the Euro-American tradition social psychology bridges the gap between cultural anthropology and sociology. In 1945, when informing social scientists about the Research Center for Group Dynamics, Lewin (1945, p. 126) had started his paper: 'The Research Center for Group Dynamics has grown out of two needs or necessities, a scientific and a practical one. Social science needs an integration of psychology, sociology and cultural anthropology into an instrument for studying group life.' Elsewhere he argues (Lewin, 1939/1952, p. 134) that sciences like sociology or psychology should feel free to use the constructs of other sciences if these are appropriate for handling their problems. It is likely that in expressing these views, Lewin was inspired by the physics of relativity. Cartwright describes this broad perspective in an interview with Patnoe (1988, pp. 14–15) and points out that the institutional environment at the Massachusetts Institute of Technology was the most productive one that he had ever experienced. Lewin's approach allowed a high flexibility in tackling social scientific problems. It was based on a combination of freedom, flexibility and high scientific standards. There were no established disciplinary boundaries at the Institute for the social sciences. 'If we wanted to talk like anthropologists, nobody was going to shoot us down.' Thibaut, too, remembers Lewin saying: 'Don't read psychology, read philosophy or history or science, poetry, novels, biographies – those were the places where you would get the ideas. Psychology at this point – it will stifle your imagination' (ibid., p. 56).

Sherif's view of social psychology as a social science, too, was always linked to other social sciences like anthropology and sociology (Moscovici, 1992, p. 108), attempting, just like in Lewin's perspective, an integrative approach to the study of social phenomena. Sherif refers to anthropological and sociological literature, in particular in the context of small groups, social movements, attitude changes and acculturation (Sherif and Sherif, 1956). He explains how his interdisciplinary approach was born. When he took his first course at Harvard University, the text was Allport's *Social Psychology* (1924),

> as it was in many major departments of psychology at the time. The important contribution of that text – namely, its persistent effort to bring social psychology firmly into the camp of experimental science – made its shortcomings all the more difficult to

assimilate. In view of his own experience in different cultures, this student in the course found a lack of perspective on cultural values, institutions, and ideologies as these affect the viewpoints and tastes of the human individual. The lack amounted, so it seemed, to ignoring sets of stimulus factors confronting the individual in any culture, thereby conducive to a social psychology that could not help being ethnocentric, even though unwittingly (Sherif and Sherif, 1969, p. viii)

Though we will not pursue this issue any further here, we are not aware of any question-begging claim against 'cross-disciplinary' approaches to social phenomena or better, against 'bridge-sciences'. A bridge-science is not simply 'interdisciplinary' in the sense that it combines knowledge of different disciplines about a specific subject matter. Instead, it is a single discipline that *builds* new knowledge about a specific subject area using knowledge of other disciplines. It is no drawback for social psychology to be a bridge-science when exploring phenomena like social influence, language, innovation or conformity. In fact, bridge-sciences, for example biophysics and statistical mechanics, have today become more the rule than the exception.

The static and the dynamic

What conclusions can we draw from what we have just said about the scientific nature of social psychology? Simply, that it does not make sense to search for a general definition of a scientific theory independently of the context to which it refers. One cannot envisage the rules of a statistical or verbal language that would, in one way or another, capture phenomena or objects in reality in their entirety. In other words, science can never explore reality as a whole. It can only draw attention to characteristics that, according to Heisenberg (2003), are thought to be 'essential'. However, if we ask how we know what permits us to say in what sense certain characteristics are 'essential', the response is quite disappointing. To give a comparative example, the human eye as a whole is not capable of very clear observation of reality. It is only through a very small zone of the retina that the human eye is capable of exploring and searching for the most marked images of reality. Similarly, human thought can only grasp clearly a very small content of reality while the rest is left in obscurity.

Until now we have used the term 'a scientific theory' in the singular, as if there were only one kind of theory. But it is fundamentally important that we distinguish between two kinds of theory: *static* and *dynamic*.

Static theories treat concepts as unequivocal and follow rigid rules with respect to the application of these concepts. Such rigid rules link concepts to one another and they also link their content to reality in such a way that the scientist can decide on the basis of a hypothesis whether the theory in question is 'correct' or 'false'. Among theories of this kind, one of the most well known is the physics theory of classic mechanics. But such theories also exist in social psychology, for example, Kelley's (1967) theory of attribution based on Heider's work. Just as in classic mechanics, for example, Kelley views human attribution and inferential processes in static terms. Attribution, he says, 'refers to the process of inferring or perceiving the dispositional properties of entities in the environment. These are the stable[4] features of distal objects such as color, size, shape, intention, desire, sentiment, and ability' (Kelley, 1967, p. 193).

Since Kelley considers both human cognitive processes and characteristics of the environment as static, the logic of his analysis is 'obviously akin to that employed in analysis of variance' (ibid., p. 195). In his view, a simple cube model can cope with all the complexities of causal attribution about the self, the need for information about the self, credit and blame, trust in interpersonal relations, as well as with socialization and 'language training'.

For twentieth-century scientists like Heisenberg, Poincaré and Einstein, among others, static theories can be opposed to other, very different kinds of theory: *dynamic theories*. In order to explain the difference between the two kinds of theories, we shall follow here the ideas of the great physicist, Heisenberg (2003). Dynamic theories do not presuppose the existence of a grand reality that consists of a network of connections between *objects* in reality that intertwine and maintain life. Instead, Heisenberg presupposes the idea of different 'regions of reality' with respect to the phenomena that the science in question examines. In other words, a scientific theory can be defined only with respect to the relevant 'region of reality'. Regions of reality are not based on *objects* but on *relations*. The idea of the difference between *objects* and *relations* also defines the opposition between classic physics and quantum physics. Classic physics uses hypotheses and concepts that are 'precise' and that stand in a rigid relation to reality. Quantum physics, instead, creates hypotheses and concepts that are not in the most 'exact' or the most 'faithful' relation to reality but, rather, these hypotheses and concepts form the embryos of other kinds of hypotheses and concepts within the 'region of reality'. In other words, what is important here is not the precision of concepts but their fruitfulness: 'Through the various modes of relation one thought combines with another one, producing new thoughts. These give rise to yet other thoughts until the wealth of their content in the space grasped by these thoughts is saturated and gives birth to a faithful portrait of the region of reality to which it aspires' (Heisenberg, 2003, p. 20, our trans.).

In social psychology, the most famous dynamic theory is Lewin's field theory. Strongly influenced by both Cassirer's theory of knowledge and the theory of relativity, Lewin, just like Heisenberg, emphasized the opposition between static and dynamic approaches in science and therefore the difference between concepts based *on objects* and those based *on relations*. His field theory was originally developed as a dynamic approach in individual psychology and it examined interdependence between the individuals and their life space. Dynamic concepts like tension, level of aspiration and motivation later fired the imagination of group dynamics and action research.

Another example of dynamic theory is Heider's theory of attribution. This theory does not concern groups but rather interpersonal relations. Heider thought that 'interpersonal relation was the most important thing psychologists should talk about. But they were busy with verbal learning, sensations, and those other topics that are still around in so-called experimental psychology' (Heider, 1976, p. 6). Although Heider's primary interest was the person as a unit of study, he presented the person only in relation to, and interacting with, another person. As he states, 'generally, a person reacts to what he thinks the other person is perceiving, feeling, and thinking, in addition to what the other person may be doing' (Heider, 1958, p. 1). All underlying concepts of Heider's theory, for instance subjective environment, perceiving, experiencing and belonging, are based on relations between the person and the social environment in which he or she acts. Attribution theory involves explications of common-sense notions, interpretations and representations of others' actions and use of everyday language in making attributions. Using the Lewinian concept of life-space, Heider assumes a direct connection between the individual and environment, in particular in interpersonal relations. Heider's aim is above all conceptual and language-based: in order to carry out empirical investigation, one must first develop a clear theory underlined by concepts and one must understand the meaning of words used in daily language. Concepts like trying, intention, wanting and belonging are at the centre of Heider's attribution theory. This is why for him, data are meaning. Although Heider talks metaphorically about 'factor analysis' when referring to diverse interpretations and to data as meaning, under no circumstances can meaning be reduced to simple variables. Instead, meaning is filled with intention, affect, evaluation and motive which need to be explicated.

Thus we see the contrasts in analysis between the two kinds of eminent social psychologists, Kelley on the one hand and Lewin, Sherif and Heider on the other. These contrasts illustrate the polarity between the static and the dynamic to which Heisenberg referred. In the final analysis in his philosophical treatise on the nature of scientific theory, Heisenberg exemplifies the contrast between static and dynamic theory in a very intuitive and concrete manner. In static theory, the scientist always chooses between 'true' and 'false' propositions or between the 'exact' and the 'false' proposition which are mutually exclusive and incompatible. In contrast, in dynamic theory, the opposite of the 'true' proposition will be another 'true' proposition (think of the wave and corpuscular propositions). They are in a complementary relation and one does not exclude the other. Moreover, in 'static' thought the scientist's ultimate aim is above all *clarity and precision*. In contrast, in *dynamic* thought one *interprets*; interpretation involves a search for infinitely varied relations with other regions of reality that are to be explained by interpretation.

Two emblems: attitudes and social groups

We do not take the liberty here of criticizing what social psychologists make of their science. And above all, we do not sustain the idea that one tradition should be deprived of the authority that science has attributed to it because, in that case, the very notion of 'tradition' would lose its significance. The fact that the Indigenous-American tradition is more individualist or that the Euro-American tradition is more social may be viewed as indices of their originality. However, the true contrast between them is perhaps best expressed in their conception of 'the social'. We may recall that Floyd Allport sharply rejected the group as a unit of analysis: 'There is no psychology of group that is not essentially and entirely a psychology of individuals' (Allport, 1924, p. 4). According to this perspective, the real is only the individual and his or her cognition. Consequently, the tradition which Allport follows defines 'the social' or 'the group' as a simple aggregate (ibid., p. 6),[5] which serves to indicate an ensemble of individuals who come together (who find themselves in a situation of a special proximity in the case of masses). They can share common interests, and above all common opinions, without even interacting among themselves, just like voters when they come together in the polling station. Here is the crucial point: public opinion may appear either as an aggregate of the will or as the beliefs of individuals.

In order to shorten this account of such well-known approaches, we need to remind ourselves that in the Indigenous-American tradition opinions are considered as close to, and stabilizing themselves as, attitudes; attitudes, in turn, articulate themselves as stereotypes and prejudices. Theoretically, attitudes are expressed *as if* they were 'social'. They are considered as social and as being presented by hypothetical groups representing a purely statistical reality. In any case, attitudes are emblems or, according to Allport, 'the primary building stone in the edifice of social psychology' (Allport, 1954/1968, p. 63).

Hence it can be seen that in this tradition the group is a vicarious notion and a fiction shared by an aggregate of individuals. As Deutsch comments, this is why '[t]he concept of "group", as well as other concepts relating to social psychological phenomena, had little scientific status among social psychologists in the 1930s and 1940s when Lewin was turning his attention to social psychology. He believed "the reality" of these concepts would be established only by "doing something with them" ' (Deutsch, 1999, p. 9).

The Euro-American tradition not only questioned the concept of the social as an aggregate of individuals and viewed it as a fiction. It also regarded as fantasy the idea that attitudes and opinions reflect common psychosocial realities shared by the individual and the group. This was why the concept of a group as a dynamic interdependence of members became the emblem of this tradition. Group interdependence is not a new concept (Bartlett, 1923) but the Euro-American tradition affirmed and testified to its internal dynamics and to the two characteristics that the aggregate conception excluded: homeostasis and interaction. Lewin is clear on this idea. Basically, he views group or culture as a living system, composed of countless social interactive forces that aim to establish equilibrium in the system. For Lewin, these forces consist of 'established norms' or 'accepted ways of doing things'. The system, that is, the group or culture, functions as a whole; disturbance in one part has an effect on the entire system. This does not mean that for Lewin a system in equilibrium is without tension. However, it presupposes a certain firmness of boundaries. Lewin elaborates this theory in groups, culture and personality. What is notable above all is the attention he gives to the idea of equilibrium and to the homeostasis of the group. Furthermore, he gives prime consideration to the interdependence among individuals in the group and therefore to their interaction.

The Sherifs take a slightly different approach. Discussing the segregation between the study of attitude and the study of groups, they point out that the former does not integrate theory and empirical findings. It is the study of groups that provides the basis for assessing individual attitudes because groups prescribe the limits of acceptable or objectionable behaviour in matters of consequence for the group. Norms in various groups provide an objective baseline for assessing individual attitudes (Sherif and Sherif, 1956, p. 344). In contrast to social psychology, studies in the fields of sociology and anthropology of small groups, social movements and acculturation are 'filled with case studies of attitude change over time in a group context' (ibid., pp. 476–7). While the latter studies are not usually conducted under the title of attitude, they were originally conceived in terms of attitude formation and change. These studies show that attitudes are formed in groups during interaction and they take shape and function in problem situations.

Our brief exposé of two emblems begs the question: is there a trait or a principle which justifies the difference between the two competing traditions? Of course, there is the principle of limited artificiality, as one might call it, in order to restore the significance given to it by Lewin's successor, Leon Festinger, in the recent literature. Festinger says:

> We learned [from Lewin] that one could, indeed one must, do studies both in the real world and in the laboratory . . . it was vital not to lose sight of the substance in the quest for a greater precision. Precision is highly desirable but only if one has retained the reality and essence of the question. Thus, a tradition grew of bringing very complicated problems into the laboratory. The tradition also included maintaining, always, mixture of laboratory and field work. (Festinger, 1980, p. 239)

That was what Festinger did in his study of prophecy failure. Similarly, Sherif did the same in his robber's cave group experiment. Up to a point, this perspective was also illustrated by Milgram's obedience studies and by Zimbardo's research on prisons. In any case, only by respecting this principle can one claim that at least in Lewin's and Sherif's work social psychology is independent of individual psychology, both as a science and as a reality. We can also agree with what Thibaut said in a different context: 'The rest of it is not really social psychology, only marginally so. It is individual psychology in a social setting' (Patnoe, 1988, p. 59).

This definition of group dynamics was beneficial. It created a theory that was meaningful both in and outside social psychology: it separated the 'real' from the 'fictive' group. The latter was based on the assumption that individuals assemble in a group because they are similar to one another. In other words, as we know from the Allports, groups are defined by similarity or by the mathematical similitude between their members. They can be similar to one another in terms of some real or imagined category, such as age or political view. The degree of similarity can be measured, therefore, by the degree of cohesiveness; for instance, we may obtain information as to how many members vote in the same way. Group research, for example, social perception, influence, decision and prejudice, is still based on the presupposition that it is some kind of similarity in categorization that defines group membership.

In contrast, in a 'real' group we have cohesiveness in terms of homeostasis and interdependency. Thibaut singles out Lewin's position on this issue and emphasizes the importance that he himself attaches to this issue: 'This is something Kurt saw very clearly and spoke of – the group is not composed out of similarity, out of categorisation, but out of interdependence of fate' (Patnoe, 1988, p. 59).

Lewin and Sherif not only presupposed but showed that social entities are real entities, at least as real as individual entities. This hypothesis, it goes without saying, did not have any currency in social psychology before the emergence of the theory of group dynamics. Its profound impact can be seen in the tradition it has created and in the method of research, towards which we shall now turn.

The factual and the real

For many people, the point of interrogation which figures in the question 'Is social psychology a science?' concerns exclusively the phenomena that our discipline studies. Concerning science in general, we are supposed to know what it is. And, it is all the same if the definitions differ. Some scholars, following Popper, evoke the criterion of 'non-refutability'; others use the notion of the 'paradigm' given to us by Kuhn. Nevertheless, there is some objection to labelling social psychology as 'science' because there is either not enough or too much science in it. In truth, the fact that we hardly know what the science is, what *our* science is, does not have the immediate effect of rendering the question void or attributing a lack of interest to it. Such a question makes sense only in the specific contexts where it poses itself most sharply.

In the case of social psychology, the question of science is carried by the experimental model. To be or not to be an experimental science, that is the question. Or, in more concrete terms, who was the pioneer of experimental social psychology? Was it Triplett, as the American textbooks claim? Or was it Lewin, as Festinger claimed at the Royaumont conference (as we shall see)? To acknowledge a pioneer also means to acknowledge the tradition of that science and, furthermore, the definition of the notion 'phenomenon' authorized by that science. This is a general rule in the history of science.

We have already referred to Triplett's experiment in 1898, which made him the forefather of experimental social psychology. This story, 'à la Popov', which consists of identifying the first researcher in one's own nation, would be different if told by a Frenchman evoking the brilliant work of Binet on suggestibility, also one of the classic studies. It would, of course, be different again if told by a German or an Englishman. Each of these stories would have something in common. In each case they would bring everyday experience into general psychology, simulated social phenomenon and compared effects of the present or absent variable, preferably in the laboratory.

Lewin's originality – and to some extent that of Sherif – was the discovery of experimentation that was deliberately adapted to social psychology. Lewin showed that it was possible and legitimate to obtain social reality by means of experiment. This is what Festinger wanted to emphasize when he referred to Lewin's experiments on group atmosphere as the first summit in experimental social psychology, although, in comparison with general psychology by which such experiments were inspired, they appeared somewhat sloppy. However, they had all the features of general psychology. First of all, they reflected on social phenomena provoked by contemporary reality oscillating between demonic belief and totalitarianism. Second, Lewin brought into play the theory that affirmed the interdependence of 'variables' in a situation of collective behaviour on the one hand and of 'field' theory on the other, thus achieving a total metamorphosis in the global situation he studied. This transformation concerned manipulation at leadership level in groups and the style of execution of responsibility by the 'leader' where the leader received precise instructions as to how to act. Lewin broadened these instructions to experiments under conditions of authoritarianism, of laissez-faire and of negotiation. These experiments do not make reference to authoritarian personality, submissiveness or other individual qualities but only to the nature of the relationship between group members.

Such intervention or 'manipulation' could be judged excessively schematic. However, it is no more schematic than an ethologist who, in an attempt to decipher intelligible responses from a studied 'group', observes a 'group' of animals and takes care to intervene as little as possible so as to minimize the disturbance of the ordinary group dynamics. In order to observe, the experimenter intervenes in a heuristic and exploratory manner. No doubt, one can criticize the sloppiness of 'dependent' variables and can criticize them amply. But, as Delbruck, one of the founders of molecular biology, argued, sometimes when we explore certain kinds of phenomena, it is necessary to accept the principle of limited sloppiness.

If we remember here that the subjects of Lewinian experiments that were carried out by Lippitt were boy scouts, we can conclude that the horizon of psychosocial experience was, in this case, just as in Lewin's other cases, natural experience. That is to say, it was experience that did not aim to simulate or miniaturize the real world but to demonstrate, amplify and finally invent new phenomena. In the long run, the scientific character of a discipline does not lie in the number of phenomena that it accumulates but in the number of boxes it succeeds in opening and closing. In other words, it lies in the number of real phenomena that it destroys and creates. Subjects and experiences of this kind illustrate Lewin's deep conviction that the problem with which social psychology should occupy itself rests, in the last instance, in the 'ethical' character of culture and in contemporary civilization. What the scientist should try to do in this field is not just describe symptoms or identify causes but aim to 'heal'. This is why nothing is as practical as a good theory. But a good theory meant to overcome the taboo of the Indigenous-American tradition.

Moreover, this Euro-American tradition tends to have a more general goal. It insists on the conception of psychology and of the social that knows how to annihilate a taboo established by the Indigenous-American tradition: the taboo of accepting the reality of social entities. As Lewin argues,.

The taboo against believing in the existence of a social entity is probably most effectively broken by handling this entity experimentally. As long as the scientist merely describes a leadership form he is open to the criticism that the categories used reflect merely his 'subjective views' and do not correspond to the 'real' properties of the phenomena under consideration. If the scientist experiments with leadership, and varies its form, he relies on an 'operational definition' which links the concept of a leadership form to concrete procedures of creating such a leadership form or to the procedures for testing its existence. The 'reality' of that to which the concept refers is established by 'doing something with' rather than 'looking at', and this reality is independent of certain 'subjective' elements of classification. (1947, p. 193)

This point demands our attention because in experimental studies it is necessary to choose variables, to find the causes which have social significance and to show not only that they are real but also that they produce real effects. Thus the theory must show the evidence on which it rests. It must also demonstrate that what it upholds is not an artefact. This is why Lewin wrote:

It has already been emphasized that the validity of social-psychological experiments should be judged not by the properties of isolated events or single individuals within the field but mainly by whether or not the properties of the social group or the social situation as a whole are adequately represented. This implies that one of the foremost tasks of fact-finding and observation in social psychology is to supply reliable data about those properties of the field as a whole. (Lewin, 1939/1952, p. 193)

We might be wrong, of course, in making the above claims about the two traditions. It is very difficult to make assessments about specific traditions in research if one was not at their initiation. But these judgements have some plausibility when we consider an elementary contrast between the two traditions. Specifically, we have in mind the contrast that existed at the time between the empirical approaches of the Yale Communication Program, directed by Carl Hovland, and The Research Center for Group Dynamics that was Lewin and his students. The former approach developed studies on attitudes and communication and was illustrated by its monumental work on the American soldier. Hovland attracted many talented social psychologists and followed a well-defined approach which Zimbardo summarized as follows:

> Hovland's approach was very behavioral, rational, very categorical, descriptive, non-theoretical and was really not that different from what we were doing with rats in one sense. You analyse what are all the input variables, what are all the output variables, what are the mediating variables and you set up a study where you vary one or two at a time. (Patnoe, 1988, p. 120)

In contrast, Lewin's Research Center for Group Dynamics introduced a totally different approach, based on a plethora of conceivably possible ideas and on foolish as well as wise theories. It tried to make non-obvious predictions and, as Deutsch remarked, 'that was very exciting'. Before focusing on Lewin's ideas, Deutsch occupied himself with social problems related to conflict and justice. 'I have continued,' he wrote, 'to believe that these foci are essential to understanding social life and also that a "social" social psychology rather than an "individual" social psychology would have as its fundamental concern' (Deutsch, 1999, p. 28). Just like Lewin's Research Center for Group Dynamics, Deutsch was interested in 'applied' and 'pure' research questions and hence in 'real social groups'. Festinger acknowledged not only that one of Lewin's major contributions was his 'insistence on trying to create, in the laboratory, powerful social situations that made big differences' (Festinger, 1980, p. 239) but also his extraordinary inventiveness in finding ways of achieving this goal.

Nevertheless, we are aware of two questions that might be raised. Are we justified in making the distinction between the factual and the real in order to symbolize a difference between two competing traditions that established themselves in American social psychology? Is there, after all, such a huge contrast between a method based on testing hypotheses on the one hand and one trying to understand and discover real phenomena on the other? We shall expand our affirmative responses to these questions by drawing attention to the motivation and ethos of Euro-American tradition.

Grandmothers' Tales

Our topic is tradition, not theory. People may share the same tradition while entertaining different theories. Those who shared this tradition were checked by one prohibition: no 'bubba social psychology'. This was not just an aphorism along the lines of Valéry's 'everything that is not strange is false'. This was a bend of the mind and behavioural style. This imperative expressed itself as impatience with the study of the obvious and as boredom provoked by trivial hypotheses. The propensity of the Transnational Committee was to discuss a project with a precision more customary among physicists than among 'pure' psychologists (Patnoe, 1988). This contrast is even more marked if we consider social psychologists who, as is the case with Triplett, did not object to the testing of common-sense hypotheses in the laboratory. If someone in the Transnational Committee succeeded in developing an idea that might constitute 'bubba psychology', there would very quickly have been repercussions from colleagues.

'No bubba social psychology' was an epistemological stance which became an ethical one. Let us explain. The crucial problem in traditional epistemology was the transformation of common-sense knowledge into scientific knowledge. It was accepted, of course, that common-sense beliefs are not necessarily erroneous and may indeed be grounded in empirically verifiable facts. But as evidence, they may be contradictory and are not usually established under carefully standardized conditions. This is why science attempts 'to introduce refinements into ordinary conceptions by the very process of exhibiting the systematic connections of propositions about matters of common knowledge' (Nagel, 1961, p. 6). The underlying view is, of course that there is contiguity between common-sense beliefs and scientific hypotheses and that the main difference between the two is that sciences are mainly 'organized' or 'classified'. In a nutshell, this perspective suggests that scientists do by systematic method what laymen do arbitrarily and/or without method. This difference is succinctly expressed by 'the dictum that the conclusions of science, unlike common-sense beliefs, are the products of scientific method' (ibid., p. 12). One understands why this perspective is so convincing: science selects from common-sense propositions and from obvious facts the 'true facts'. In the case of social psychology, laboratory experiments and quantitative surveys are methods that lead to the discovery of 'true' facts. This, however, is 'bubba psychology' or 'scientified' common sense.

The science of the twentieth century made a radical break with this position. It affirmed that scientific hypotheses cannot be derived from ordinary common sense (e.g. Farr, 1993; Wolpert, 1992). Moreover, scientific hypotheses are often counter-intuitive and cannot be established by examining familiar phenomena. Instead, they are usually outside common-sense experience. The first test of this science is to produce 'strange' ideas and 'strange' phenomena. Science accounts for the obvious and the ordinary in terms of the non-obvious and the extraordinary. Under the influence of physics and mathematics, this tradition of the strange, if one can call it that, has spilled over into all fields of inquiry and strangeness has become *sigillum veri*. We can remind ourselves of Bohr's famous question about a new theory, 'is it sufficiently crazy to be true?', suggesting that a theory grounded in common sense might not be relevant to science or truth.

We must assume that this way of 'doing' science became a bone of contention when the Transnational Committee came into existence. And it is not by chance that Kelley wrote: 'In its reaction to the charge that it was "bubba psychology", in the early 1960s social psychology developed a strong theme – one might say an ethos – of "demonstrating the non-obvious" ' (Kelley, 1992). Here we have the pertinent word, 'ethos'. Avoiding the commonsensical 'obvious' and 'the quest for a result that will surprise Bubba' (ibid., p. 14) was the ethos that those who came into contact with the Transnational Committee quickly discovered. It can even be argued that the edict 'no bubba social psychology' influenced the choice of projects and the everyday interaction among members of the 'invisible college'.[6]

So why did a part of the Euro-American school make a break with the classical world? It could be that Lewin and Festinger envisioned social psychology in the same light as mathematics and physical sciences. However, at that time neighbouring social sciences, such as sociology and anthropology, had already made that break.

'No bubba psychology' is synonymous with the Yiddish saying 'no grandmothers' tales'. How can one believe tales which merely repeat what is taken for granted? How should we treat 'new information' that is actually old and which everybody knows to be the case?

The last point: the ethos of 'no to bubba psychology' is related to another 'no' that imposes one of the strongest biblical prohibitions. This says that when you judge, you must avoid siding with the majority in following their judgement. For a researcher, at a deeper level, the imperative 'no bubba psychology' entails 'do not follow the crowd' but instead, make your own judgements. A unanimous consensus is always suspect because some things may have been left unexamined or because individuals may not have made up their own minds. Of course, it is necessary to relativize these remarks. Nevertheless, they give an idea of the ethos of the Transnational Committee and why it inspired its members. It was the exposure to independent scientific judgement, the style of cooperation with others while continuing individual research and the concern to follow a path without seeking consensus in one's own field or winning the approbation of institutions. It was this confidence everybody had in their work that allowed the Committee to exist. Ironically, this confidence also cost the Committee its existence. But this is another 'grandmothers' tale', another strange story. The strange nature of that story would probably escape other storytellers' accounts of the small and apparently ephemeral character of what was not expected to happen. As we shall see in this book, the Transnational Committee became a 'shadow' research group in social psychology.

II

The West European Experiment

3

Americans and Europeans

The Pleasure of Meeting Other Mavericks

Although the first conference for European social psychologists took place in Sorrento, Italy, it started of course as an American event. It was 'a family affair', a negotiation among American social psychologists, and it is difficult for a foreigner to speak about it diplomatically. It was not only the difference in point of view between two institutions as we saw in chapter 1. But it was also the difference between the two traditions. This difference was inevitable, given the prominence of the Lewinians in the Transnational Committee from its establishment up till its end. But we will return to this point.

The initiative of the ONR played a decisive role. As we know, Lanzetta represented the London branch of the ONR. One cannot say that before he arrived in London he had travelled extensively in Europe or that his interest was provoked by cries for help from European social psychologists. The latter were absorbed by problems in their own countries. And except perhaps for a few English and Dutch social psychologists, most had little interest in international scientific exchange. Despite his limited knowledge and the initial lack of demand, John Lanzetta was motivated to achieve his goal with total success. He also had a clear perspective based on two ideas of social psychology in Europe. These ideas were perhaps debatable but expressed sound intuition.

It was clearly important at the time that Festinger and Lanzetta sketched out the international perspective. Lanzetta's perspective was based on two premises. They were perhaps presumptuous but they were not far from the truth. The first was that applied social psychology was developing more successfully than academic social psychology. 'In such a social climate', Lanzetta wrote,

> the social psychologist interested in theory and experimental methods finds himself an isolated deviant. Marginal to the applied group and not yet wholly accepted by his academic brethren in experimental psychology, he stands alone – unsupported and unheard. Students are not attracted to him, because he has few facilities and little support to offer . . . Experimental psychologists remain aloof because the social psychologist is not in a position to earn their respect – the body of 'respectable' work required for acceptance demands better support, more people and adequate facilities. Under such pressures social psychologists gradually become 'assimilated', i.e., they turn to applied problems of interest to society or to more 'traditional' problems of interest to academic departments, and the prospects for the development of a viable experimental social psychology are further reduced. (Lanzetta, 1963, p. 2–3)

This situation applied both to Americans and Europeans. Academics learned about social psychology first and foremost from professionals and researchers working in applied psychology. Leavitt, about whom we shall speak later, summarized the situation two years later in similar fashion: 'In fact the whole profession of social psychology is something of a maverick on the European scene'.[1] However, Lanzetta expressed his second premise with some optimism, observing that capitulation was not complete:

> there remains a small but energetic and productive group with predominantly theoretical and experimental interests. They are scattered throughout Europe with heavier concentration in some countries than others, but with almost no country unrepresented. Only hazily aware of the work of other Europeans they have tended to look toward the U.S. for encouragement and support. Very often they have been trained in the U.S. or have been influenced by American social psychologists who have spent sabbatical years in their countries. These investigators are well-trained and are doing interesting and important work, but their voices are uncoordinated and thus feeble. Singly they have not convinced their applied colleagues or policy makers who control research funds that experimental methods and basic research . . . have a contribu-

tion to make. No doubt their impact would be greater if their own links were stronger. (Lanzetta, 1963, pp. 3–4)

This quotation is momentous. It was in fact the first occasion that someone had spoken about social psychology in Europe in such terms. Despite some inaccuracy, the general sense of Lanzetta's ideas expresses something that was substantially true for both Europeans and Americans. Lanzetta touched here on a problem common to social psychologists on these two continents, although it seemed that he paid little attention to the obstacles that lay ahead for his initiative. Or at least he gave that impression, because notwithstanding the good relations that were likely to be established with the American SSRC at the scientific level, the idea of a conference organized and financed by the Navy aroused a great deal of resistance. Whatever the attitude of individuals, the political climate and norms of the scientific community were not favourable to cooperation with American military research.

When Lanzetta issued invitations for the Sorrento conference, he did not wait for responses from invitees. Instead, he visited many of them to explain his intentions, to calm and silence foreseen and unforeseen objections and to bring into the open the purpose of the conference. He was an extraordinarily sympathetic, friendly, honest and open-handed person (Nuttin, 1990). His most characteristic personal feature was self-confidence that made an immediate impression on others and was combined with a determination to pursue his task. He had excellent reason to display confidence. At that time, conferences were rare and did not play any role in researchers' careers. His initiative in organizing the conference in Sorrento was a mark of genius. It was a stylistic and prestigious enterprise.

The invitees could not resist the temptations of Sorrento. One can hardly imagine a more magic and famous location in Europe. Sorrento is the place where Le Tasse was born, where Byron stayed for some time and which many creative individuals such as Walter Scott, Goethe, Leopardi, Stendhal, Verdi and Musset visited on various occasions. But we can equally reverse this portrayal of Sorrento. One can also say that the *genius loci* influenced the necessity for holding such a conference. In that case, the novelty of the event contributed to its success.

Sorrento

The Sorrento conference took place from 12 to 16 December 1963. Most participants came from more northern parts of Europe.[2] On arrival they were charmed by the view of the Bay of Naples and its peninsula with oranges and lemons in flower. Pagodas and gardens encircling the large hotels embellished the place during the day and enchanted the calm nights. The brisk breeze and warm sunshine fostered a good atmosphere and facilitated interpersonal contacts. Iacono, himself from Naples, booked into a prestigious hotel, Il Tramontano, and it was here that Americans and Europeans endeavoured to give the social psychology of the Old Continent a new look.

In principle, participants represented ten countries. In another, more realistic, sense there were only four groups present: the Americans were observers at the conference, while the British, French and Dutch were contributors. In a sense, discussing European social psychology at that time meant discussing these three nationalities. The presence of only one or two individuals from Belgium, Germany or Italy demonstrated its absence from the major part of Europe. Thus it is true to say that the participants did not represent merely a sample of European social psychologists but their whole population at that time.

The programme was organized for five full days (Lanzetta, 1963). It consisted of ten formal sessions, each devoted to a distinct topic. Eight sessions involved an invited paper with several researchers delivering shorter notes relating to appropriate sections. The other two sessions were panels, in each case followed by submitted papers and discussions. There were also informal meetings during which ideas were further elaborated and discussed. These lasted well into the night.

In order to give an idea of the scientific preoccupations of the participants, let us mention the main topics, without going into detail. Robert Pagès gave the opening lecture, outlining what might become the programme for experimental social psychology in Europe. How could European psychology develop in an innovative direction rather than remaining a digest of findings imitating American research? How could Europeans free their creative energies and what was to be the trigger for revitalizing their science? According to Pagès, the main source of scientific revival lay in questions and hypotheses derived from practice.

The panel on cross-cultural studies focused on the problem of comparison and generalization of results obtained in different countries. Despite its apparent consistency, when regarded from a distance, Europe was a mosaic of cultures and nations. Economics, sociology and anthropology had always been preoccupied with descriptions and explications of their differences. Social psychologists had now joined the debate. De Montmollin from Paris drew up a list of three types of inter-cultural studies: anthropological, the study of differential social psychology based on questionnaires and attitude scales, and the replication of experimental studies. She concluded that, due to methodological problems, proper comparative studies were rare.

Iacono maintained that it was necessary to define the relevant aspects of culture in comparative studies. This is why, before undertaking experiments in a specific region, for example, in Southern Italy, it was important to observe and describe the culture under study. Anthropological knowledge was an essential prerequisite for replication in different countries.

Rabbie from Utrecht presented a cross-cultural study involving parent–child relationships in the USA and Germany. In the light of his experiences in Africa and his anthropological knowledge, Gustav Jahoda from Glasgow attempted to tease out the objectives of cross-cultural study and sounded the alarm concerning its methodological pitfalls. In his opinion, social psychologists should not feel 'apologetic about generalizations that are likely to hold only within a given culture' (Lanzetta, 1963, p. 20). Otherwise, the bulk of current research would have to be condemned. To counter-argue this possibility, Jahoda outlined comparative studies broadly, asserting that their aims were not only to achieve universal generalizations but also to discover phenomena restricted to specific non-Western cultures. The example of his studies in Africa illustrated this point in a practical way. His observations concerned relations between researchers and subjects, the problem of language and the period the researcher stayed among the inhabitants of the studied culture. The ideas and questions about cross-cultural psychology expressed in this panel seem to be just as actual today as they were in Sorrento in 1963.

As for the remainder of the papers, we shall only give an idea of the kind of research being pursued in Europe at that time. Argyle presented a paper on the socialization of children, Tajfel spoke about social perception, Mulder about power relationships, Lambert was concerned with intergroup conflict and Rommetweit raised questions about language. Moscovici explained his media research on communication genres and Flament presented his work on mathematical models. Another panel, consisting of Faucheux, Koekebakker and Hutte, highlighted the relationships between laboratory experimental approaches and the study of organizations.

At first sight, this catalogue of interests may seem somewhat obsolete. However, it was here that for the first time the outline of themes that were subsequently developed in European social psychology, like social categorization and social representation, were already on display. Researchers from different countries discussed them both in plenary sessions and in informal meetings.

Unsurprisingly, the participants at first had difficulty in understanding one another, either because their research traditions were different or because every researcher tried to defend the ethos of their own national laboratory. Let us not forget that the majority of Europeans had no experience of this kind of conference. It was to be expected that early contact was made in an atmosphere of embarrassment and nervousness. After all, the work of every participant who delivered a paper was not only discussed but also judged. This apprehensive climate was intensified by the relationship between Europeans and Americans. It was state-of-the-art social psychology in Europe that the Americans were evaluating and, although this was unpleasant, everybody was aware of it.

If one reads correctly the documents about the conference at Sorrento, its organizer, Lanzetta took a favourable view of the quality of research and discussion across the different presentations and panels. In contrast, in his report to the SSRC, Staff Officer Willerman[3] observed that the papers were of an uneven quality, some much too packed with data and others with rhetoric. It seems to us that both commentators were right. The same observation could be made about any conference today with justification. Lanzetta was aware that, in the relatively uncertain conditions of researchers and laboratories, one could not expect miracles. Willerman was aware that, despite his criticism, 'enough of the papers and most of the discussions were of such high scientific caliber that the participants' exposure to them may have had the important effect of introducing them to models of high quality research and to fruitful ways of thinking.'[4] This diagnosis applied equally to informal meetings. The participants had not previously had much experience of such gatherings and were discovering their virtues. Here they could expand on issues that no one had the courage to confront during formal sessions. It was easier to clarify ideas on the terrace or in the hotel bedroom with three or four interested colleagues of different nationalities. Questions posed during informal sessions allowed people to lose their inhibitions and spell out basic principles, querying the direction of work and suggesting how research should proceed. For example, could experimental methods be profitably integrated into research? Some judged this inevitable, others unacceptable. The argument, according to which experimental method made social psychology more respectable in the eyes of other psychologists, was not convincing. Instead, it was the intrinsic fertility of the experiment and its theoretical justification that counted. Yet it was the latter that the majority doubted. They were faced here with a real problem: experimental social psychology was isolated even within the field itself.

Informal communication sessions entertained a great deal of enthusiasm and warmth. If there was not enough discussion about group dynamics in the participants' papers, there was a lot of it in their interactions. As a result, the beginnings of small 'transnational' groups started crystallizing their personal and intellectual affinities. This was a visible evolution which was why Willerman could write in his report: 'It was interesting to note the change in composition of groups during the formal and informal sessions, and at mealtimes, from homogeneity of nationality early in the conference to maximum internationality during the last half.'[5]

It was of no real importance to the participants that this conference was organized by the ONR. The fear that it would provoke an unfavourable response, which had worried the organizers, was no longer there, given the charm and enthusiasm of the meeting to which all participants were susceptible. What they might feel the next day, once they returned home, was a different matter. But they could always remind themselves of Sorrento, of the people whom they had met and of the events they had experienced in magic and colourful style.

After Sorrento

In trying to grasp a historical event, in this case what happened in Sorrento, one would normally search for a founding institution or association, or even a set of events that could be seen as the date of its inception. One does not usually consider the possibility that answers turned up may be no more than a myth established by the founding group which has little to do with historical reality. Whether one likes it or not, the future of an institution or an association, as a result of the actions of an individual or a group, is a consequence of events that can rarely be predicted at the outset or later. Neither can one predict the implications. The same is true if we examine events that took place after the Sorrento conference. Archival evidence shows that the majority of participants believed that this first conference would be followed by another conference, that its planning group would take on that role again and would have the freedom to do that.

For Lanzetta the situation was relatively clear. Given the universally acknowledged success of the Sorrento conference, he proposed, as anticipated, organizing a second conference: Sorrento II.

There were of course questions to settle. Should the same participants be invited? Lanzetta's planning group believed it was quite reasonable to propose that the participants in the second conference should be those from the first one. However, he did not want to give the impression that the conference was reserved for an exclusive group. He therefore suggested that younger and more active researchers should also be invited. This proposal expanded the list to 45–50 participants. 'The SSRC however took an opposite stand recommending that[6] any decision concerning a second conference with ONR funds be indefinitely postponed . . . that the Sorrento planning group be enabled to meet as requested, but that no further meeting be authorized until after review of a proposal from the new committee on desirable next steps.' At first glance it appears that the need to establish the Transnational Committee, chaired by Festinger, acquired a peculiar urgency. And from the same documents it seems quite clear that Willerman, who had attended the meeting of the Sorrento I planning group, would not agree to Sorrento II. Willerman

> strongly urged the planning group that instead of increasing the number of participants to 45 or 50, as was proposed, the number should be held to 25, as at the first conference, by inviting only persons actively engaged in research. It was noted that the proposed title of the conference gave the impression of a convention, and the SSRC urged the Planning Committee to rephrase the subject of the conference. The Planning Committee was also advised to extend the participation geographically by including qualified social psychologists from Greece, Turkey, and the Middle East, if they could be found and perhaps to invite two or three Americans.[7]

It was further demanded that these changes should be made on the basis of administrative decision and not by increasing the number of participants. The insistence on expanding the geographical boundaries was not unreasonable. However, it was unrealistic to expect to achieve this in the time available before the second conference, especially given that Lanzetta's project was focused on Europe. Thus it was not for the first or last time that the question 'Europe or not Europe?' was posed.

As far as we know, and according to Tajfel's[8] testimony, 'after considerable discussion and consultation with the SSRC', the planning committee yielded and modified the formula and composition of the invitees. Following the advice given, the planning group agreed that:

> the criterion for extending invitations was active work in experimental social psychological research . . . the desirability of including some persons who were younger . . . and . . . some attention to geographical representation. . . . 26 persons will be invited of whom 13 were not participants in the 1963 Sorrento conference. Nine persons, including 6 Europeans and 3 Americans, who participated in the Sorrento Conference, will not be invited.[9]

The desire to reach an agreement with the SSRC prevailed and harmony triumphed over the risk of dissent. This compromise was particularly important at a moment when the Transnational Committee was in the making.

The Second Conference

The planning of the second conference was therefore more delicate and took longer. However, once the problem of participation was solved, invitations were sent out, announcing that the conference would take place in Frascati, near Rome, 11–15 December 1964.[10]

No praise is sufficient for the small town of Castelli Romani. Struck by dreadful air attacks during 1943 and 1944, the town rose from its ruins after the war and the houses of the aristocracy recovered their glory. The conference took place in the magnificent sixteenth-century Villa Falconieri which was the property of the Italian government. In addition to the British, French and Dutch 'veterans', the list of social psychology participants included Germans, Israelis, Italians, one Belgian and one Lebanese.[11] Apart from the representatives of the Transnational Committee and the ONR, there was only one American invited, who was in Europe on sabbatical leave. Europe was therefore represented better from a geographical point of view than from the point of view of social psychology.

In retrospect, we can say that the conference in Sorrento had been about the past and the distant future, and the philosophy of experimental social psychology. By contrast, the Frascati Conference was more about the contemporary state of affairs and the 'here-and-now' of the field. The presence of 'veterans' facilitated contacts with newcomers. It was easier to reach consensus about factual issues. It allowed the participants to familiarize themselves with existing research on cognitive dissonance in Europe through the papers by Nuttin and Irle. Equally, interest in the study of processes of influence was apparent in the presentation by de Montmollin or in the studies on eye contact by Argyle. Group dynamics also stimulated some research. This included Duflos' work on groups, Schild's research on leadership styles and

Lambert's work on group decision making. The reported research on practical and social problems was very lively. The papers by Himmelweit on 'Social Facilitations of Delinquent Behaviour', by Israel on 'Film Leadership and Audience Reactions', by Iacono on 'Attitude Change in Industrial Groups' and by Spaltao on 'Analysis of Risk-taking Behaviour' all showed specific perspectives and methods used in the study of social problems. Methodological concerns also attracted attention. Diab presented 'Some Limitations of Existing Scales in the Measurement of Social Attitudes', Foa treated 'Hypotheses on Cultural and Environmental Influences on the Development of Interpersonal Behaviours' and Schönbach spoke on 'Language Effects on Attitudes: the Specificity of a Phenomenon'.[12]

On the whole, these papers exemplified normal science in a Kuhnian sense, facilitating exchanges between Europeans and non-Europeans. After each session, the participants discussed with the author some possible grounds for collaboration and acquainted themselves with research in the author's country. They were surprised to discover the existence of social psychology in Germany, Italy and Lebanon. Optimism filled the air as participants from different countries initiated new and long-lasting relations. It is important to remember that these relationships were particularly welcomed by Germans who had remained relatively isolated since the end of the war.

Without attributing too much weight to various subtle exchanges, we can say in passing that the organizers had intended to reduce the 'metaphysical' and 'epistemological' aspects of social psychology. If it was present at Sorrento, it was because it was tolerated as a European foible. But as they say 'You can drive out nature with a pitchfork, but she just keeps coming back.' Although this 'metaphysical' aspect was not present at formal sessions, it nevertheless dominated informal small-group discussions which took place late into the night. The threads of interrupted conversations came back after Sorrento to be woven into new material. New themes that had been absent from the first conference were introduced, in particular, whether social psychology was an experimental science. More precisely, was the only way that social psychology could become a science for it to become experimental? It is impossible to give a detailed account of all these debates. To conclude, let us simply say that in the small hours of the night ideas were crystallized that later proved essential to the creation of the European Association of Experimental Social Psychology (EAESP).

What Next?

Nothing illustrates better the difference between Sorrento and Frascati than the manner in which they each ended. In general, the participants did not have any clear idea about the administrative background to these two conferences, the planning group, and so on. They might well have imagined that it was an ONR project because Lanzetta and Petrullo were there. And despite their generosity and the evident interest in European social psychology which these two Americans expressed, the participants did not attempt to guess their long-term intentions. In any case, rumours started to circulate among participants as to what might happen next. Only the British and the Dutch – who seemed to have had more contact with each other and with the Americans – seemed to understand the situation. Nevertheless, the participants were surprised to learn from these rumours that there would not be another conference after Frascati. It was not that they had expected to be invited to a third one but a pattern had started to emerge. When one receives a gift on two occasions, one wants an explanation as to why a gift is not offered a third time.

Hence, during the last session of the Frascati conference, participants raised the question that was on everyone's mind: what next? That this question was posed at all signalled the hope of a common future, of doing something together. The 'what-and-how' should be done was unclear that evening. It seemed like a manifestation of the general will in Rousseau's sense. At such exceptional moments, everybody wants to partake in the general excitement and to declare publicly their commitment to the idea or to the group.

For everyone that evening that had the privilege of taking part in the collective brainstorm, there remained an image of a packed room and a tense group. One sensed the wish of the majority to develop the relations established in Sorrento and Frascati without really knowing how they had come about. There were many ideas put forward for the future, differently inspired, and they were admirably defended. In his report Tajfel enumerated[13] these suggestions: 'training institutes, exchange visits, a clearing house of information about research, a form of organization for continuity' and so on. But he was also cautious to warn against the impression of unanimity that one might retrospectively assume: 'With regard to some points of discussions previously enumerated, it is a little risky to attempt a summary which may give an impression of a consensus in which many divergent views need to be represented.'[14]

These preliminaries by no means exhausted the particular interests of the group. But they had gone far enough for the immediate purpose. And as is usual in these kinds of meetings, it was proposed to elect a committee with no specific task to which the general will would be entrusted. There were no candidates for election: the participants voted only by indicating a preference for a person to become a committee member. It was quite late in the evening and was a very quick procedure. The elected members were Gustav Jahoda, Serge Moscovici, Mauk Mulder, Jozef Nuttin and Henri Tajfel. Needless to say, all events can be viewed and judged from divergent perspectives and this election was no exception. But the result of the ballot came as a surprise to some of those who were elected and a disappointment for others who were not and who judged themselves, quite rightly, as more representative of their countries and of contributing to the success of the two conferences. The composition of the committee was astonishing and looked at first sight like a Rorschach test. If the group had wanted to assure its continuity and realize plans made during the assembly, it should have voted for university heavyweights like Hilde Himmelweit, Robert Pagès and Martin Irle. Instead, it voted for university lightweights of the time, such as Jahoda, Moscovici and Tajfel. Obviously, several conclusions were drawn. Some participants wondered whether the vote signified a compromise between experimentalists and non-experimentalists. Moreover, there was a further and more delicate point of representation. Let us acknowledge candidly that in academia and in scientific milieus, nationality does count. Recent immigrants are hardly ever considered representative of the country in which they now live and work. It is not a question of discrimination but of symbolism. If we look at the list of elected persons, we see that the committee was a transnational one *de facto*, since it comprised, with Jahoda, Moscovici and Tajfel, a majority of recent immigrants to their respective countries. Would one bet on this committee of 'mavericks' becoming overnight an efficient committee to organize the building of European social psychology?

Yet once the vote was cast, everyone was relieved. The danger of being separated was over. Everybody promised to keep in touch, to do what they could so that the group could continue. Tajfel wrote in his report that the general feeling was that one could conclude on a note of cautious optimism. But who could say, that evening in Frascati, whether all those discussions, elections and plans would end 'with a bang or with a whimper'?

4

The Transnational Committee: from New York to Rome

Welcome on Board

The members of the Transnational Committee – a committee about which so little is known – belonged to the same generation and shared many experiences. The war had finished a while earlier but people still felt its repercussions. Many participants at the Sorrento and Frascati conferences had experienced war's devastation, exile, military service, the terror of fascism or prison camps. Those experiences had moulded their personalities and their lives. What brought them closer together and allowed them more immediately to understand one another were their common histories and field of study. There were many more things they shared to which they attached importance than there were things that divided one from another. One can say of them what was once said about Lewin's students: they were hard-headed idealists. In order to understand what happened at those two conferences and in their aftermath, we need to consider some characteristics of that epoch, as well as the thoughts of individuals who played an effective role in that unique enterprise: building a science. Without such an understanding, we would be left with only a superficial idea of the history of our discipline, implying perhaps that it had been shaped solely by institutional forces.

The Frascati conference finished and Moscovici, like others, was packing his bags to go home. But something else happened. Moscovici (1999) describes his first encounter with the Transnational Committee as follows. After the conference in Frascati, he found himself being transported by Petrullo, quite unexpectedly and without explanation, to the Hotel de la Ville in Rome, at the top of the Spanish Steps. To his great surprise, Lanzetta introduced him to another two Americans, Festinger and Schachter, neither of whom Moscovici recalled seeing at Frascati although their names appeared on the list of participants. He knew of them but he had not met either previously. In fact, at that time he knew very few social psychologists. Anyway, in the luxurious hotel lobby that day, Festinger came up to him and, having paid him a compliment, started a conversation. They were stuck with a thorny problem. Among the Americans who were hoping to promote the development of social psychology in Europe and worldwide, two leading factions were emerging. One party favoured comparative studies, based on the replication of those designed in the USA. These studies enabled both the teaching of young students and the generalization of the theories in question. The other party, however, was looking for creative researchers; it supported work in existing laboratories and was attempting to raise standards. Festinger and Schachter spoke among other things about the 'seven countries' experiment and about comparative studies in cognitive dissonance.

Those who observe others playing cards often allow themselves to be drawn into play. Moscovici let himself take part in the game by explaining why he did not see any advantage to the first option and explaining why he thought the second alternative might attract young researchers seeking something new to social psychology. Perhaps it was Moscovici's use of numerous arguments from the philosophy of science that evoked a *cri de coeur* from Schachter: 'too French!' For many years Moscovici was convinced that this discussion was just a kind of social diversion until he saw from the minutes of the SSRC[1] that such questions were being asked at that time about the role of the Transnational Committee. For example, was it the intention to foster comparative research, in which scholarly experience and data from several cultures would be brought together? Was it primarily to bring social psychological research in Europe and elsewhere more into line with standards in the USA? Alternatively, was it 'that the committee be . . . concerned with raising the level of research and the quality of personnel in other countries so that good research there would ultimately benefit the development of theory in this country [the USA] as well'?[2]

But recalling these questions is to make a virtue of necessity because it is acknowledged that in well-established science imitation or 'following the crowd' is a good formula. However, a marginal science *in statu nascenti*, as social psychology was, only receives attention for its creative research.

So although in appearance this was no more than a casual conversation, Moscovici had the impression he was being tested when asked 'What are you doing these days?' He spoke of his experiments on language (Moscovici, 1967). This started another round of questions and answers about research and language. This topic did not enjoy much favour among social psychologists. Finally, Festinger got irritated. With a vehement gesture, he took out a pen from his pocket and challenged Moscovici: 'Do you want to make me believe that it is not the same thing if I show you a pen as if I say: "here is a pen"?'

It was an improvised rite of passage. Festinger and Lanzetta explained that they were to hold a meeting of the Transnational Committee. Moscovici had been a member for several months. He did not question this. Yet he had been nominated to the Transnational Committee without having been consulted, just like Rommetveit,[3] for whom the news of his membership equally came as a revelation. However, with hindsight, this was not at all surprising, given the conditions under which the Transnational Committee was taking shape. But so much for the first impressions of a new member.

The First Meeting Outside the USA

Whatever the ways in which the SSRC conducted its business, for the Transnational Committee the moment had come to find its own way, to live in the real world. Perhaps because its original members had wondered for several years whether the Transnational Committee would ever come about, there was a sense of relief when they met in Rome. There were a handful of participants: Ancona, Festinger, Koekebakker, Lanzetta, Moscovici and Schachter. Willerman was present as Staff Officer and Petrullo as observer.[4]

The first item on the agenda was unexpected, at least for the newcomer. Originally, many people shared Lanzetta's concern about the lack of communication and contact between social psychologists in Europe. Therefore, it seemed that the task of the conferences in Sorrento and Frascati was to create a European network, combining researchers from different countries, much in the way of the American melting-pot. Nonetheless, once the meeting in Rome had begun, it was apparent that there were already many contacts between European social psychologists. In fact, there were two associations with which the Transnational Committee had already established ongoing relations.

First, there was the European Board, the members of which were Novak (Poland), Jezernik (Yugoslavia), Iacono (Italy), Ardoino (France), Tajfel (England), Thorsrud (Norway), Hutte and Koekebakker (Holland) and Irle (Germany).[5] This group intended to plan and organize summer training institutes in 1965 and 1966. Festinger was at the International Congress for Applied Psychology in 1964 in Ljubljana.[6] He met representatives of the European Board, learned about their projects and we suppose that he encouraged them in their efforts. And second, there was the European Foundation for Summer Schools, which had been set up in England in 1964 by Marie Jahoda, Emery and Tajfel.

To be sure, these two associations were not highly developed but the nature of their projects, the quality of their membership and even their financial resources in the early 1960s gave them a headstart in planning their activities.

Then there was a third group, the Provisional Committee elected in Frascati. One might expect that the conference in Frascati that had just finished and absorbed so much energy would form an important part of the agenda. However, minutes from Rome indicate nothing of the sort. The first item on the agenda was concerned with the European summer training institutes. Moscovici, who was present at the first meeting of the Transnational Committee, did not know what the rules were or how it worked. When he became aware of the existence of the three 'entities', he was left with the problem of puzzling out how to raise the question of their role before any major decisions were taken. In the political arena, with which he was more familiar, it would not have been a problem. But here he had to be neutral and, moreover, in a committee that was still provisional, he had no mandate to speak for others whom he scarcely knew. On the other hand, the question of 'this third group' had to be tackled vigorously as part of the first item on the agenda. And so, as a member of the Transnational Committee, he expressed his surprise at his discovery of the existing European committees and indicated that he had a responsibility towards those who had elected him in Frascati. This started a very lively discussion about these groups and the European situation, which, until then, had not been taken into account. Some members of the Transnational Committee had long-standing connections with British and Dutch social psychologists. Others expressed their uncertainty as to what the Frascati elections meant; and what the chances were that this 'elected group',[7] as they called it, could achieve something. Finally, a compromise was proposed. This allowed for the combination of commitments, vis-à-vis the European Board and the Foundation for European Summer Schools, with the lurking existence of the Provisional Committee, which after all represented most European social psychologists. It was recommended to start with that the programme of two training institutes be launched in 1965 and 1966. And it was agreed that 'Moscovici and Schachter would be added' to the planning committee for the European Foundation for Summer Schools.[8] The compromise concerning the Provisional Committee was an 'iffy' one. One reads that

> The Committee agreed to urge this group to concern itself also with possible future summer training institutes. Should this 'elected group' become actively functional, the Committee would strongly recommend that the previously mentioned European Board yield to this elected group. It was agreed that the group elected at the Frascati Conference should be encouraged. While it was expected that this group would become self-supporting in due course, the Committee *recommended* that the SSRC provide funds for the initial costs of organization and travel of this group.[9]

One needs to read the P&P minutes to get an idea of the fictive character of this compromise, the lack of clarity of the situation and the Gordian knot created by the Frascati election:

76   *The West European Experiment*

It was not known which group would be developing in these plans, the self-constituted European Board, whose members were largely unknown to the P&P, the 1965 planning group as augmented by the committee's recommendation, or the group elected by the Frascati conference participants, and the political problems presented by this situation were recognized. Provision of the suggested funds to aid organization of the third group might help to avert or resolve some of these problems, since if this group becomes 'functional', relinquishment of planning responsibility by the self-constituted board would be encouraged.[10]

All this is past; it is history. But these extracts represent the initial compromise allowing the Gordian knot to be cut so that the EAESP could be born. There was nothing here to object to, either by those who doubted or those who believed in what they were creating. The essential point was that the 'elected group' got the help it needed to begin its task.

The Trouble with the Rest of the World: Armchair Speculations

The second point on the agenda of the Transnational Committee meeting in Rome concerned the two conferences, Sorrento and Frascati. The Committee reviewed the course of events and, of course, everybody agreed that the conferences had been successful in bringing European social psychologists together. Subsequently, it was decided not to sponsor any more such conferences in Europe.

The third point on the agenda concerned the possibility of expanding the field of action outside Europe and reaching the rest of the world. Was there any specific ground for this plan of action or was it no more than a fascinating proposition by the Transnational Committee? The Committee reviewed the situation in different countries in the Near East, Asia and Latin America. This review also covered the question of finding European colleagues who could establish contacts in other parts of the world through correspondence or other means and identify students from remote communities studying in the USA or Europe. Should these explorations be successful, then a conference could be organized involving those individuals.

Of all these proposals, Tajfel's letter to Festinger was the most concrete, investigating the Air Force Office of Scientific Research for its potential for 'social psychological research concerned with new and developing countries'.[11] The Committee favoured the project and agreed 'to explore the possibility of SSRC's cooperation'.[12]

Ironically, however, now that the Committee had started its practical work, some of its members began to wonder whether this 'hit-and-run' strategy was really advisable. How realistic was it for this small committee to extend its international wings in unknown territory? Why should one expect that social psychology was universally known? Why should one imagine that one could find social psychologists in Southern Asia or Latin America when they were so scarce in Italy or France? Further problems were considered relating to 'developing experimental psychology in various countries'. It was thought that the main difficulty was related 'to the lack of clear identity of social psychology as a field'. It was considered whether 'creating an international organization and having international congresses of social psychology would promote such identity and help development of the field'. And to set the wheels in motion, 'Moscovici and Lanzetta were appointed a subcommittee to investigate and think through the pros and cons'[13] directed towards the creation of an international organization of social psychology. And this subject would 'be on the agenda of the committee's next meeting'.

A Brief Conversation Before Leaving Rome

The meeting in Rome was coming to an end. Reflecting on what had happened there and at Frascati, Moscovici felt uncertain about the implications of these events for his own situation when he returned to Paris. Moreover, being the only member of the Transnational Committee who was also an elected member of the Frascati provisional committee, what should he say to other members if they chanced to meet? Time passed and he could not get to grips with the subject matter with which he was intensely preoccupied. It must have also worried other Europeans to whom the Frascati meeting sent mixed signals. Moscovici thought that only Festinger could bring some clarity to the matter. It seemed to him that there was one last move he could make. He decided to risk telling Festinger about his concerns. Taking advantage of a private conversation in the lobby of the hotel, Moscovici revealed to him his impression: The Transnational Committee was like Buridan's ass, hesitating between the three European committees and not knowing which of them to choose. It was difficult to understand how the Frascati group could become functional. Anyway, who would decide whether it was functional or not? This was similar to the question often asked about foreigners: who is to decide whether they have been assimilated by their new country or not?

At first this conversation was arduous. Festinger's reputation for toughness was not without grounds. He listened with the focused attention that was so characteristic of him and so difficult to describe. And so he learned that it was desirable to alter the assumptions dominating the debate that assumed that Europeans were isolated. For example, the French were not isolated because there were networks in France which brought together competent and institutionally powerful people. Moscovici spoke about another assumption that the Committee seemed to embrace. It considered its main goal to be the dissemination of social psychological knowledge throughout the world and the provision of better training. Training institutes and teaching were the leitmotif of the Rome meeting. It was as if the main question, at least in Europe, was whether or not there was enough training. Training in what and why? Was it to produce good specialists and professors? If the main objective of the Frascati group was adult education, then there was not much prospect for the future of social psychology.

It was quite clear that Festinger would react strongly to such criticism. It was also certain that training institutes were not his cup of tea either. Otherwise, he would have told Moscovici quickly what he thought and the dialogue would have come to an end. Instead, he expressed curiosity and asked Moscovici what he was driving at? Moscovici responded that if the Frascati group and even the Transnational Committee were to fulfil their real mission, they would have to shift their focus of attention from the diffusion of knowledge to the advancement of knowledge, that is, from training to research. It was a priority to enable social psychologists to cooperate but not in order merely to resolve problems of isolation, but to create a critical mass of research. It was to be hoped that in that way a few new productive individuals or groups could be found and encouraged in their research, and that a genuine contribution to European social psychology could be made.

This of course was a leitmotif for Moscovici then and later. We can look here at Tajfel's (1972, p. 315) presidential report, delivered at the plenary conference of the EAESP in Louvain 1972, saying that '[w]hen Moscovici presented his presidential report in Louvain in 1969, he insisted that our undertaking will have to be judged, in the long term, on the criteria of its intellectual creativity. I entirely agree with this view.' Festinger also agreed at that point and asked that Moscovici explain himself more fully. Moscovici answered that the only issue that appeared to him to be exciting was the concept of international social psychology.

There is an observation to be made from the point of view of the history of science. In the beginning, a science attempts to become international by borrowing ideas, by replicating the results of others, and by diffusion and comparison. However, science becomes truly international when it acquires the capacity to form a number of research groups which compete and communicate with each other. In other words, it turns international when research becomes, so to speak, multi-centred. This was the case with mechanics in the seventeenth century in Italy, France and England as well as with quantum physics in the twentieth century in Germany, Denmark, France, England and central Europe. Each centre had its style, its themes and also its method of progress. And this, too, was the case with psychology during its great epochs. Therefore, it would be unreasonable to believe that social psychology would be an exception. It would become international by creating centres with their own specialisms, adapted to their tradition and their milieus.

That reference to the history of science triggered a long chain of questions and answers. And it seemed that what Festinger expected the Frascati group to do was above all to provide the proof, a symbolic gesture that the Europeans would involve themselves and would maintain cooperation with the Transnational

Committee. Moscovici promised that this was possible and Festinger assured him concrete support, at least at the beginning. And they agreed to meet in Paris in order to inaugurate *la belle époque* of social psychology. On leaving Rome, everything appeared to be in place and there was reason to be satisfied: the sympathy, help and cooperation of Festinger. History is always richer and more surprising than any effort to reconstruct it imagines.

5

The European Map of Social Psychology in the Mid-1960s

A Traveller's Account

While one might imagine John Lanzetta as someone like Graham Greene's eponymous hero in *The Quiet American*, full of naive realism, his perceptions of European social psychology, just like those of Ben Willerman, were profound and largely correct. He considered social psychology from the point of view of an actor, and more specifically, of a policy maker. The question was not 'What is it?' but 'What to do?' with the map of Europe.

Fortunately, we also have a map drawn by an observer and traveller in the person of Harold Leavitt. Leavitt is not only well known for his studies on small groups, but also as a Professor at Stanford Business School and an international expert in applied social psychology and education. Leavitt's account, we shall see, is relevant to the continuation of our story of European social psychology.

In the spring of 1965, Leavitt undertook a trip to Europe to collect information for the Ford Foundation about the application of social psychology in organizations and management. This was a sign that Ford was taking a new look at Europe and, more specifically, that it had become interested in establishing relations with management and business schools. This was Leavitt's second visit to Europe. He had made a similar trip ten years earlier as a training consultant in human relations for the European Productivity Agency (Leavitt, 1957). Now, during his second trip in 1965,

Leavitt re-evaluated the European situation. He reserved a specific part of his report for the UK and France.

Leavitt's account emphasized the many positive developments which he observed in applied social psychology. He carefully described the role of the Tavistock Institute in London which, after the Second World War, became famous all over Europe. This was due to several fields of specialization in which the Institute had become engaged, like the group selection of officers, new forms of the theory revolving around groups and organizations and civil resettlement, which was designed to facilitate transition between citizens' wartime experience and civilian life (Sofer, 1972), among other things. The Tavistock Institute not only inventively synthesized Lewinian group dynamics and industrial psychology but was also concerned with applications of psychoanalytical theories. We may recall the work of individuals like Emery, Jaques, Bion, Sofer and Trist (e.g., Trist et al., 1963) among others who were associated with the Tavistock Institute. The Institute also consulted and ran training groups. Leavitt noted the very positive impact of the Tavistock Institute on many European countries like Denmark, Norway and Sweden. He also briefly described the work of the Imperial College in London and the London Business School and referred to research at the universities of Leeds, Manchester, Edinburgh and Liverpool.

Having visited numerous institutes and universities, Leavitt nevertheless concluded that, in general, social psychology in the UK appeared to be rather weak. Although the Tavistock Institute was scientifically stronger and livelier than other places, it too, according to Leavitt, required more discipline. He argued that the major movers in applied social research were those institutes that were not affiliated to universities.

In addition to the Tavistock Institute, he spoke highly of other remarkable places in Europe: the Institute for Social Research in Oslo, the Institute of Preventive Medicine in Leyden and the Institute for Personnel Research in Stockholm. Leavitt was quite astonished to find that social sciences at European universities generally played 'a surprisingly small and sometimes downright impeding part in the development of modern work'.[1]

Leavitt then turned to France, which meant Paris, where practically all social psychology was concentrated. He did not find the

situation any better here than elsewhere. He noticed few substantial changes since his last visit ten years earlier. However, he
described the new Business School in Fontainebleau and similar
establishments in France in more flattering terms. He evoked his
meeting with Max Pagès, one of the most original specialists in
training groups whose work he appreciated.

'One Important Break in the French Academic Scene'

Let us remember that Leavitt's account was written for officers
of Ford when the Foundation was undergoing change. During the
years 1965–6, American policy shifted: Rockefeller was with-
drawing from its financial commitments in Europe while Ford
was creating a special branch in Europe in the field of higher
education.

In retrospect, however, what seems striking is that Leavitt
devoted some lines to what he called 'one important break in the
French academic scene'. What made this event interesting in
the year of Leavitt's visit was that in carrying out post-war reconstruction in France, the state encouraged the creation of new
establishments at the periphery, or outside, the existing educational system of traditional universities. These new establishments
did not follow the same rules for the recruitment of professors
and researchers that applied to universities. It is no exaggeration
to say that everything that was forbidden at universities was permitted in great establishments like the very old Collège de France
or the new Centre National de la Recherche Scientifique. At this
point, Leavitt's general comment about the major movers in social
science at institutes not affiliated to universities was perceptive. It
applied equally to France as it did to other European locations.

More generally, 'one important break in the French academic
scene' according to Leavitt's report included the rejuvenation
of the Sixth Section of the École Pratique des Hautes Etudes
(EPHE). This had been in place since 1947. This revival was
facilitated by returning social scientists, like Fernand Braudel who
had survived the prison camps, or who, like Koyré, Lévi-Strauss
or Gurvitch, came back from New York where they had been
teaching during the war. The core of the Sixth Section consisted

of historians belonging mostly to the École des Annales of which the medievalist Marc Bloch, shot by the Gestapo, was an emblematic figure. Their goal was to establish a faculty of social sciences in Paris. And since 1956, Braudel, with the authority of a great historian who inspired young historians everywhere (Hobsbawn, 2000, p. 294), was also able to attract other social scientists, inviting them to this new intellectual milieu. Thus he could write in a preliminary report that 'In the new domain of social sciences, we still have the advantage of presenting the best ensemble of scientists and institutions in Europe' (cited by Gemelli, 1995, p. 292). He surrounded himself on the board of the school with scholars like Aron, Friedman, Le Bras and Lévi-Strauss, who contributed to the Sixth Section both their reputation and scientific rigour. And although the Sixth Section was of modest size, its laboratories attracted a large international audience, were active and produced internationally interesting scientific work. Again Hobsbawn writes: 'From about 1960, I was increasingly drawn into the Parisian academic life, and especially towards the new academic empire of Fernand Braudel' (Hobsbawn, 2000, p. 331). The novelty and the institutional vista of the EPHE had a special affinity with the Graduate Faculty of the New School for Social Research in New York and with the London School of Economics and Political Science in London.

To be sure, to foster international relations is a difficult and exhausting task. It was mainly Clemens Heller who took on this tough assignment. He was an American of Austrian origin and someone who 'may be best described as the most original intellectual impresario of post-war Europe' (Hobsbawn, 2000, p. 331). He was a sort of administrative genius who not only invented and grasped new ideas with incredible speed but who knew how to realize them. Heller deserves special recognition in the history of European social psychology for helping it to accomplish its activities, whether it was at the Royaumont Conference, the establishment of the *European Journal of Experimental Social Psychology* or the European Laboratory of Social Psychology in the Maison des Sciences de l'Homme (MSH).

Writing about 'one important break in the French academic scene', Leavitt also referred in this context to the election of

Moscovici to the Sixth Section of the EPHE. Moscovici worked closely with Faucheux and they hoped, Leavitt notes, 'to develop an active research and training program'.[2] It was in 1964, between the Sorrento and Frascati conferences, that the EPHE decided to take a gamble on a new discipline: social psychology. Moscovici was elected as the Director of Studies, which carried the title of professor. He was put in charge of creating a new laboratory and establishing international scientific connections. His programme included a seminar for doctoral students and researchers. In the EPHE, each Director of Studies was independent and could shape his field as he saw fit, providing that he was successful. That impressed Leavitt and was what inspired his confidence that this appointment would open a window of opportunity for research of interest to his American colleagues.

When Moscovici returned from Rome, he was, to some extent, anxious. Since he had been an immigrant in France, he had been abroad only once as a Fellow of the Institute of Advanced Studies in Princeton and did not participate in the life of academic institutions. This was not only because he was a refugee but because his job as a researcher in the Pagès laboratory had no such official duties. The only social psychologists he knew at the time were those from the Latin Quarter. Moscovici of course was familiar with Italy, Germany, Austria and Hungary, but he had been in these countries at a younger age – and in camps (Moscovici, 1997). Now he was charged with opening a new forum for social psychology at the EPHE where he had eminent colleagues. This task inherently implied competition with the Sorbonne. Clearly, it required a total investment of energy. This is why his election to the Provisional Committee appeared to be a daunting task, demanding a great deal of perseverance to grasp its nature and meaning. Yet at the same time it was tempting to develop relations with social psychologists in other countries and to contribute something worthwhile to the science to which Moscovici had decided to devote his life. Soon there was to be the first meeting of the Provisional Committee in Louvain. As preparation and to help organize his ideas, Moscovici wrote a 'memorandum' which, if need be, he could present to colleagues. It included the following points:

1. Social psychology represented a follow-up of intellectual movements such as folk psychology, mass psychology, collective psychology, the psychology of public opinion, group psychology, that is, fields defined around a common object, for example, the economy around the market or child psychology around the child.

2. Social psychology presented, at the same time, a societal point of view similar to economics or history, and this is why it had not been accepted as a specialism of either psychology or sociology. It should hence occupy a specific niche in the university system. Its present marginality was a major obstacle to its development.

3. The participants at Sorrento and Frascati were a mixed-generation group which included both older, established researchers and very young ones. Hence the Association must also be generationally diverse.

4. The Association should not be a 'learned' society recruiting and reuniting its members from time to time because it would not necessarily foster research. The desire to create an Association that would above all promote research in a voluntarily created scientific community had already been proposed at the Frascati and Sorrento conferences. Unfortunately, unlike sociologists or anthropologists, social psychologists could not rely on an existing tradition of such a scientific community and they had to create it.

5. In order to make the Association durable and lively, appropriate changes had to be made so its conduct was not 'maverick' or deviant, but active and relevant. Hence attention had to be paid to the membership of the Association, its size and distinctive quality. One might imagine it as a 'mobile think-tank' in which collaborating researchers would shape European social psychology. Group meetings, exchange units and similar activities could all be organized within such a framework.

One might expect that every member of the Provisional Committee would be raising similar issues in preparing their imaginary proposals. Moscovici was the only member of the Transnational Committee and he knew that a good programme was not sufficient to bring about the desired outcomes. That would only prove that the 'elected group' functioned but not that it was functional. What was needed was to give a concrete indication of 'what next'. If left to its own devices, unlit by the spotlight of distinct purpose, the community would not survive. The participants of Sorrento and Frascati certainly -expected token activity. If the answer to the question 'what next?' was not forthcoming, all that would be left would be good memories. Moreover, the Americans needed proof that the European group had made progress. Such proof was necessary not only for morale but also to encourage the SSRC. One might imagine that the only proof of success of the first two conferences would be the scheduling of a third conference. As there was not much time to consult each member of the Provisional Committee, it was necessary to act at once. So Moscovici made an exceptional request to the administration of the EPHE which authorized him to discuss with Heller the prospects for such a conference. Although no one could promise it at the time, the discussion had one main outcome: the choice of the Abbaye de Royaumont as the location for any such conference. It was not so much a choice but the only location worthy of such a historical conference. For that era and that generation, it was an eloquent symbol.

All these events make it clear that if we are to understand why the conference of the European Association took place in 1966 in Royaumont, how the 'elected group' became functional so quickly and how the laboratories in Bristol and Paris could be created only a few years later, it is necessary to turn to the EPHE and to Ford. As everybody knows, by contrast with Athena who was born fully grown from the head of Zeus, academic associations are born neither from the heads of planning committees, nor from isolated relevant institutions. Rather, they are born from actions and from funds made available by one or two interested institutions. However, institutions follow their own policies. We are not saying that without these conditions the EAESP would have never come into being. But we are not writing a hypothetical history. The fact is that, if we look at the sequence of events from close quarters, we can see that the EPHE and Ford were crucial to the founding of the EAESP.

6

The Second Milestone for European Social Psychology

A Quiet Historic Meeting

The first meeting of the Frascati Provisional Committee took place on 5–7 February 1965 in Louvain. Members were excited by the importance of the event and some were intimidated by finding themselves in one of the oldest universities in Europe. They were conscious of being surrounded by a peaceful, contemplative and private atmosphere that one hardly ever experiences in a city university. Jozef Nuttin had reserved a large, white-walled, comfortable room. Did he believe that the meeting would be a memorable one? Or was he simply concerned about hospitality and a relaxing atmosphere? He opened the meeting with manifest pleasure and an element of irony. Inevitably, the Committee had to start by skimming through the proposals made in Frascati. Tajfel who, more than anyone else, was used to such meetings and who had prepared the report on Frascati, read the list of items: 'short exchange visits, research training seminars, newsletters,' etc.[1] (Tajfel, 1965). This list was approved straight away. It was more difficult outlining a common vision for social psychologists and imagining how this vision could enrol the discipline in the scientific space. Each member occupied a specific position, carved out for them by the tradition of the country to which they belonged. In some cases, social psychology took its place next to psychology and in others next to sociology, depending on how different universities organized their social sciences. All this explains why the

Provisional Committee was aware of the necessity of coming up with something original and attractive in order to make its mark on the European scene. During that epoch, it was hard to identify a significant trend in social psychology at a European level.

But in the meantime, the task of the meeting in Louvain was down to earth. To start with, it was necessary to find the point of departure because without that it would be impossible to form the Association. It did not take long to gather what every participant had been thinking, in what way and what the reasoning was behind their thoughts. The discussion was at first passionate, if a little disorderly, but it brought about a better understanding of 'who was who'. It was obvious to all that it would not be a good idea to try and impress. As it was, Mulder spoke very little and Jahoda preferred to listen. Tajfel was a historian; he had been in touch with several groups from the moment they were established. There is a mysterious pleasure in entering a history and a group where people already know one another and this was what Moscovici enjoyed. Only Nuttin, the youngest member, had to maintain a certain distance in order to fulfil his role as host. Perhaps under the influence of the European spirit of Erasmus, who had lived in Louvain some centuries earlier, there was no disharmony among the members of the Provisional Committee and each was convinced that they had together started something really promising.

It is difficult to remember or summarize what was said during the two days of the meeting.[2] Each shared with others his opinions and expressed his position. One may see in exchanges the essential gains of these encounters. Moscovici presented the main ideas from his 'memorandum' which was in line with his discussion with Festinger in Rome.[3] He proposed that the association of social psychology should not be either a 'learned society', like the psychological societies representing the establishment, or a network of specialists, but an active collective promoting the advancement of knowledge. This was particularly important because universities lacked both laboratories and training facilities. But what was particularly urgent was to establish a strong link with the Transnational Committee to which the 'elected group' still had to show that it was 'functional'. What Moscovici suggested in order to strengthen this link was to organize, after Sorrento and Frascati, a third conference near Paris. He did not make any commitment but he was quite sure that the EPHE would help. And then, of course, each participant made other proposals. The fact was that the conference near Paris was the only one that had the backing of an institution on which they could count.

It is also part of the accomplishment of the Louvain meeting to have baptized the future scientific community 'The European Association for the Advancement of Experimental Social Psychology'. The key word 'advancement' indicated immediately its goal – to advance research. This meant of course that it could not claim to represent all the social psychologists in Europe. It made it clear that the envisaged Association would not overlap with the two existing associations, namely, the European Board and the European Foundation.

Finally, the 'elected' group chose Moscovici as President and Mulder as its General Secretary. There comes a point in the arduous task of finding direction when one finally touches base. That was what happened at the meeting in Louvain. Its pioneering and novel character provoked enthusiasm from all members. Nuttin reports:

> Within one week, stationery was distributed with the first name of the new association: *European Association for the Advancement of Experimental Social Psychology*. Le Président, Moscovici, had the privilege to also use the French stationery of the *Association Européenne pour l'Avancement de la Psychologie Sociale Expérimentale* (Nuttin, 1990, pp. 366–7).

The planning committee also expressed 'gratitude to the Transnational Committee for making a grant which insures the continuing functioning . . . for this year'.[4]

Meeting in Oxford

Tajfel organized the second meeting on 1–3 May 1965 in Oxford, aware of the impression that the university would make on others. What made this meeting easier was that the members of the Committee started to understand each other and a group spirit developed. The minutes[5] recorded some good news, like the invitations from the SSRC and the NSF in the USA to apply for a grant to support exchange visits. That was an important and symbolic gesture. There was also the promise of a grant from the Royaumont Foundation where the conference might take place.

The most important, even essential, item was the preparation of the Royaumont conference to which the meeting was devoted. We will not attempt to summarize here the discussion about the choice of participants and so on. On the other hand, the preliminary decisions concerning the programme for the conference are of historical interest. The first thing about the five invited papers was that they were all theoretical in nature. And the second point is that most of them were intended to be written by two or three authors. Such an idea has its risks but it also expressed the importance attached to future intellectual cooperation between social psychologists in Europe. The list of these papers was as follows:

Festinger will prepare a lecture on a subject in social psychology of his choosing;

There will be a joint paper by Tajfel and Moscovici on perceptual and inter-cultural aspects of conformity;

A joint paper by Mulder and Flament will focus on communication networks and group structure;

A joint paper by Jahoda and Frijda will explore methods and problems in social psychological cross-cultural studies;

The fifth paper will either be by Rommetveit on the subject of his choice or a joint paper by Lanzetta, Pruitt and Faucheux on experimental studies in conflict resolution.

Another aspect of the Oxford meeting was the discussion of the expansion of the Committee's activities in relation to different institutions. First, of course, there was the close collaboration with the Transnational Committee in preparing two training institutes. In the scientific arena, Tajfel made contact with social psychologists in Eastern Europe and attended a meeting of the ISSC in Paris devoted to problems of comparison in social sciences. Despite having incomplete records, we can see how rapidly the agenda grew. Some of these issues quickly became obsolete; as with any innovation, it is often uncanny and obscure in its consequences. There was a problem with multidisciplinary effects on similar organizations and initiatives, like the creation of a foundation for social psychology in Mannheim, to which Irle invited Tajfel.[6]

Be that as it may, the Oxford meeting brought to light a strong and unmistakable feeling that the 'elected group' had become what its members had aspired to. Even the Transnational Committee felt obliged to acknowledge its strength.

Royaumont: As One Association Ends, Another Begins

Whether or not one manages to identify a precise date matters very little. Let us remember that in February 1965, at a meeting of the Provisional Committee in Louvain, everything about the third conference was still obscure. Royaumont had been proposed as the venue for the conference but members were invited to make alternative suggestions. It was not until the meeting of the Planning Committee in Oxford that everything was clarified. The family Gouin-Lang, who owned the Abbey of Royaumont, were willing to make a grant with the assistance of the EPHE if no financial help was available from elsewhere. Two years later Jahoda and Moscovici (1967) stated the facts: 'Thus the Third European Conference of Experimental Social Psychology was organised in 1966, with the assistance of the Fondation de Royaumont pour le Progrès de Sciences de l'Homme' and of the EPHE (Sixth Section) (ibid., p. 300). For some, Paris was the place to be. It was internationally very active; one could meet there with social scientists from all over the world representing universities and foundations, as well as delegates from different countries in UNESCO. The extent to which the EPHE functioned as an open house and played its role in the international scene is hard to envisage. The British sociologist, Platt, portrays the EPHE as follows:

> The EPHE . . . was a part of the network of interrelated Parisian institutions. It had a close relationship with the Ford, a very big player in the social sciences in the USA foundation world in the 1950s and involved with the high-level interest of the period in improving USA knowledge of foreign countries through comparative and area studies also manifested in its contribution to SSRC

funding. Ford provided substantial funds toward the creation of the MSH as a centre for social-scientific research, at which the EPHE has been based. Some ISSC activities were carried out at the EPHE, under formally joint sponsorship. (Platt, 2002, p. 10)

But although the Planning Committee now had the green light, curiously, this was not the end of the matter. For some, holding the conference in a twelfth-century abbey near Paris was not an attractive idea and they expressed some reservations. As we know, the French–Anglo-Saxon asymmetry certainly existed well before the battle of Waterloo and has a good chance of outlasting the first manned landing on Mars. The Transnational Committee, which had decided at its December 1964 meeting in Rome not to organize any more conferences in Western Europe, now expressed the view that perhaps the conference should be held elsewhere in Europe. Even some months after the meeting of the Planning Committee in Oxford the Transnational Committee voted in July 1965[7] 'to explore the possibility of having the conference at the Rockefeller Foundation's villa Serbelloni in Italy. If this is possible, it is the Committee's first choice. A second choice would be at Royaumont near Paris. If this site is selected, Mr Moscovici will make the arrangements.' Therefore, the small administrative group in Paris found itself destined to wait. It decided, however, not to wait because, as Shakespeare says, 'in delay there lies no plenty'. After the Oxford meeting the Planning Committee left the hand of the chairman untied by any condition, except to succeed. The conference site could not be anywhere other than Royaumont, about 30 km north of Paris.

The twelfth-century abbey was founded by Saint Louis. Parts of the original abbey still exist such as the 'abbatial palast', the cloister, the refectory and the former kitchens. It was a well-known meeting place for the Parisian intelligentsia and it was a beautiful spot for concerts and conferences. Writers, philosophers, researchers and academics often retreated to the abbey to work in tranquillity or to enjoy a weekend in an enchanting place. And after all, who knows? Social psychologists, too, might count as intellectuals! The Planning Committee met there on 13–15 October 1965 and agreed that the medieval abbey would become the birthplace of the future EAESP.

This was at a time when the given word and written text served as a guarantee and were trusted. Clemens Heller kept the promise of the EPHE by providing a grant for the travel expenses of the thirty participants. He also made an agreement with Gilbert Gadoffre, the Director of the Centre Culturel de l'Abbaye de Royaumont, to schedule this rather exceptional conference. Furthermore, la Fondation Gouin-Lang generously offered a grant for the board and lodging of participants. Last but not least, one could count on the experience and fine organizational skills of Denise Jodelet from the new laboratory of social psychology in Paris being used to advantage in preparation for the conference.

The Royaumont Conference took place between 27 March and 1 April 1966. Twenty-eight European social psychologists and two American guests were present.[8] One American was Festinger. He gave a lecture on the current state of social psychology. His participation demonstrated the links between the EAESP and the Transnational Committee. The other American guest was Rasmussen, at that time Liaison Officer of the ONR in London. His report (Rasmussen, 1966) on the Royaumont Conference will serve here as the testimony of an independent observer.

The seven main presentations dealt with the following themes:

On the scope and method of cross-cultural research: Frijda and Jahoda started by highlighting the methodological problems encountered in cross-cultural research: adequacy and comparability of descriptive categories, research and sampling procedures; functional equivalents of studied phenomena; and problems of interpretation. The proposed conclusion carefully considered approaches to solving methodological problems.

Linguistic and non-linguistic components of communication: Rommetweit emphasized the manner in which cognitive social psychology could serve as a meeting point for linguistics and social psychology. He argued that the interaction between linguistic and non-linguistic aspects of communication processes showed the ever-growing contribution of social psychology to psycholinguistics. 'Regardless' of the degree to which one might be interested in psycho-linguistics,' Rasmussen wrote in his report, 'the thoughtfulness, systematic formulation and clarity of Rommetweit's presentation certainly commanded attention'.

Origins of ingroup–outgroup attitudes: The paper by Rabbie reported research directed towards a definition of the inimical conditions needed to elicit discrimination in ingroup-outgroup attitudes. The findings showed that, regardless of experimental conditions and of whether or not the group was rewarded, the differentiated treatment in each of the conditions is more positive in in-group and out-group valuation.

Preliminary observations for experimental studies of identity: Zavalloni opened her presentation by pointing out that the concept of identity has a long history, yet there was little empirical support for any theory. She proposed various hypotheses that could be tested in this emerging topic in international studies.

The effects of structure of task and group on productivity: Cohen reported a series of experiments concerning the effectiveness of central versus non-central structure in problem solving. As predicted, centrality becomes increasingly important in group productivity as interdependence within the group increases. At the same time, an inverse relationship appears between non-centrality and interdependence.

The dependency of organizational centrality: Faucheux contended that most tasks used in studies of group organization and structure were of an analytic nature, so that if appropriate effort is expended, solution is predictable. He hypothesized that groups will tend to follow a leader when dealing with deduction tasks. They will be more democratic if the task is of an inductive and inferential nature.

An overview of social psychology: Festinger's lecture was a major event, both on account of his personality and the candour with which he addressed his audience. Speaking without any notes, he outlined the history of experimental social psychology over the past 25 years. After a brief discussion of Allport's and Sherif's work, he dwelt in more detail on the leadership studies of Lewin and Lippitt, which in his eyes constituted the beginning of experimental social psychology. He described how the Lewinian School was founded at the Center of Group Dynamics at MIT and then transferred to Ann Arbor. Continuing the historical approach, Festinger examined the situation current in 1965, which required theoretical development. Among the possibilities he outlined, two fields stood out: a serious theoretical

EUROPEAN ASSOCIATION FOR THE ADVANCEMENT OF EXPERIMENTAL SOCIAL PSYCHOLOGY

PLANNING COMMITTEE

MARTIN IRLE
UNIVERSITY OF MANNHEIM (WIRTSCHAFTSHOCHSCHULE).

GUSTAV JAHODA
UNIV. OF STRATHCLYDE (GLASGOW).

SERGE MOSCOVICI (CHAIRMAN)
ECOLE DES HAUTES ETUDES. UNIV. OF PARIS.

MAUK MULDER.
UNIV. OF UTRECHT.

JOZEF M. NUTTIN JR.
UNIV. OF LOUVAIN.

RAGNAR ROMMETVEIT
OSLO UNIVERSITY

HENRI TAJFEL
UNIV. OF OXFORD.

SECRETARY:

PROF. DR. MAUK MULDER
UTRECHT UNIVERSITY
INSTITUTE OF SOCIAL PSYCHOLOGY
CATHARI.JNESINGEL 28 B.
UTRECHT. NETHERLANDS

Figure 6.1   The Association's headed letter paper before . . .[10]

EUROPEAN ASSOCIATION FOR ▮▮▮▮▮▮▮▮
EXPERIMENTAL SOCIAL PSYCHOLOGY

PLANNING COMMITTEE

GUSTAV JAHODA
UNIV. OF STRATHCLYDE (GLASGOW).

SERGE MOSCOVICI (CHAIRMAN)
ECOLE DES HAUTES ETUDES. UNIV. OF PARIS.

MAUK MULDER.
UNIV. OF UTRECHT.

JOZEF M. NUTTIN JR.
UNIV. OF LOUVAIN.

HENRI TAJFEL
UNIV. OF OXFORD.

MARTIN IRLE
UNIVERSITY OF MANNHEIM (WIRTSCHAFTSHOCHSCHULE).

RAGNAR ROMMETVEIT
OSLO UNIVERSITY.

SECRETARY:

PROF. DR. MAUK MULDER
UTRECHT UNIVERSITY
INSTITUTE OF SOCIAL PSYCHOLOGY
CATHARI.JNESINGEL 28 B.
UTRECHT. NETHERLANDS

Figure 6.2   And after[11]

consideration of the vast area of 'influence' and an exploration of the biological aspect of social behaviour. These last remarks made it clear that he was alluding to new ongoing research in Europe and America.

Festinger's lecture was one of those inspiring moments that recompense researchers for their efforts to accomplish something with others and which make them feel unforgettably privileged to be part of that exceptional moment. Festinger had prepared his talk carefully as he makes clear in his letter to Moscovici:

> It seems like a very simple request to ask me to give you the title of my talk for the Royaumont Conference. Actually, it is not simple at all since I am not clear in my mind what I am going to say and how I am going to fulfill the role of a wise old man which you have given me.[9]

According to Himmelweit, who chaired Festinger's presentation, the speaker fulfilled this role perfectly. Our privileged witness, Rasmussen wrote: 'In some respect Festinger's presentation may have been less scholarly than many participants had anticipated. On the other hand, it may have been quite appropriate for this extremely energetic and active group to pause for a moment and obtain a long-time perspective from an individual who has been identified with this field almost from its inception' (Rasmussen, 1966, p. 11). Major presentations took place in the morning. The afternoon sessions were dedicated to meetings of three or four small groups. This allowed detailed discussion of ongoing research as well as debates on theory, the choice of research topics, and so on. On several occasions, the liveliest exchanges among participants extended well into the small hours. Rasmussen concluded 'This was a well-organized effectively-managed and clearly successful conference. With one or two isolated exceptions, all papers and formal discussions were well prepared and meaningful' (ibid., p. 3).

During conference debates it became clear to every participant that the new era had just begun. The participants expressed their will to shape the new Association and to develop its independence, and at the same time to maintain common bonds and foster the spirit of research and creativity. One did not have to be a great anthropologist to recognize that giving or changing a name was an act of baptism and a celebration of the birth of fellowship. As Jozef Nuttin writes 'Halfway through this Conference, the "General Assembly" held its first "business meeting" . . . All members of the European Planning Committee were re-elected and, together with M. Irle and R. Rommetweit, they became the formal "Executive Committee" of what was, from now on named the EAESP' (Nuttin, 1990, p. 367).

This action was taken without any objection or judgement about for instance, American social psychologists. Rasmussen found that significant. 'Rarely was there any tinge of hostility toward or depreciation of American leadership (or domination) in the field. Rather, the message conveyed was one of desiring to develop some sort of mature professional identity and sufficient resources to establish a significant European position in the world of experimental and theoretical social psychology' (ibid., p. 2). The participants accepted the proposal that the new Association was not to be conceived of as a learned society or a professional network. The Association was to become 'a special milieu', in which something unique was to be created, a milieu fostering new ideas and research. And, in the wake of two dreadful wars, European social psychology should develop at the same pace as other sciences, such as sociology, anthropology and linguistics, if it wanted to become one of them.

In light of this, it was necessary to encourage more active communication among researchers and to hold a general conference at least every two years. And to give priority to originality, it was suggested that new members should be recruited on the basis of triple sponsorship, according to the key criteria of participation in research. The number of new members should be limited to approximately ten per year. Evidently, everybody felt that it was possible to maintain a high degree of interaction and the means of support for an active scientific community.

Although everybody was conscious of the obstacles that were bound to arise in this fragile new venture, the prevailing feeling of belonging to an avant-garde movement embraced the group. Their mission was to shape European social psychology in the decades to come. Rasmussen sensed this anticipation when he wrote in his report 'If the Sorrento and Frascati Conferences are considered the first milestones in the development of European social psychology, the Royaumont Conference well might be considered the second' (ibid., p. 4).

Spring in Paris

The Transnational Committee met in Paris immediately after the Royaumont Conference on 3–5 April 1966. The meeting took place at 4 rue de Chevreuse, 'Reid Hall', a grand and beautiful property owned by the University of Columbia in Montparnasse. It rented one part of this building to the EPHE and this was the first home of Moscovici's laboratory. Of course, the Committee discussed the items on the agenda, but Royaumont was on everybody's mind. The members felt relieved and compensated for all the ups and downs of past struggles. The promise given to the SSRC that the EAESP would become autonomous had been fulfilled. The Executive Minutes of the SSRC stated: 'The activities of the Transnational Committee illustrate not only the effects of moral and financial support of social science in Europe, but also the ability of Europeans to gain the confidence of local sources of support'.[12]

But there was an added significance to these events. It was the politically charged agenda of the Cold War that made Europe the primary focus of many American agencies and foundations. And from this point of view it meant that the Transnational Committee was not only present in Europe but also that, after the creation of the new Association, it became its reliable partner. Although there were many points to discuss during that meeting in Paris, the Transnational Committee was already preparing itself for a new start. This posed the question as to what should be its *modus operandi*.

At first, the Transnational Committee searched for contacts among social psychologists who might know someone in the Middle East or Asia who would be willing to take part in a training institute. But after the Royaumont conference, members of the Committee took a less ambitious view of their mission. They appreciated that time was needed to accomplish these tasks and to organize a training institute successfully. This would involve not only individuals but also universities. One could say that the Committee opted resolutely for what might be called 'nation building' or rather, here, association building. In years to come, the Committee no longer had to scan the illusory map of social psychology for imaginary locations. It dedicated itself to designing it. Spring in Paris has always held the sap of new life.

7

The Louvain
Summer School

History has Many Cunning Passages, Contrived Corridors

Just after the Rome meeting in December 1964, let us recall, Festinger found himself back in the USA with a more definite vision of what had made him move so resolutely towards Europe. It seemed he needed to rethink his part-idea/part-dream of an international social psychology for it to become a reality. As most pathfinders, he was not certain where he was going and who could accompany him on the road. The Transnational Committee was after all composed of people who did not know one another well, did not live in the same country and did not have much institutional experience. Before the other members of the Transnational Committee, an astonishing and lively group, could be of any help, he had first to come up with a clearer definition of their task. But in the meantime, he realized that the central figure to the whole endeavour was himself. What made cooperation easier was that Festinger, who was respected and admired, was also remarkably patient, willing to understand and compromise. In addition, he was very trusting. He was not what some people assumed him to be – brash, critical or distant. That reputation was false.

Let us remember that at the meeting in Rome it was agreed that two summer training institutes would be held, one in 1965 and the other in 1966. The European Board was to organize the first of these. The Transnational Committee had made the initial request to the NSF for sponsorship for a summer school in the autumn of 1964.[1] Meanwhile, as we know, the 'elected group' in Frascati was not only developing the Association but also announcing a European conference in Royaumont. That made a favourable impression on the SSRC who recognized that the organization of the European Association of the Advancement of Social Psychology was functioning well and raised money for a third conference.[2] This required that the 'elected group' become functional and that following the compromise made in Rome the European Board would have to yield to it. When discussing the proposal to the NSF for sponsoring a summer training institute, the P&P remained firm on this point.[3]

> Provision of the suggested funds to the Frascati group to aid the organization of the third group might help to avert and resolve some of these problems, since if this group becomes 'functional', the relinquishment of planning responsibilities by the self-constituted board would be encouraged. It was proposed that the Council specify that support for the 1966 Institute would be contingent upon cooperation with the elected group and control of the funds by the Transnational Committee.

Nonetheless, relinquishing the European Board was easier said than done. There was the following problem.[4] On the one hand, there were already several groups in Europe: the European Board, the European Foundation for Summer Schools and Irle intended to create a foundation of social psychology in Germany. On the other hand, the Transnational Committee and the 'elected group' wanted to bring together all social psychologists and put an end to the splintering of the academic discipline. The problem came to a head when all the European groups became keen to define their special role, raise funds and organize training institutes. We can read in the minutes of the SSRC Council. 'This illustrates one problem likely to be encountered by an international committee: when it decides upon an undertaking in a foreign country, it may find more than one indigenous group with similar interests and must deal with public relations and administrative as well as substantive questions.'[5] The Planning Committee could not do much. Nevertheless, at the Oxford meeting it decided that overlap of membership of several committees would be unwise but agreed that Tajfel, who was invited to a conference in Mannheim, could 'explain our position and . . . resign from the Board of the

Foundation'.[6] In a confidential report to the members of the Planning Committee, Tajfel said that it was useful to discuss the matter 'in the sense of preventing what could easily develop as confusing competition' between committees. He mentioned that a foundation had been created in Mannheim which would like to co-sponsor the second summer school and he proposed a meeting between Moscovici and Hutte in Paris and with Koekebakker in Amsterdam. We cannot summarize here that rather long report and the reasons why, in Tajfel's opinion, cooperation between the two bodies was desirable. But he claimed 'it is certainly more fruitful to cooperate than have a permanent and useless split. You will have noted above that I was able to obtain an agreement for limiting the aims of the Foundation to the organization and financing of future summer schools in cooperation with our Committee'[7] But this did not lead to any enthusiasm or response from the rest of the Committee. It was perhaps why the letter from van Giles to Moscovici, suggesting a meeting with the representatives of the European Foundation, was somewhat disconcerting, even more so as the letter stated that the purpose of this meeting would be to discuss 'the integration of the activities of both organisations . . . especially in regard to the co-sponsorship of the Foundation to the 1966 Summer School organised by the Association and in regard to long-term planning of future training programs in Europe.'[8] It was, to begin with, an inadvertent letter, since most of those involved were representing only themselves and could not commit themselves to collaborating in a future that did not in fact depend on them. Furthermore, collaboration in the context of the summer school was not a priority for the EAESP because it could profoundly alter its goals stated above. To cut a long story short, it was felt that no decision could be made without involving the Transnational Committee. A meeting was arranged with the representatives of the European Board and Foundations. It took place in a friendly atmosphere as Festinger, who was present, was well acquainted with the Dutch participants. The contradiction between what was agreed in Rome and the existing situation was discussed once again. It was left to the Transnational Committee that met afterwards in July 1965 in Amsterdam[9] to decide on the best solution. The Chairman explained that it would consume too many resources if the Committee were to be involved with several groups in Europe as well as being primarily responsible for the summer schools. He clarified the position of the SSRC concerning the summer schools in The Hague 1965 and Louvain 1966. The proposed solution was, of course, a negotiated compromise. As stated in the SSRC Council Minutes:

> The problem of relations between the European Foundation and the new European Association for the Advancement of Experimental Social Psychology has been satisfactorily resolved: the former has changed its name to European Foundation for Summer Schools in Social Psychology and is now affiliated with the Association, so that the 1966 summer training institute will be sponsored by the committee in co-operation with the Association 'through' its Foundation.[10]

One may notice the carefully punctuated 'through' in inverted commas. The Association finally achieved consensus by including the European Foundation as one of its specialized 'branches'.

The recognition of the 'elected group' by the Transnational Committee was now apparent. The Committee co-opted Tajfel as a new member, following the resignation of Ancona. And the symbol of the new relationship was the common responsibility for the organization of the Louvain Summer School, a symbol showing better than anything else how this story changed from grandiose ambitions to easier targets, from near-conflict to reasonable solutions to difficult problems. This is what intrigues the historian. While the German proverb says *Aller Anfang ist schwer* (every beginning is difficult), an answer to that is the French *tout est bien qui finit bien* (all's well that ends well). The story's end is recorded in the minutes of the P&P:

> In accordance with P&P's stipulation in January 1965, the proposal for a 1966 summer training institute, prepared by the planning group (Moscovici, chairman, Nuttin and Schachter) named by the Transnational Committee and the European Association for the Advancement of Experimental Social Psychology, has been submitted to the Council and circulated to P&P.[11]

In Search of a Research Training Device

Preliminary brainstorms

The preparations for the Louvain Summer School took a full two years. A subcommittee consisting of Moscovici (chairman), Nuttin and Schachter was in charge of accomplishing the task. As a preliminary move, Moscovici and Nuttin attended the Summer School in The Hague, Holland, 15 July–11 August 1965. The programme focused on the social psychological aspects of organization. Koekebakker was the director, surrounded by a distinguished international faculty. The flexibility of the programme and the eagerness of the participants from Eastern and Western Europe were very encouraging features. Nevertheless, students evaluated the programme as too heavily weighted towards an experimental approach, whereas the real-life phenomena of power and conflict should have been given a more prominent role (van Gils and Koekebakker, 1965).

Right at the start of organizing the Louvain Summer School, Festinger explained to Moscovici that the goal was not just to run the summer school but to find a training formula for young social psychologists that would turn them into experimental researchers. The formula was to be tested in Western Europe and hopefully then applied elsewhere. With this in mind, Moscovici wrote a long letter to Festinger, who was to come to Paris in November, proposing among other things that the professors were chosen on the basis of their age and reputation. 'This is necessary,' one reads in the letter, 'in order to attract advanced researchers.'[12] On the other hand, it was desirable to let young researchers perceive the training institute as a forum for personal improvement and, at the same time, as providing an opportunity for them to meet researchers with whom they could establish a continuous scientific dialogue and cooperation. Festinger, who could not come to Paris after all, answered immediately: 'The changes that you and Jozef Nuttin made in the proposal for the summer school are perfectly fine as far as I am concerned. If you feel there should be an equal number of Europeans and Americans, then your choices of Elliot Aronson, Morton Deutsch, and Harold Kelley are excellent. I agree also with your choices of Europeans. Also, the way you propose to organise the curriculum at the summer school seems very sensible.'[13]

The subcommittee and its proposal

It was good to get Festinger's vote of confidence. But today if we look more closely at the subcommittee, we see that it was composed of relative novices in the area of training institutes.

Moscovici until then had never taught advanced students. The only experience that he had was his own, as a student at a seminar with Alexandre Koyré, the well-known philosopher of science, at the EPHE. Moscovici's idea of training was that of apprenticeship, central to which was the choice of a student by the master or vice versa. Yet, beyond this, he had a more 'theological' view of the evolution of the individual's libido. That is, one is born with an *erotic libido*, à la Freud. Between twenty and thirty years of age, one develops a *libido sciendi*, and eventually, when one is between forty and forty-five, one acquires a *libido dominandi*. Moscovici thought the theory of selecting students for research on the basis of academic criteria was therefore useless. One had to consider, primarily, whether prospective students had developed the *libido sciendi*, their love of the pursuit of knowledge that would endure and, in any case, outlast their PhDs.

Nuttin, the junior member of the subcommittee, already had a teaching career, both in Africa and Belgium. He was the only member who was familiar with European universities and their rules and administrative channels. This is what enabled him to create the greatest laboratory for social psychology in Europe at the time. He always insisted on an extended summer school, and on the necessity for professors and students to perform experiments during the summer school, something that had not previously been given enough thought. One sensed in him a well-established willingness to honour his laboratory and his university. All this facilitated preparation, the method of teaching and the choice of professors and students.

Last but not least, Schachter displayed above all the attitude of an artist. He had a very long experience as a researcher and professor. One could believe that he was born in the laboratory. His vision of a training seminar could perhaps be subsumed under the notion of the 'research climate'. He often described the details of life in his laboratory, how he chose his students and their PhD topics. He was sharp and insightful and chose the students who loved the climate of hard work and its seductive atmosphere. One of his students, Singer, described Schachter's attitude toward his students:

> It's if you are good and have a certain kind of personality that I am going to enjoy being with, that is fine, then we can be friends. If I call you schmuck and I yell at you and all the rest, it is only because I have granted you a fundamental degree of respect. People I am polite to I have no use for. It's a Jewish family – you yell and scream at each other – but of course you wouldn't do that to a stranger, that would be crude. (Patnoe, 1988, p. 149)

Such diversity of experience could easily bring about a clash. But the task had to be done and points of view reconciled. Moscovici met Nuttin and Schachter separately in Paris. And they all met before the Hague Summer School. Much of that was an exercise in brainstorming, an unfreezing of ideas.

In September 1965, a proposal was drafted by Nuttin to be sent to the SSRC on the basis of the subcommittee's discussions.[14] The draft was edited in good English and Webbink, the Vice-President of the SSRC, sent it to the NSF for their reactions. The proposal contained the following statements:

- It is planned to select 30 young researchers as students and a full-time faculty of six eminent experimental social psychologists.
- The objective of the institute is a) to provide an intensive and first-hand experience in research; b) to attempt to demonstrate the process and procedures by which experimental social psychologists translate problems into testable forms; c) to help students solve their individual research problems. In order to reach these objectives, the summer school had been conceived as a research apprenticeship.
- Each of the faculty members will work with a group of four to six students throughout the five-week session. The selected problems will be research topics of current interest to faculty members. Their relationship with students will be similar to

that with assistants in their own laboratories. In that sense the summer training institute was conceived as a normal work setting.

- Each student's experience will be primarily with a single faculty member. This embodies the idea of apprenticeship that the subcommittee considers essential.

- In selecting students, the summer institute faculty will ask colleagues at all major centres of social research in Europe to suggest the most promising young researchers already engaged in social psychological research.

It is clear that the aim of the proposal was the training of researchers and the production of knowledge and it was expected that the results of each group would be the product of working together. And certainly this summer school had all the more reason to succeed, as it would take place in a seat of learning, the University of Louvain, a university that was a phalansterian community. This is why it is important to underline the delicate nature of the task for the director of the summer school, Nuttin, who was chosen by the two committees that sponsored it. It was a period during which the SSRC started to place more confidence in the perspectives of the Transnational Committee and, by implication, of the European Committee.[15]

Training for an intercultural habitus

The Transnational Committee realized that it needed a new definition and a new purpose for the training institutes. It is now difficult to trace the process by which this idea came into being and how it was formulated and accepted. In the proposal addressed to the NSF,[16] it is clearly stated that it was not known to what extent a finding in social psychology is universal and to what extent it is 'culture bound'. Its author, Festinger, wrote:

There was a time when many social psychologists thought that the solution to this problem was easy. They proposed to select particularly important, theoretically strategic, experiments that had been conducted and replicated in the US, repeat these experiments in other areas of the world, and see the extent to which the earlier findings were verified. This solution, however, turned out to be at best a partial one.

How does one 'repeat' an experiment in another country? Does one simply 'translate' everything, or does one attempt a conceptual replication suited to that culture in accordance with one's intuitive ideas about that culture? Rarely have attempts of either kind proved to be fruitful . . . It may be assumed that the only way to make sure that social psychological knowledge rests on an international factual basis is through the research of trained indigenous experimental social psychologists, working in various parts of the world on the problems and ideas that seem important to them. Reconciliation, on a theoretical and conceptual level, of the diversity of resulting data will guarantee that generalizations are not 'culture bound'. In the process something may be learned about 'culture' as an independent variable.[17]

This text deserves to be quoted in full because it challenges the received view that internationalization of social psychology was a form of Americanization. Moreover, it shows what was disturbing with the natural generosity of American colleagues who wanted to raise the rest of the world to a higher level of science – that is, to theirs. It was exporting science, not discovering it.

The Committee started posing questions about the comparative view from the beginning. Could it be applied to experimental social psychology? And if so, how useful would it be? There were no answers to any of these questions. Though it was not specifically excluded, students were not encouraged to replicate an American or European study in their own country. The focus was on ways to communicate, to pool idiosyncratic ideas and to invent something new from them. If the subcommittee can be faulted at all for its brainstorming, it is because implicitly it hoped to create an *intercultural habitus* that would cross-fertilize the work of future generations of social psychologists. At the same time this term was a good metaphor for what the Transnational Committee intended to achieve.

A meeting of the faculty in Santa Monica

Looking back, one is struck by the amount of theoretical investment in the Louvain Summer School, as well as by the attention to every feature of its material and intellectual development. No wonder that the subcommittee felt it necessary to reunite the prospective faculty at a meeting in Santa Monica, California, on 15–16 November 1966. It was hoped that such a meeting would revive interest in the Summer School, which had been postponed from 1966 to 1967. It would not be easy to reconstruct the verbal account of the Santa Monica meeting without the minutes drafted by Zimbardo,[18] which clearly report the proceedings. Moscovici opened by stressing the long-term goal of this seminar: 'Encouraging the establishment of a milieu which would support the "basic" research activities of young social psychologists and imparting both additional research training and concrete research experience to advanced social psychology students.'[19] Nuttin emphasized the role of the teaching staff, referring to the proposal made to the NSF. He restated his firm conviction 'that what the seminar participants required most was the opportunity to develop, in close collaboration with a master, an original hypothesis from its creation origin, through its operationalization and execution, analysis and written exposition'.[20]

And after that the differences between the Hague Summer School and the Louvain Summer Research Training Institute were set out as in table 7.1.

Finally, a major difference between the two summer schools was the amount of preparatory work demanded of both students and faculty. Nuttin drafted a seven-page letter[21] setting out the

Table 7.1 The Hague Summer School and Louvain Summer Research Training Institute

The Hague	Louvain
Younger research students	More advanced research assistants
Two senior staff, changing every week	Seven permanent senior staff
Lecturing each morning	Formal lecturing minimal
Staff of permanent workgroup: leaders (5) and assistants (5)	Senior staff as workgroup leaders
Direct recruitment with concern for geographical representation and broadening of the field	Recruitment via directors of centres

principles of the summer schools, and the preparation, including reading, expected of candidates. The colleagues in the various universities and laboratories in Europe who had been invited to nominate candidate participants all reacted very positively to a request to provide a minimum of half a day per week for the nominees' specific preparatory work.

All this fine tuning was necessary in order to change the attitude to learning at that time. Until then, learning meant basically assimilating existing knowledge while research was considered a 'secondary' activity. Most research took place outside the university, for example in special institutes like the Max Planck in Germany or the CNRS in France. Therefore, the difference between learning – that is, assimilating knowledge – and discovering new ideas, or phenomena – that is, producing knowledge – at universities was blurred. It was during the epoch of the mid-1960s that it became desirable to set young social psychologists the goal of knowledge production. That is to say, it was important to instil in young scientists the awareness that in order to bring social psychology to life they had to become 'knowledge producers', and not just 'knowledge consumers'. One of the implicit tasks of the Louvain Summer Institute was to achieve such a change.

As Zajonc remarked during the Santa Monica meeting, students in Europe (he himself had been a student at the Sorbonne) were very eager to learn and they were critical of ideas and research in social psychology. This Summer Institute, however, was designed for 'artists', not for 'critics'.

Kelley, a new member of the Transnational Committee in 1966, proposed a very effective schedule for each group to follow, combining group work and individual effort:

- problem area set by staff;
- preparation by each participant of parallel formulations of hypotheses and experimental design under close individual supervision of staff member;
- group confrontation of individual formulations and agree on one proposal;
- preparation of parallel first draft of the problem and method of the report resulting in a group report;
- piloting and running of one experiment (minimal programme);

- analysis and interpretation of data, implying again both individual responsibility of each participant and group discussions and decisions;
- drafting of parallel first individual reports of results and discussion of results;
- group responsibility for a 'finished product' group report.

The Louvain Summer Research Training Institute: 31 July–2 September 1967

The Summer Institute took place between 31 July and 2 September 1967. It was one of the most carefully planned and charismatic events to take place in the history of European social psychology. In the end the faculty comprised Gerard (California); Kelley (California); Rabbie (Utrecht); Rommetveit (Oslo); Zajonc (Michigan); and Zimbardo (New York). There were thirty students, most of whom worked as research, teaching assistants or lecturers at their universities.

Gerard's team worked on dissonance theory, and more specifically on forced compliance. Kelley's team was concerned with negotiation and bargain in the context of mixed-motive games. The focus of Rabbie's study was intergroup relations. More concretely, it examined the idea that the expectation of future interaction with other people could be regarded as a minimal condition for differentiating the in-group from the out-group. Rommetweit's team explored the joint contribution of linguistic and extra-linguistic contexts in the communication of messages. Zajonc's team worked on social facilitation, showing the energizing and directive effects of the presence of another person on behaviour. Zimbardo's team studied de-individuation phenomena. In particular, it focused on the anti-social consequences of losing personal identity in a group setting (Nuttin and Jaspars, 1967).

As the faculty consisted of distinguished social psychologists and because the chosen themes represented current research, the Summer Institute concentrated on some fundamental topical questions. As envisaged, each team acquired direct experience of the complete research process from expression of theoretical idea to conclusion. It accounted for methodological problems from the submission of an idea, to subjecting it to an experiment and managing the study. The Laboratory for Experimental Social Psychology at Louvain, equipped with adequate facilities, was on hand and satisfied all needs and interests. Participation in the common experience of the Summer Institute also provided a good opportunity to experience contact with other cultures. Exchanges during group work enabled students to learn how ideas are transferred and how to understand the problems others experience. In other words, the participants learned how to free themselves from the rigid principles of their own backgrounds. That may seem trivial, but it was essential to 'defreezing' European social psychology and thinking interculturally. One thing is sure: the students who participated at that Summer Institute evaluated it, both personally and intellectually, as a most enriching experience. Each step in the subcommittee's proposal entailed forming a new social psychological *habitus* and a new practice of 'promoting and encouraging good standards of training and research' (Tajfel, 1972, p. 313).

The first American and European common endeavour worked well and proved fruitful. And from its hunter-gatherer beginnings, the Transnational Committee within a few years was reaping a harvest. It had now a 'device' for initiating and raising new generations of social psychologists from different cultures and traditions.

8

The Ford Foundation and Fundraising for Europe

The New Policy of the Ford Foundation

We may not have an exact record of all the attempts during the late 1960s to secure funding for social psychology. No doubt, well-informed circles have such knowledge. But knowledge so obtained will necessarily be selective: what was significant in the past is unlikely to be significant now and vice versa. This preamble will appear more understandable if we clarify the circumstances that led to the grant awarded to European social psychology by the Ford Foundation. This grant was an unintended consequence of the report by Harold Leavitt, mentioned previously.

At the time when the EAESP was born in Royaumont, the policy of the Ford underwent a decisive change. Marshall Robinson, who was appointed the Director of the programme on Higher Education and Research, recollects that 'the Foundation's activities in Europe changed sharply in early 1967 when McGeorge Bundy, its new President, closed the Foundation's program called "European Affairs" and urged its domestic program in Science, Education, Research, etc. to deal with the European organizations, as they do with those in the US'.[1]

These modifications in the activities of the Ford Foundation corresponded to changes in American strategies of influence. 'We have seen,' wrote the Italian historian, Gemelli,

> that the strategies of influence of the Rockefeller Foundation were particularly centred on the exportation of a model of research. On the contrary, Ford has as its objective the official recognition of the third level [i.e. the doctoral level, *authors' note*]. It is in this context,

in my opinion, that one has to inject an enormous effort of organization into European business schools, and in a more limited
organizational and financial perspective, the grants made in 1967
to the EPHE for an experimental programme of training at the
third level in social science (Gemelli, 1995, p. 340, *our translation*).

These strategic moves became apparent when Ford showed an
interest in creating business schools in Europe and in 1967 chose
to sponsor an experimental programme at the EPHE in Paris for
training doctoral students in all social sciences. However, nothing
demonstrated Ford's policy better than its financial and intellectual commitment to the project of building the MSH in Paris as
a centre of coordination of research in social science and in international exchange. This was one of the most innovative projects
in Europe after the Second World War.

Conversations with Marshall Robinson

We now come to the beginning. After all those years of trial and
error during which the Transnational Committee was attempting
to create international social psychology, the vision and all (or
nearly all) the ideas were still only in the minds of those concerned and had yet to be realized. To counter the belief that the
past is more or less like the present, let us recall one relevant fact.
In 1966–7, the EAESP was not much more than a letterhead, a
novel idea, although probably a unique one. Its few members were
scattered all over Europe. Its activities depended on the good will
of individuals and the help of the Transnational Committee. It
seems wonderful that such an active minority had the same
unselfish interest in fostering research and spreading the gospel
about the different ways in which social psychology could be
practised.

Serge Moscovici was President of the EAESP and a set of con-
comitant events played its role. He was one of those who, since
the war, had, as the French say, 'a fear of shortage'. One of his
worries, which he shared with Tajfel, was that the EAESP could
become insolvent and incapable of pursuing its goals: it could even
disappear. The legitimacy bestowed on it by the Transnational

Table 8.1 Income of the EAESP

Membership dues	$1,500
General Electric Grant	$3,000
Volkswagen Grant	$20,000
EPHE	FF 12,500
Royaumont Foundation	FF 12,000
Remainder of the grant from the ONR	FF 2,500

Committee might not be sufficient to save this inspired idea from such a sad destiny. Let the figures speak for themselves (table 8.1).

The needs of the EAESP were far greater than could be met by these sums and, in any case, most of these grants had little likelihood of being renewed. What could be done in these circumstances? In pondering this, Moscovici never considered the possibility of a grant from an American foundation. Such an idea was unthinkable.

Yet during the autumn of 1966 Moscovici was invited by Pierre Tabatoni to meet his American colleague. Tabatoni was a professor of economics in Aix-en-Provence who founded there the Institut d'Administration des Entreprises, the first establishment of its kind in France. Actually, it was the American colleague who wished to see Moscovici. This invitation could be explained by the fact that Marshall Robinson, Tabatoni's colleague, was also an economist and was acquainted with Harold Leavitt. He also knew Claude Faucheux, then a visiting professor at the Carnegie Melon Graduate School of Business Administration in Pittsburgh. As they all had a common interest in encouraging the creation of business schools in Europe, it was not surprising that these shared incentives meant the meeting with Moscovici was easy, even friendly. The conversation with Marshall Robinson revealed his interest in social psychology. He asked questions about some of the items in Leavitt's report, which he had presumably read, dwelling on this person or that institution, so that he could learn more about them. He seemed to want to obtain an impression of social psychology generally, and of the laboratory at the EPHE specifically. He also spoke with Moscovici on various aspects of the ongoing research.

Though it was left unsaid, Robinson wanted to know about the relationships between the EAESP and the Americans. Thus they spoke about the creation of the EAESP, about the conference in Royaumont that had taken place earlier that year and about the hopes which rested on a pioneering group of scientists. There was no mention of a possible request for funding from Ford. Afterwards Robinson asked Moscovici to be more specific about the future. Moscovici replied that he did not believe in the viability of a European centre of research in any social science. As in the past, it was likely that such a centre would fall into the hands of someone not doing research himself, but who had political and administrative skills and ambitions. As far as social psychology was concerned, it was a teaching subject at only a small number of universities. With regard to active research, Moscovici pointed out that only three or four moderately-sized research centres had any chance of prospering. Afterwards Robinson requested Moscovici to draft a memorandum about all these issues. Before leaving he added: 'We cannot tell, of course, what shape these things may take.' Not long after the meeting, Moscovici wrote to Robinson as follows:

> You will doubtless recall that when you were in Paris, we discussed the possibility of contacting the Ford Foundation in the name of the European Association for Experimental Social Psychology. At the same time, you were kind enough to offer more than your assistance and advice when the need arose, and in particular you suggested that I submit my proposed Ford project to you before taking up any official correspondence . . . I should be most grateful if you would examine the project and let me know your opinion, as well as any modification or change which you feel should be made.[2]

Considering the explorative character of the first conversation with Robinson, the content of this letter might be judged as too presumptuous and its author as taking too much of a liberty. An answer to such a letter might be thought unlikely to come soon, if ever. Yet it did come and very quickly. 'I want to acknowledge,' Robinson wrote, 'the proposal that you sent and to say that so far, I have only had an opportunity to skim through it.'[3] Taking the reported circumstances into account, it is easy to understand that this was an opportunity not to be missed. But Moscovici was too much of a novice and was not ready to hit the mark. Following

Moscovici's trip to New York in November 1966, Robinson did not commit himself to anything but asked for a report about the centres of social psychology in Europe. Nothing more than that! Not that there were many such centres, but their level of functioning was very variable. Early in 1967 Moscovici described the whole situation to Jozef Nuttin as follows:

> Robinson, the Director of the Department of Social Sciences at the Ford, whom I saw in November in New York, will be in Paris on 7th and 8th March and we should see him. As I have already told you personally, my meeting with Robinson was positive but he did not give off any idea or a concrete proposition. He simply demands that this year we prepare a report about the centres and the individuals who concern themselves with social psychology in Europe.[4]

Moscovici therefore asked Nuttin to write such a report about research institutions in Belgium because he knew that Nuttin would do it well and in time. But he also said at the end of his letter to Nuttin: 'Be careful, we should not speak about the purpose of this request. Robinson wishes that at present all takes place at an informal level.' As with any informal negotiations, one did not know whether or not to say something, and if so, to whom, when, and how.

Two Proposals to Ford

Anybody who thinks or believes that it is easy to obtain a research grant either lacks experience or has no concept of the way funding bodies function, or of their policies and procedures. Following his conversations and correspondence with Robinson, Moscovici decided not to take the initiative and, instead, to rely on the advice and expertise of the relevant individuals at Ford. And the advice was 'write a personal letter'.

At that time, the Transnational Committee was no better off than was the EAESP. Though it was one of the Committees of the SSRC in New York, it had to compete for finances to carry out any initiative. Every time it planned a conference or a summer school, the Committee had to request money from foundations and especially from the NSF. Whatever the request, the Transnational Committee could never rely on a positive answer. Only a significant grant would consolidate its relations with the SSRC and allow the Committee to plan long-term initiatives.

The Transnational Committee was aware of Moscovici's contact with Robinson and in the spring of 1967 Ford received two requests for grants in support of social psychology. The first one came from the EAESP in the shape of a personal letter from Moscovici of 28 April 1967[5] to Robinson requesting $275,000 (in today's value approximately $1,650,000) for a period of four years. Two months later, on 13 June 1967,[6] another proposal came from the Transnational Committee requesting $500,000 over a period of seven years (today's value is approximately $3,000,000).

Fundraising for Europe

Moscovici's letter to Robinson described the developmental prospects for European social psychology. He also summed up discussions he had previously had with Robinson and outlined 'what might be contemplated for the future'. This outline concerned the reinforcement of the EAESP's activities regarding centres of scientific research. He felt that the idea of a European institute did not have much to recommend it. The main obstacles would be the choice of location, of a person capable of leading such a centre, and of students whose status was problematic due to the differences between European universities and the degrees they conferred. All these factors could become a source of conflict.

What Moscovici proposed was in his opinion much simpler: to develop the three existing research centres. These included Nuttin's centre in Louvain, his own, recently established laboratory in Paris, and Tajfel's future laboratory in Bristol, which he was just moving to from Oxford. This choice did not imply that these three laboratories were centres of excellence but they were three laboratories that could collaborate. Their cooperation with other laboratories would bring young researchers closer together. The functions assigned to these centres would be threefold:

Research function: The principal task of these centres would be to promote continuous and intensive scientific research. Serving as types of productive cell, they would be foci of attention and interest for other researchers. Their sphere of operation would extend beyond national boundaries, ending the isolation and dispersion of various research efforts.

Training function: One task would be to seek out and train talented young people. Such education, reserved for a limited number of 'trainees' would be intensive and would take place in the frame of concrete research.

Communication function: The centres would improve or facilitate communication between Americans and Europeans. At the European level, they would also facilitate communication between East and West European countries. Thus, in response to some demands formulated in Vienna in 1967,[7] each centre would specialize in the distribution of documents related to research results, new projects and bibliography.

In order to accomplish work of real value or to show the weight of the discipline, it would be necessary to support each centre during the four-year period. Effective teams would be set up and stability for the future assured. Moscovici requested $80,000 per centre to cover expenses for the invited research staff, students, research costs and a secretariat. He ended by writing:

> I believe that your decision must be oriented, in one direction or the other, solely on the basis of the objective facts which are accessible to you, coupled with the opinions of those, such as Leon Festinger or Harold Leavitt, who have contributed to the development of social psychology and know the European situation intimately. If I permitted myself to emphasize one point . . . the existence of the very real problem of the time factor . . . to respond at the opportune moment . . . by a movement whose far-reaching effects risk being solely limited by the absence of means.[8]

Another proposal in Moscovici's letter was that the EAESP itself receive $35,000 as a small and regular income for several years. It was important for the EAESP to look ahead and not worry about what would happen from day to day. It would take responsibility for consolidating social psychology in Europe and developing a more productive research. Moscovici did not think it was

the EAESP's responsibility to establish more extensive relationships with the Americans. Instead, it was imperative that the
EAESP did something new in Europe.

If we read between the lines, we can see that the main reason
for requesting an independent grant was to legitimize the very
existence of the EAESP in Europe. A science in the making and
an active minority are both eager to possess the means which
ensure that they can work undisturbed by external problems.
When writing to Robinson, Moscovici had a hunch that, should
Ford offer a grant, it would be modest and a one-off. So he thought
carefully about the amount he should request.

In his reply, Robinson reassured him that if an idea appealed
both to him and his collaborators, then an officer in charge of the
EAESP's case would contact him to test the feasibility of the
project.

The seven-year proposal

The proposal for a seven-year programme that the Transnational
Committee launched in June 1967 was remarkable and different
in nature from Moscovici's proposal. It was a programme of
research and training orientated towards the development of
international social psychology as a scientific discipline.

The Committee[9] devoted considerable time to discussing the
proposal, which the SSRC Executive Committee[10] supported.
Festinger put all his energy into drafting the proposal, inspired by
his vision of what the Committee could do in the future, and the
members participated by providing suggestions and contributing
to the text. Jerome Singer, the Staff Officer who succeeded Ben
Willerman after his death, coordinated the work.

The proposal began with the observation that American social
psychology had experienced, intellectually and geographically,
a period of unparalleled expansion. These developments had
attracted widespread attention both in the USA and in Western
Europe. They promised to bring many central topics to experimental research, such as social influence and conformity, the
dynamics of group decision making, conflict, its resolution, bargaining, negotiation, attitude formation and change, risk-taking
and creativity, among others.

The proposal had nine main goals. First, there was a request for $45,000 to support conferences which promoted research contacts. The proposal referred to Sorrento in 1963 and Frascati in 1964 that had brought West European social psychologists together; the widening to Eastern Europe through the Vienna conference in 1967; the planned conference in Prague in 1968; and the two envisaged Latin American conferences.

The second target was research developmental conferences. Their purpose was to establish social psychology as a scientific discipline and, specifically, to assist researchers to explore the properties of an idea, to conduct mental experiments, confront methodological problems, generate theoretical explanations of phenomena and the like.[11] The Transnational Committee anticipated 'developing some "culture bound" areas, from having an international group of scholars to share their thoughts and effort'.[12] It was envisaged that five to ten scholars would meet intensively for one or two months to explore the research problem in question. The first such topic was Moscovici's inquiry about 'how small minorities are able to induce changes in a large society'.[13] Another topic was based on Schachter's ideas in developmental social psychology concerning social behaviour change through the life cycle.[14] The Committee planned another three research development conferences. It was estimated that $25,000 would be required for each conference.

The third issue concerned specific topical conferences. This initiative would explore a field in which 'there has been a substantial discovery or an accumulation of findings that need to be pulled together'. For instance, methodological or technical innovation opens up new research opportunities, requiring exploration in connection with a well-defined topic, for example, the borderline between linguistics and social psychology which Rommetveit was developing at that time.[15] Another possible topic was Tajfel's on acceptance of racial or elitist ideologies. The Committee proposed four or five conferences of this kind and the funds requested were $55,000 in total.

The fourth item on the proposal concerned training institutes. The Committee stated that training was difficult at that time because there were only a few social psychologists involved in research and, although research assistantship was valued and common in the USA, it was not easily available in other countries. The proposal suggested expanding training facilities in Latin America and Africa[16] and requested funds for three research training institutes in these regions, estimating a total expenditure of $95,000.

The fifth item was the preparation of monographs and curriculum materials with an estimated expenditure of $35,000.

The sixth point referred to exchanges and scholarly visits facilitating meetings of two to three persons to discuss and share ideas, plan the collection of data or agree on analysing and interpreting results, particularly among Latin Americans and East Europeans. The proposal estimated that this would require $15,000.

The seventh item comprised the Committee travel for pilot projects in new professional and geographical areas, estimating the need of $5,000.

The last two items concerned the Committee meetings ($55,000) and the Staff Officer's work ($70,000).

The proposal ended by saying that 'In a discipline where, by necessity, the subject matter is cross-cultural, the Committee represents international disciplinary effort without the overtones of "intellectual imperialism" or mere export of US research products. It is worthwhile to encourage this both for its own sake and as a model of international collaborative efforts.'

This account shows the common points of the two proposals, the seven-year one and Moscovici's, and the difference in their outlooks. The reader might wonder what the importance was of the two proposals. In science as in life, it is an advantage to possess the means of constructing bridges across open spaces separating those who wish to be united by common action and who share a vision which they aspire to. These proposals, we could say, represented efforts to build bridges at that time, allowing collaboration to take place, although neither its known nor its unknown effects could be assessed.

Social psychologists who wish to acquaint themselves with their discipline's past will find in these accounts the stuff of history. Although some readers might find them too long, placed in the context of the period in which they were written, they are astonishingly imaginative. Whether these proposals were successful or not, they were not only thought out and written up, but also developed and applied, as far as was possible, in the course of the years that followed. The vision of an international social psychology had to be matched by reality.

Conversations with the Programme Officer at Ford

Let us return to the course of history. In early May 1967 Robert Schmid, Ford's programme officer, wrote to tell Moscovici that Marshall Robinson had shown him his letter of 28 April 1967 and asked him to get in touch to talk about it. 'I wonder, for example, if you could have lunch with me on Thursday, May 18. I shall be staying at the Hotel Pas-de-Calais on the Rue des Saint Pères, and we ought to be able to find a good restaurant in the neighbourhood.'[17]

We learn from an inter-office memorandum at Ford that the meeting between Serge Moscovici and Robert Schmid took place in Paris on the evening of 17 May 1967. It did not take much more than ten minutes to run through the project. The rest of the evening was dedicated to exploring the status of social psychology in Europe. Needless to say, the start of the discussion was friendly, if a little mysterious and unusual. The memorandum specifies what was really under discussion that evening: 'Why should we support [Moscovici's] social psychological association when there are many other branches of the Sixth Section which are doing work which is called either social psychology or sociology?'[18]

The memorandum states that Moscovici explained how the groups in the Sixth Section at the EPHE differed from one another. He also clarified to Schmid something that, as he pointed out, had not previously been understood. Specifically, under 'social psychology' in the centres 'that he was proposing we set up, he included not only *experimental* social psychology . . . but any and all of the other branches including observational kind of work which, for example, Donald T. Campbell is known for. Moscovici pointed out that his own work has not been limited to the experimental field.'[19]

The memorandum affirmed that Moscovici was to move to the MSH. He would therefore appreciate it if the decision about funds from Ford were made soon so that he could plan space in the new building for his laboratory.

The memorandum indicates Schmid's hesitation over including 'observational' social psychology. He thought that Moscovici

> might as well include some sociology and some behavioural polit-
> ical science. My personal view is if we take these centers seriously
> we should not design them as social psychology centers but as
> behavioural science centers. The important exclusion . . . ought to
> be this: to keep out the descriptive, literary essay types . . . ones
> who masquerade in France as social researchers.[20]

In fact, the talk was about three prospective centres, three laboratories, in Louvain, Bristol and Paris, of which only the last two
were in *statu nascenti*, and which were at that time recruiting new
researchers and students. Moscovici suggested that Schmid get in
touch with Nuttin and Tajfel. Tajfel had been newly appointed at
Bristol. Both Nuttin and Tajfel knew about social psychology in
north-west Europe and they would also be able to inform Schmid
about their programmes.

The question about experimental social psychology was very
easy to answer. A small number of researchers devoted themselves
to experiments alone but most carried out observations as well.
This indeed is how one should proceed: observation and experiment should be combined, just as Lewin and Festinger did in their
laboratories. Moscovici's own laboratory insisted on both these
approaches.

In order to grasp Schmid's concerns, it is necessary to bear in
mind that he was already in charge of a very large project, the
construction of the MSH in Paris. The construction was on the
historical site of the prison, Cherche-Midi, notable for incarcerat-
ing Captain Dreyfus some decades earlier. The French government
and the EPHE were participating in this project jointly with Ford.
This is why, as we shall see, Schmid had on many occasions to
consider this big project alongside Moscovici's proposal for the
three centres.

Following his memorandum, Schmid wrote again[21] regarding
Moscovici's proposal requesting further information on items in
that letter, for example, the meaning of terms such as 'invited
research staff' and 'students', and how much money could be spent

on each item. Schmid also made a general comment regarding the Transnational Committee's request for $500,000, which was to be submitted shortly. He questioned how serious the overlap would be between the two existing proposals. Perhaps Moscovici's proposals should not be incorporated into those of the Transnational Committee? That would have been a reasonable solution to the dilemma because the EAESP was quite dependent on the Transnational Committee; even their membership overlapped at the time. Schmid also had to take the MSH into account, hence his following questions for Ford in the same memorandum:[22]

1 *The Maison:* If we do not support the social psychology that Moscovici is proposing, will he go into the MSH in any case? What kind of facilities will he command without support, and what improvement would there be if he had a four-year grant from us along the lines he suggests?
2 *Future Financing:* What sources of support for Moscovici's centres are likely to replace Ford funds at the end of four years?

Schmid raised these issues because it had already been decided that the social psychology laboratory would be among the first to enter the MSH, and he probably wondered whether failure to get the grant would alter this decision. He also feared that the grant might entail a long-time commitment for Ford.

The relationship between Schmid and Moscovici was quite peculiar. Schmid liked talking about his life and was a highly cultivated person who enjoyed exchanging ideas and discussions. However, at the same time he did not disclose intentions, nor did he reveal what his impressions were. Consequently, Moscovici thought that a modicum of reserve was necessary on his part. He avoided asking Schmid direct questions about individuals, about his meetings with Nuttin and Tajfel whom he had seen several times, and even about Faucheux who, as Schmid was well aware, was a close friend of Moscovici. While his personality was open, he also had a secretive side, bearing the caveat 'no trespassing'. It was impossible for Moscovici to get an inkling as to what Schmid thought of the different proposals that came to him and what was his frame of mind with respect to Ford. He never said a word about the Transnational Committee proposal, although he knew that Moscovici was a member and that he was very close to Festinger. It was as if the issue did not exist or as if he knew nothing about it. Thus their conversation always stopped at the threshold of these important topics. Moscovici listened with the utmost attention to what Schmid said about others, being aware that his responses to Schmid's comments would have significance for his interlocutor and that they would play a role in crucial decisions. It is difficult to describe the atmosphere surrounding these conversations. It was a kind of a seductive rather than Machiavellian relationship between the two of them, each with his private thoughts. Moscovici felt anxious, just as he often had felt in his years of exile, because his fate, or the fate of his proposed centres, was in the hands of others. However, he understood perfectly that Schmid's role required discretion about matters that could have easily become gossip.

In 1967 time seemed plentiful. In fact, after the first encounter between Schmid and Moscovici, Schmid and probably Robinson too had an opportunity to talk to Tajfel and presumably also to Nuttin. They most probably discussed the 'Moscovici's Centres' as they called the project and the grant sums which some judged too modest.

As one would expect, Ford envisaged counter-proposals from others attempting to expand the field of social psychology. Indeed, the EAESP gave these proposals legitimacy. Among the interesting alternatives was Tajfel's request for finance to build international projects around a network of researchers. Another proposal was for training and research in developing countries, for example in Africa.

Until the autumn of 1967 there was almost no communication between Paris and New York. Moscovici saw waiting as a good strategy, believing that interference in the ongoing game could be disruptive. Thus he did nothing and did not get in touch with either the Europeans or the Americans involved in it. However, inter-office documents in Ford show that in the autumn of 1967 Schmid thought that they should finally respond to Moscovici in some way. He exchanged a little memorandum with Robinson (figure 8.1)[23]:

THE FORD FOUNDATION

MEMORANDUM   DATE 9-5-67

TO: MAR

FROM: ROBERT SCHMID

SUBJECT:

Do you owe a sign of life to Moscovici?

Yes

MAR:
Perhaps the
EPRASS grant will
cheer him up?

Figure 8.1 Do you owe a sign of life to Moscovici?

Schmid: Do you owe a sign of life to Moscovici?
Robinson: Perhaps the EPRASS[24] grant will cheer him up?
Schmid: Yes.
Robinson: What comes next?

This was followed by another inter-office memorandum entitled 'What next?' (figure 8.2) which Schmid sent to Robinson.[25]
This much is clear

a) We have to dispose of transnational SSRC soon – (and negative?)
b) then we can decide whether to revive Moscovici scheme
c) But I feel you owe him a kind of personal 'hope you're well again' note.

Following this exchange, two things happened. First, the Ford Foundation decided not to support the seven-year project of the Transnational Committee. Sadly, Singer reported at the P&P in January 1968 that 'the Council's request for funds for the over-all program of the committee approved by P&P in June had not been successful because of the Ford Foundation's wish to maintain more direct relations with experimental social psychologists in other countries.' This decision did not alter the Ford Foundation's interest in supporting the conference which the Transnational Committee proposed to hold in Prague in 1968.

The second consequence was more long-lived. Robinson[26] wrote a letter to Moscovici, saying how sorry he was that they could not meet in the summer and that he hoped his health had improved. After this introduction, he wrote:

We continue to study a great many proposals; we have taken no further initiatives in international social psychology. You have probably heard of the grant we made recently to support the experimental training and research program of the Sixth Section of the EPHE. I hope that in due course some of these grant funds will find their way into your area of operations. Meanwhile, I trust that you will let me know if you have any further thoughts about strengthening social psychology in Western Europe. Bob Schmid joins me in sending best personal regards.

THE FORD FOUNDATION

MEMORANDUM   DATE   10 - 9

TO: MAR

FROM: ROBERT SCHMID

SUBJECT: What next ?

This much is clear

(a) We have to dispose
of trans national SSRZ
soon – (and negative ?)

(b) then we can decide
whether to revive the
moscovice scheme.

Please
draft.

(c) But I feel you
owe him a kind
of personal "hope you're
well again" note.

Figure 8.2   What next?

Moscovici responded to the above point: 'According to what you wrote me, you have been studying numerous proposals but have not taken any initiative with regard to international social psychology. I imagine that this is due to the abundance of alternatives, and I dare to hope that the day is drawing close when you will make your decision!!'[27] No further correspondence was exchanged during the winter 1967–8. However, towards the end of March 1968, two letters crossed the Atlantic at the same time, one from Paris to New York and the other from New York to Paris. The former letter was from Moscovici[28] to Robinson, motivated not merely by the fact that there had been no reply from Ford to his proposal. As early as 1964, Moscovici had received an invitation to be a scholar of the Center for Advanced Study at Palo Alto in California. Due to his commitments in his laboratory and the impending move to the MSH, he kept postponing this fellowship. But he could no longer delay his departure. In his letter to Robinson, Moscovici referred to the lapse of time since they had corresponded, then he described the situation in Paris with respect to the MSH and explained the purpose of his letter. He wrote:

> I must therefore forecast and consolidate the functioning of my research and training group in Paris, and this advance planning assumes that I be fully aware of the material bases and possibilities at my disposition, also taking into account available resources. With this in mind, and in view of our previous conversations on several occasions – with Bob Schmid as well – concerning the help which the Foundation could give to research and training centers, I should be happy to know if you consider the possibility to act in my direction at some future date . . . It is for this reason alone that I take the liberty of writing so frankly, and asking you to let me know your intentions in this respect, thus permitting me to set up my program in consequence.

The other letter crossing the Atlantic was from New York, written by Schmid.[29] Schmid planned to spend a week in Paris towards the end of April and hoped to meet Moscovici there. He wanted to 'talk with you for a couple of hours' and then 'see you again later in the week, after I have talked with a lot of people'. He also wished to see Faucheux separately and asked Moscovici to arrange that. Only later in the letter did he come to the question of social psychology, however, without any explicit reference to Moscovici's proposal of April 1967:

> Among other things, I want to talk to you about social psychology in Europe. As you know, we are expecting to make a grant to support most of the cost of the Prague conference on which you have been busy, and I will want your advice on some other projects in social psychology as well. Incidentally, it would be helpful if you could send me within the next ten days a brief up-to-date statement on the European Association for Social Psychology. What are its plans for 1968–1969? What was its budget last year, and what is it this year? Where does its money come from? Finally, is the EASP incorporated as a non-profit association? Obviously, we can talk about these things when I see you, but it would be helpful to have some hints, especially on the financial situation, before I leave here.

Moscovici received this letter at the beginning of April 1968 and he immediately responded.[30] He was pleased to have, once again, the opportunity of meeting Schmid:

> You are doubtlessly aware, I wrote to Robinson quite recently concerning several questions which have been on my mind, and which I rather imagine are not unconnected with the object of your visit. Our letters seemed to have crossed in the mail. Needless to say, I am truly delighted to be able to talk over a number of matters with you personally.

Moscovici responded to all the questions that Schmid had asked in his letter and also arranged the meeting between Schmid and Faucheux. Schmid[31] reported the discussion with Moscovici and with Faucheux in an inter-office memorandum at Ford. His report reflected his positive view that he had formed of the progress made by the EAESP. Specifically,[32]

> Moscovici expressed the conviction that the most significant role of the Association would lie in 'legitimizing' social psychology in the eyes of the fund-disbursing agencies in most European countries. He is convinced that research money for the social sciences exists but the social psychologists, for instance, will not be able to lay claim to it until, through the activities of an association with a

serious record of achievement, they can present themselves, to the CNRS for example, as legitimate claimants.

It is quite clear from the memorandum that Ford was slowly moving towards providing the grant for the 'Moscovici's Centres'.

The report on Schmid's meeting with Faucheux was different in tone. One has the impression that Schmid was exploring social psychology in Europe in relation to American psychology. Thus he asked Faucheux if he 'shared the view that was becoming prominent in the US, that there were grounds for disappointment in the work in experimental social psychology'.[33] Indeed, Faucheux agreed and thought:

> that it is not unprophetic that such giants as Festinger and Schachter are leaving the field. Experimental social psychology had become increasingly arid, irrelevant and trivial. It is uninformed by the insights which other social sciences are drawing from new discoveries in biology, genetics, neurology and animal behaviour. Unless a new set of basic assumptions is developed he sees a global decline in the field . . . it is indicative of the situation that the most important work on dissonance is Festinger and Lorenz's book, *Deterrence and Reinforcement*, published in 1964, which is based on the study of the behaviour of rats, not human beings.[34]

Slow Progress

Ford was now prepared to award the grant. However, if this choice had been made more or less publicly, the final decision was taken behind closed doors. It is here that one can examine in detail the motives behind the decision, the agenda of the officers involved and the consequences of the grant for Ford. 'Our decisions,' wrote Robinson, 'about which institutions and programs would be included in this first serious Ford Foundation engagement with the social sciences in Europe were made slowly, based on discussions with staff and with many others outside the Foundation and eventually, with my bosses at the time – Ward and Bundy. None of the latter generated written memoranda.'[35]

The inner members of the staff asked unconventional questions, much like sceptics in a philosophical dialogue, or gatekeepers in an organized group. In order to avoid anachronism, let us recall some facts. Peter de Janosi[36] of the Higher Education and Research section at Ford raised 'brief and ignorable' comments such as this appeal to caution:

> Before we can evaluate the effectiveness of the three social psychologists you cite we ought to know more (or do we already?) about where the other half-dozen or so European social psychologists are and why they were not selected for our blessings. After all, once they hear of this grant we will have to face them also.
>
> I would think that we could do more than simply hope that the small grants to T, M and N would serve as 'bait to attract roughly equal amounts and perhaps more from their universities'. Why not try blackmail instead of bait? If we don't, we are sure to have these three worthy scholars back on our necks in four years' time. (See my memo dated January 30 on Marshall's and my meeting with Tajfel in London.)

De Janosi was not the only one to hold such strong reservations. They are echoed in the note addressed to Schmid by Chamberlain: 'My reaction to your memo of May 17th was similar to Peter's, that I did not know enough about Moscovici, Nuttin and Tajfel to what they stand for in social psychology and hence did not find . . . adequate grounds for selecting these three.'[37] Although it may not have been very pleasant for Moscovici, Tajfel and Nuttin to learn that they were complete unknowns, in some sense these observations were fair for a number of reasons. It was difficult in the USA to obtain information about any of them. But Schmid already had a response available because, very soon after Moscovici had written his personal letter to Robinson in April 1967, he had made his own investigations. He sought information[38] about Moscovici from some individuals in the USA, like Tumin and Campbell. The information that these social scientists provided was highly satisfactory.

Finally, Schmid[39] wrote to Moscovici that Ford had awarded the grants for the Centres and the EAESP. Moscovici[40] expressed gratitude on behalf of the EAESP to Ford for the decision they had taken: 'The aid that you have offered will insure that in the course of the next few years we shall be able to organise, effectively and fruitfully, very important activities in the development of social psychology in Europe.' In the late summer of 1968, Ford initiated negotiations with the Universities of Bristol and Louvain concerning their readiness to match the Ford grant with their own contribution. The negotiations with Paris were simplified by the fact that the new laboratory was part of the MSH. By that time Moscovici was a Fellow in the Center of Advanced Study at Stanford and Tajfel had become the Acting President of the EAESP. He handled the financial negotiations with Ford, establishing an impressive correspondence which gives an idea of the work done inside Ford's Higher Education and Research Section.

Looking back, one is astonished how much patience was required and how much had to be done to endow the EAESP with its second limb! One can never use the word 'final' in matters of fundraising. As late as in 1969, when Schmid[41] wrote to Moscovici announcing his visit, we can read the following postscript: 'Miss Bishoff has shown me your letter . . . I think I can clear any remaining questions about the grant payment schedules.'

However, this still was not the end of the matter. With regard to accounts and financial control, the EAESP at that time was still no more than a romantic fiction. Who could serve as a financial guarantor for the grant? Several solutions were sought. It was the programme officer from New York who found the obvious solution when raising a rhetorical question:[42] 'Could this grant be made to the Marc Bloch Association?' The Marc Bloch Association was related to the EPHE and managed its finances, including those from Ford. The letter from Tajfel informed Schmid that 'the Association is at present legally registered in Holland, but I would need further information from Mulder in order to deal with the legal aspects of the questions and also reach (together with him and Serge) the decision whether it would not be more convenient to use the Association Marc Bloch as a fiscal agent.'[43]

The grant was indeed eventually administered through the Marc Bloch Association in Paris which served as fiscal agent for the EAESP and the laboratory of social psychology grants.

At last, at the end of November 1968, Howard Dressner of the Higher Education and Research Section at Ford sent an official letter to Fernand Braudel, the President of the Marc Bloch Association,[44] informing him of the grant of $35,000 for the

EAESP. In December 1968, Moscovici wrote to Schmid,[45] saying that he and his colleagues were 'grateful to you personally for the kindness and tact with which you have treated our problems, something so rare and striking . . . the happy decision of your Foundation, will allow us, I hope, to create the stream of exchanges of research which will allow us to establish a solid basis of social psychology in Europe.'

Moscovici also wrote to Dressner,[46] thanking him for the grants both in his own name and as President of the EAESP.

It took a full two years to achieve this result. It was a useful learning process during which, contrary to what he had thought, Moscovici started to understand that the process of decision making by Ford would not be any simpler or faster than that of the French administration. It would only be more personal and friendly.

What was most intriguing during those years was the discreet character of the manner in which these grants were awarded. Everything began with the personal relationships which allowed those in charge of Ford to develop the idea of social psychology in Europe. However, the game got gradually more and more serious even though there were two years during which nothing much seemed to happen. The game was dependent on the one hand on the investment of Ford in the MSH in Paris and the choice of the three European centres. On the other hand, there was the proposal of the Transnational Committee which, for obvious reasons, was very difficult to refuse. One could see that the idea of three centres made relatively good sense. As time went on, Schmid became more open and Moscovici more overtly and directly involved the members of the Committee of the EAESP in the 'game'. From Tajfel's letter above, one gets a sense of the solidarity among them.

At that historic moment, things suddenly looked brighter. The following is at least clear: the task in which the researchers were engaged was well managed and had a long-term effect. Working with these documents, we have found a final evaluation of the grants awarded, written ten years after these events began. The final sheet of the last paper contains nothing but an astonishing and reflective quotation from De Janosi, casting a backward glance at the event:

In the early stages of the Foundation's interest in the European social sciences we assisted a number of centers of training and research in experimental social psychology. It was then thought that experimental social psychology was a discipline ready to flower in Europe, an expectation only partially fulfilled. Related to an effort to assist the building of centers of advanced training and research a grant was also made to the EAESP's program of exchange visits and conferences. It was thought that the Association would give the individual centers and scholars an opportunity to develop a network and thus facilitate the flow of information and people.

The modest funds provided to the Association were used frugally and effectively. The Association is now stronger and more effective and while we have had considerable difficulty in obtaining narrative reports, it is evident on the basis of individual conversations with participants in the Association's activities that the grant was indeed a useful one.[47]

To this, there is nothing else to add.

Bridge Passage

How can we evaluate the development of European social psychology at that time? As far as we know, there were not many grants awarded by Ford. The fact that the EAESP obtained several of them placed it on the social science map in Europe. It was recognition for an intellectual project of the EAESP. The Ford document accompanying the grant award stated that 'When the Ford staff began studying the state of health of the social sciences in Europe and England, it was immediately apparent that experimental social psychology was one of the liveliest, most productive, least nationalist and best organized in the social research discipline on that side of the Atlantic.'[48]

It is hard to understand today what it means, in social scientific terms, to live from day to day. It is difficult to appreciate that, having obtained grants for four years for the three laboratories and for the Association, one could start looking ahead, organize group meetings, establish exchanges and free the energies of each of the involved individuals in order to create mutual relations. The Ford

Foundation was much concerned with the uneasy nature of the relationship between Americans and Europeans. There was indeed some irony in American sermonizing about peer relationships in scientific communities, given the lack of intellectual respect for their European colleagues who, in turn, accused them of callousness and domineering attitudes. Given the situation of social psychology in Europe at that time, clearly these grants represented recognition of the need for European social psychologists to become independent, and encouragement to them to keep going in their own way. 'It was natural,' stated the above Ford document,

> under these circumstances, that European social psychology developed under a dependent and 'colonial' status with reference to US researchers – but the Europeans have rapidly moved towards independence. One of the marks of this independence is the present tendency of the Europeans, both as individuals and collectively, to approach US funding sources directly rather than simply as participants in research programs originated by American scholars.[49]

This was an extremely strong and courageous declaration. To the extent that Europeans represented a weaker discipline, they always had to defend the independence of their field and its creation. And now they were assured both of their doing well and of the motive for their project's approval. The above Ford document explains why it took two years to choose between this European proposal and other proposals. 'About a year ago,' the document states,

> the Transnational Committee submitted to the Foundation a proposal for a substantial seven-year grant much of which has been spent in collaboration with European scholars. This otherwise attractive proposal was rejected largely because in the staff's view it left too little initiative on the part of European scientists. The four grants recommended below represent an effort to help a thriving segment of the social research community in Europe strengthen its training and research capacity by making its own decisions.[50]

One knew that such truth was not yet acceptable (indeed, is it today?). Those who read these lines may have shrugged their shoulders and said that it was no more than circumstantial truth.

However, they were witness to at least one thing: the awareness that social psychology in Europe had entered the stage of maturity, in that year, 1968, and in those circumstances.

And this maturity signified that, in a very short time, the Transnational Committee had largely and successfully carried out its mission in Western Europe. Obviously, the rejection of its proposal for a seven-year grant weakened it. However, it had acquired strategic experience and the awareness that association building was the proper way to achieve its goals. Moreover, the Committee had a partner and a scientific community which made all its efforts meaningful. This was something of which the Committee members could be proud and could apprise others of and even offer it up as an example. From now on, they were entering unknown territory. And Eastern Europe was the bridge to this new terrain.

III

The East European Experiment

9

The First Encounter of a Small Science with Big History

The Royaumont conference in 1966 represented the clearest case of success for the Transnational Committee. It inaugurated also a lasting alliance between North Americans and West Europeans. One self-evident sign of this was their readiness to go ahead in two directions: towards Eastern Europe and towards Latin America. Shall we blame the Transnational Committee because it bustled with activities or because it took high risks on the road to transforming the abstract goal of creating international social psychology into the concrete and tangible one of drawing up its extensive map?

Establishing relations with Eastern Europe within the Soviet bloc was a difficult task. On the one hand, it seemed to be merely a question of reviving and reinforcing old cultural and scientific relations. And yet the military divide and the political conditions of the Cold War were a formidable obstacle for such a new and small group of scientists. Nevertheless even here changes were slowly taking place. After Stalin's death in 1953, the political show trials, arbitrary executions and the cruellest forms of injustice were replaced by less extreme ways of punishing political outcasts and dissidents.

By the 1960s, communist totalitarianism in Central and Eastern Europe gradually softened and transformed into milder forms of semi-totalitarianism. While Marxist ideologies of historical and dialectical materialism still occupied the major role on the syllabus in higher education, social sciences were now allowed a restricted existence both at universities and in academies of sciences. For example, while from the middle of 1920s until the 1960s there had been practically no sociological research in the USSR, and 'sociology' was a term that a good communist would not use, in the 1960s restricted forms of empirical sociology were allowed. Among these was the study of leisure time and time-budget studies, market research and youth culture (de Sola Pool, 1973). The Soviets even reintroduced some limited public opinion surveys. Social psychological research, where it existed, was carried out within sociology or psychology. Outside the Soviet bloc, very little was known about any social psychological investigations that might have been going on inside the USSR.

The First Encounter with the Soviet Bloc

Vienna 1967

In this situation the Transnational Committee decided that in order to find out what was happening behind the Iron Curtain, it would propose a conference involving East European social psychologists as well as West Europeans and Americans. Such a conference would enable both the latter to acquire a general impression of the East and find out how relations between Eastern and Western Europe could be established. In other words, such a meeting would explore the terrain and its potential for building social psychology behind the Iron Curtain. Most importantly, the Committee was convinced that in order to progress with that project, it was essential to involve social psychologists from the USSR. The scientific background to the meeting, at that stage, was considered less important. It was more necessary to overcome the political barriers, make personal contacts and generate an impression of uncharted territory.

The conference was to be held in Vienna in April 1967 for some twenty social psychologists from Eastern and Western Europe and the USA.[1] The Executive Committee of the SSRC voted to make limited funds available if no other financial support could be obtained. The EAESP was the co-sponsor. The task group consisted of Tajfel as chairman, Festinger, Irle and Moscovici. Invitations were extended to six psychologists from the USA, five from West European countries and fifteen from East European countries.

The principal aim of the conference was to initiate an encounter between East and West. It was hoped that participants would establish basic knowledge about each other, enabling the exchange of information between these politically remote regions. This would facilitate the development of continuing communication and future research cooperation. It was also intended to explore prospects for cross-national comparative studies.[2]

It turned out that at the beginning it was more difficult than expected. To start with, there were very few social psychologists in Eastern Europe and it was exceedingly hard to establish any contact, let alone invite them to a conference. Social psychology as a discipline received no encouragement in the Soviet bloc; in some countries it was prohibited, in others, if it existed, it was strictly censored. In order to discover potential participants, individual members of the task group undertook more or less specific jobs, based on their personal connections. For example, Tajfel had more relationships with East Europeans than the others so in June 1966 he visited Poland, Hungary and Czechoslovakia to meet with social psychologists. Moscovici was acquainted with Hans Hiebsch, an important figure in the German Democratic Republic (GDR), while others had contacts in Yugoslavia and Romania. The International Congress of Psychology in Moscow, August 1966, provided further opportunities for finding possible participants.

The second problem was political and administrative. In communist countries, professional and academic decisions, and specifically decisions with respect to travelling abroad, were made on the basis of political criteria by the institutions which employed the individuals concerned. Thus, although it was necessary to approach the individuals, first of all, it was essential to obtain the approval of the relevant higher-order bureaucracies. In practice, these two approaches were often combined. Since it was necessary to deal with academies of sciences and universities which did not have institutes of social psychology, it was crucial to identify the key individuals dealing with such problems, e.g. Hiebsch in the GDR and Janoušek in Czechoslovakia, among others.

Despite these obstacles, as the idea of the Vienna conference became a reality, enthusiasm and eagerness to take part was growing, particularly in Eastern Europe. However, the political and bureaucratic institutions were rather frosty. Of the fifteen invited social psychologists from communist countries, only eight 'accepted' the invitation. The diplomatic language that the organizers and the SSRC committees used in their memoranda and reports, such as 'accepted invitation', did not allude to the fact that the other seven individuals who 'did not accept' were simply not allowed to travel abroad. The article published in *Items* (Lanzetta et al., 1967, p. 30) stated that 'Several others, who were unable to attend, expressed eagerness to be included in any similar future activities.'

In contrast to the problem of attendance from communist countries, the choice of participants from Western Europe and the USA did not entail any difficulty in identifying suitable participants. Instead, the participants were chosen more or less arbitrarily. There were many individuals who were eligible and in the end, the Transnational Committee had only to ensure that the selected participants were actively engaged in research and represented a spectrum of different areas in experimental social psychology.

The Conference in Vienna took place on 9–14 April 1967. Meetings were held at the Hotel Intercontinental in Vienna. For a number of delegates, Vienna was a place of nostalgia and beauty. At the informal reception on the evening of their arrival, there was already clear evidence that the conference would be a great success. As Lanzetta and his colleagues (Lanzetta et al., 1967, p. 31) wrote, 'The group proceeded with the task of breaking the ice and discovered the ice was paper-thin. All the participants were warm, friendly, and eager to establish contact. By the end of the evening a few old acquaintances had been renewed and many new friendships initiated. It was an auspicious beginning.' There were several persons who particularly contributed to the good atmosphere. First, there was Hilde Himmelweit, who had excellent social skills and a subtle social knowledge of people and who therefore became the gatekeeper of the friendly atmosphere. The Soviet sociologist, Yuri Yadov, played an important role in helping break down barriers between East and West by engaging people in friendly conversation. Finally, there was the extrovert personality of Tajfel, a good ambassador for the Anglo-Saxon world, who was very sociable. Although he lived in the UK, he had earlier established relationships with many Americans. The presence of Festinger gave the conference prestige and legitimacy. Since

Festinger represented what was important in social psychology at the time, delegates from Eastern Europe could see that the meeting was not organized by a nameless group of people.

The programme was constructed to encompass a wide range of interests. The conference sessions, both formal and informal, were organized to facilitate free exchanges (Lanzetta et al., 1967, p. 30). The programme involved two main sections. The first section was devoted to the presentation and discussion of invited papers that had been distributed to the participants beforehand. The topics of these papers were concerned with characteristics of the existing trends in different countries. Harold Kelley gave the introductory paper in which he outlined four main approaches of American social psychology. The first approach concerned attitude change, following in particular Festinger's theory of cognitive dissonance. The second approach involved studies of decision making, leadership and responsibility in small groups. The third explored social perception and included the study of emotions, accuracy in person perception and the physiological determinants of social perception. Finally, Kelley was concerned with methodological problems, including physiological variables in sociological and psychological studies, the analysis of social psychological processes, mathematical models, comparative studies, relations between laboratory and real-life problems, and ethical issues. On the European side there were two lectures in response to Kelley's paper. First, Vorweg from the GDR spoke about the development of social psychology in Eastern Europe. In the second lecture, Koekebakker reviewed developments in Western Europe. These lectures were followed by more detailed accounts about general trends in Czechoslovakia (Jurovsky), Poland (Mika), USSR (Yadov) and Yugoslavia (Jezernik).

The second section of the conference included submitted papers on specific research topics. Lanzetta presented a paper on uncertainty as a motivational variable in conflict situations. Deutsch spoke about conflicts and their solution, attempting to apply the detailed analysis of conflict in small and large groups and relate this to social problems of greater significance. Thibaut discussed negotiation in games and Kelley reviewed experimental studies in mutual adaptation among people. In response several East European papers were presented, based on specific areas of research. Janoušek (Czechoslovakia) spoke about the reversibility of communication within groups. Malewska (Poland) discussed cultural and psychological determinants of sexual behaviour in women. Yadov (USSR) presented field research studying the relation between young workers. Mika (Poland) referred to the social context of punishment of children in educational establishments. Jurovsky (Czechoslovakia) spoke about socialization in the development of youth. He also commented on the differences between American and European studies. American research focused on the essential social psychological mechanisms, on laws as determinants of important social events, and on basic interpersonal processes. Jurovsky observed that methodological approaches exploring these phenomena could seem too detailed and too remote from what they actually wanted to study. Nevertheless, he appreciated the scientific value of American studies. Jurovsky also commented that European studies were more orientated towards applied social problems and that, methodologically, they were based on field studies and surveys rather than on experiments (Lanzetta et al., 1967).

The success of the Vienna conference

While hopes for the meeting ran very high, reality exceeded 'even the most optimistic expectations' (Lanzetta et al., 1967, p. 31). Yet it is interesting to reflect on the different ways in which West and East European social psychologists evaluated the conference. We must not forget that the participants came from different political backgrounds as well as from different social psychological traditions.

The delegates from the West thought that, above all, the meeting was extremely successful in reducing barriers between the East and West and in generating a friendly and cooperative atmosphere. Ideological and philosophical problems did not arise with any significance and did not play any important part in the ongoing discussions. Staff Officer Singer considered it important to comment on this fact:

> At an early point one East European questioned whether social psychology, as discussed, was appropriately Marxist–Leninist. It was the other East Europeans, rather than the Westerners, who unani-

mously rejected the question as an unnecessary intrusion. The tenor of their replies was pragmatic; abstract ideological concepts could not be made specific enough to provide help in resolving methodological difficulties or other research questions. The point, once raised and rebutted, was not brought up again nor did it hinder any of the other discussions.[3]

It was not surprising that Western psychologists would not respond to such a delicate ideological issue concerning Marxist–Leninist social psychology. Diplomacy required Western psychologists to be cautious. Any explicit show of ideological disagreement would preclude the possibility of a future encounter between East and West. Western psychologists obtained 'an extremely useful perspective on recent developments in the field' (Lanzetta et al., 1967, p. 31) in communist countries. In some communist countries, social psychology was recognized as a field of study. In the past, social psychological problems were treated by other disciplines such as sociology, pedagogy, medicine and law but now social psychology was developing rapidly, although the rate of development differed between one communist country and another. Among the most important subjects that were studied there were youth, the impact of family and institutional practices on moral development and attitudes of young people to various social issues. In addition, labour processes and decision making, small groups, social interaction and the role of mass media were becoming centres of interest.

Concerning research, there was an overlap between those that were topical in East and West European countries. However, there were differences in methodological approaches. In communist countries, social psychological problems were studied through survey or interview rather than by laboratory experiment. Lanzetta, Tajfel and Festinger (1967) surmised that laboratory experiments would 'probably be slower to develop since they are more dependent on physical facilities and equipment, and are generally perceived as more remote from application.' This comment suggests that these Western social psychologists thought that complex social problems should be studied in the laboratory. They assumed that the 'slow progress' in the East was due to lack of physical facilities and equipment. Of course, they may well have been correct in their assumption. However, they totally disregarded that what they saw as 'slow progress' could reflect a different perspective on social psychological phenomena and a different approach as to how they should be studied. This 'methodological issue', as we shall see, was a recurrent theme both in Eastern Europe and in Latin America.

Finally, the Western delegates came to understand what the main problems were for their colleagues in Eastern Europe. All communist countries had difficulties in obtaining books and journals from abroad. Isolation from the West did not allow them to learn about new publications. There were currency restrictions on foreign expenditure and a general shortage of funds.[4] Such barriers prompted proposals on how to reduce the isolation of East European colleagues. How could communication become more effective? How could they plan for future scientific collaboration and secure help in exchanging books and periodicals? How could they enable East Europeans to become members of the EAESP? Bureaucratic problems differed from country to country. There were very few generally applicable actions that could benefit all communist countries.

For East Europeans, too, the main merit of the Vienna conference was the establishment of social contacts. They were very enthusiastic about the proposal that would enable them to join the EAESP and participate in the training institute that was to be held at the University of Louvain.[5]

It could be said, though, that East Europeans had somewhat different views about social psychology and its nature. Above all, their main concern was to examine complex social problems related to youth, leisure, family and so on, but they did not consider exploring them in the laboratory. Just like sociologists and anthropologists, they worked largely in the field.

The Czechoslovakian psychologist Jurovsky (1967) characterized the differences between American, West and East European psychologists. He observed that in contrast to the USA, social psychology in Western Europe was characterized by a concern to solve issues in a speculative manner (for example, following the tradition in pre-war Germany), but not empirically. East European research, in contrast, was characterized by an effort to transform social psychological questions into problems of 'scientific socialism' and to view social psychology as part of general psychology (ibid., p. 106). This point is interesting for several reasons. We have already seen[6] that placing social psychology within the domain of general psychology was not specific to Eastern Europe. Indeed, the dominating tradition of American social psychology, too, viewed social psychology as part of general psychology. However, historical reasons for this connection were different in the USA and in Eastern Europe. In the latter, placing social psychology within the realm of general psychology served to detract attention from those social perspectives that might have been viewed as 'opportunistic' or 'bourgeois' and thus not acceptable to the regime. Regarding it as part of general psychology meant placing social psychology in a more 'scientific' framework and making it less ideologically noticeable. Thus we see that 'pure' science, for very different reasons, can become a hiding place for social science.

In his observations about the conference, the Czechoslovakian psychologist Janoušek (1967, p. 476) raised yet another issue. He noted the strengthening of research in Western Europe and its attempt to become more specific in developing goals and methods independently of the USA. Self-reliant social psychological research was developing particularly in Holland, Belgium, France, England and Norway. But collaboration between Western Europe and Americans was very important and would continue. Demand for solutions to social problems in Eastern Europe was considerably higher than available existing resources. Poland and Yugoslavia had already established contacts with Western centres founded on tradition, long-term exchange programmes and involvement in international projects.

Nevertheless, despite this very promising beginning in Vienna, it was evident that progress in establishing cooperation between East and West would be slow. In the existing international atmosphere of mutual suspicion and ideological conflicts, a full-scale programme of exchanges would not be feasible.[7] Some proposals for exchanging books and journals and staff and student visits were put forward, as well as programmes of collaborative research and joint training courses. However, certain kinds of collaboration were considered less suitable. For example,

With regard to the desire on the part of some East Europeans for research collaboration, the levels of methodological sophistication and technological knowledge are high enough in the West to militate against an immediate truly collaborative effort, but the next conference will focus on substantively oriented work groups. Specific discussion of research projects of mutual interest may be the first step toward joint research efforts.[8]

So we can see that history repeats itself. Here we have a little reminder of the beginnings of 'the West European Experiment'. Just like West Europeans some years ago, now East Europeans should first be trained or involved in 'work groups' in order to become suitable partners for their more advanced Western colleagues.

The last half-day of the Vienna conference was devoted to the evaluation of the conference and to future planning. The Vienna conference had opened up new possibilities. A very favourable sign of a bright future and cordial interchange was an offer by the two Czechoslovakian delegates, Janoušek and Jurovsky, on behalf of the Czechoslovak Academy of Sciences. They proposed that the next international conference should take place in Czechoslovakia in October 1968 at the Castle Liblice, the property of the Czechoslovak Academy of Sciences. The conference could be larger, focusing on specific research topics.[9] The proposal was enthusiastically accepted and the prospect of another conference in Central Europe was very exciting. A task group was immediately set up for the proposed conference to explore the feasibility of organizing it for the following year, 1968.

Prague 1968

Preparations

Czechoslovakia seemed an excellent choice for the next conference. In 1967 the situation there was tonic and seductive. The new party leadership started introducing changes to reform the political system. The monolithic and rigid regime was becoming more flexible and was acquiring certain diversified features; for example, there was less censorship in the media and previously forbidden literature started appearing in the press. The old regime lost its grip on social life and, instead, 'socialism with a human face' became the slogan of the day. Liberalization quickly changed the political atmosphere in the country.

The Transnational Committee started preparing the conference in Czechoslovakia with much care. Rapport between East and West was now established and the next conference was therefore to be more scientifically focused than the Vienna conference. The task group met in Aix-en-Provence in January 1968.[10] It was composed of Tajfel (chairman), Irle, Janoušek, Kelley, Moscovici and Riecken. The Transnational Committee also invited the Soviet sociologist, Yadov, who had played such an important role at the Vienna conference. Unfortunately, Yadov could not attend but it was agreed that his involvement in some way would be absolutely essential for the conference in Czechoslovakia, if Soviet representatives were to be well chosen.

The purpose of the meeting in Aix-en-Provence was to make sure that everything was very well prepared for the Prague conference. Social psychology in Eastern Europe was characterized by a kind of a 'social demand', focusing on useful and practical applications. There was some danger that unless some practical results, based on empirical work, were obtained rather quickly, the boom would not last.[11]

The Prague conference had special aims. It was seen as the beginning of a wider cooperation between East and West. It was expected that more provision would be made for East European students to be trained in Western Europe and in the USA. Also, there were hopes regarding the development of two-sided exchanges and it was planned that West European scholars and students would study in communist countries. It was expected that the conference papers would be published by the Czechoslovak Academy of Sciences as a book. This book would include papers from Eastern Europe as well as from the West and would make a visible and identifiable record promoting the field and documenting the establishment of public relations between East and West.

The procedure for invitations was carefully prepared. First, a formal letter was signed by Festinger on behalf of the Transnational Committee, by Moscovici on behalf of the EAESP and by Jurovsky on behalf of the Czechoslovak Academy of Sciences. This was followed by an informal letter, signed by Tajfel, chairman of the task group, describing the invitees' responsibilities, for example, their role as chairman, stimulator, critic, reporter, lecturer, and so on. Riecken was to ask Festinger to give a talk on the 'Usefulness of Social Psychology' and Campbell to give a lecture on 'Experimental and Non-experimental Methods from a Methodological Point of View'. Riecken would also invite all the USA delegates. These careful arrangements and the flourishing Prague spring promised a great international conference.

The crisis

Dramatic political events changed the course of history. The intention of Czechs and Slovaks to establish socialism with a human face was quashed on 21 August 1968 when the armies of the Warsaw Pact brutally invaded the country. The Brezhnev regime deeply humiliated the Czechoslovakian communist leaders, claiming that the Soviet army had to come to Czechoslovakia to defend socialism because 'the Czechoslovakian people had lost their orientation', meaning that they supported Dubček's reformist movement. From the point of view of the USSR, the invasion made sense: to maintain their territory, if necessary by force. From the other side's point of view, the invasion was unacceptable and the occupied country was not prepared to sacrifice either reason or freedom.

This political event stirred worldwide indignation and put into question the conference's future. For some, to continue with the conference would show support for their colleagues in the occupied country. For others, it represented an expression of acquiescence or, worse, legitimization of the invasion and the new regime. If the events had been less important, a compromise could have been reached. But the invasion of Czechoslovakia by the Soviet Army at that time was considered as serious as the Hungarian revolution in 1956. It was a violent event that had great international significance for the free world.

This placed both the Transnational Committee and, even more importantly, the EAESP, in a very unusual situation as scientific organizations.

At the time of the invasion, the President of the EAESP, Moscovici, was a Fellow at the Centre of Advanced Study at Stanford University and Tajfel became Acting President of the EAESP. The conference in Prague was to take place on 6–10 October 1968. The first reaction of the organizers seemed to be 'wait and see'. However, there was not much time for waiting. On

26 August, Tajfel sent a circular letter to all members of the EAESP and of the Transnational Committee,[12] requesting them to express their views about the appropriateness of holding the conference.

The line of the Transnational Committee was that the conference should be postponed 'unless further information can be obtained from Prague which would make it likely that, from the point of view of the Czechoslovak hosts, it was desirable to hold it'.[13] Yet the organizers could not make a decision. On Saturday, 6 September, Tajfel and Mulder visited Moscovici at Stanford and they agreed that the conference should be postponed.[14] The advice of Henry Riecken, President of SSRC at this point, was also to wait and to decide on the basis of the response from Czechoslovakia.

No doubt outsiders and insiders at an event always view the situation differently. In this case, the Czechoslovak organizers wished the conference to go ahead as they saw it as essentially supporting their case. A telegram from Jaromír Janoušek dated 3 September said: 'Irrespective of the present situation in Czechoslovakia, the organizing committee is able to arrange the conference under the terms given and stated before, Jaromír.'[15] And later he wrote to Tajfel,[16] 'Thank you very much for your call, kind words and efficient help. We had a rather shocking experience with international relations during last weeks and so much more we appreciate the genuine international solidarity.'[17] And the last sentence said: 'Looking forward very strongly to see you in our Prague.[18] Janoušek referred to the isolation of Czechoslovakian scientists and intelligentsia and insisted on continuing with the conference. All previously planned international meetings had been cancelled and people were desperate for international support. In view of this, Riecken thought that the conference should go ahead. It was mainly on these grounds that, in his letter to Mulder, the Secretary of the EAESP, Tajfel[19] suggested that the conference should take place.

There was, however, a split in opinion among the members of both organizing committees. On the Transnational Committee, two European members, Moscovici and Koekebakker, were resolutely against holding the conference.[20] The EAESP was divided almost fifty-fifty on the issue. The ensuing disagreement indeed threatened the very existence of the Association. Nuttin[21] decided not to accept the invitation to the Prague Conference, writing to Tajfel, 'I regret that the EAESP is sponsoring a scientific meeting which will be held at a place which, for the time being, is bound to have unambiguous political meaning . . . I'd like to ask you to relieve me from my organizational responsibility with regard to that Conference.'

The Secretary of the EAESP, Mulder, felt 'pressed' to write a confidential letter to all Committee members and to some others closely associated with the conference (Jezernik, Frijda and Koekebakker),[22] pointing out firmly that from the very beginning he had been strongly in favour of postponing the conference for at least six months. He was not aware, however, until very recently that 'independent of each other 3 members of the Committee were *against now!*' He thought that communication had totally failed and that 'important things are not handled properly between all Committee members (within the Committee)', referring implicitly to the Acting President.

Tajfel, who was chair of the organizing group of the conference as well as acting President of the EAESP, was in a precarious position. In the early days of the Soviet invasion, he found it difficult to elicit any views on the matter from members of the task group or from the EAESP. At the same time, he was receiving messages from Prague urging continuation of the conference. Europeans, like Mulder and Koekebakker, warned that other East Europeans, in particular those of a more liberal outlook, would not be allowed to go to Prague. Riecken, too, advised investigating this possibility before making a final decision.[23] This was why Tajfel described events in a chronological order in his letter of 30 September, seeking last minute guidance from members as to what to do:

I feel that I have acted as best I could in a difficult situation. The decisions I took may prove to have been wrong, but I *had* to take some decisions quickly on the basis of the information available to me. . . . On the first day of the conference in Prague, I am scheduled to give one of the three opening speeches – the one in the name of the EAESP. Now, I have no idea what I should do. If you feel that the Association should withdraw its sponsorship of the Conference, please let me know *immediately by telegram* (I am leaving Bristol for Prague on Thursday, 3rd October in the afternoon), and I shall act accordingly.[24]

tsjechoslow gewelt

AFSCHRIFT

VAN EEN AAN HET TELEGRAAFKANTOOR
TE UTRECHT
PER TELEFOON AANGEBODEN TELEGRAM

VOOR NAVRAGEN WENDE MEN ZICH
TOT HET KANTOOR VAN AANBIEDING

Telefoon-nr.
26551

Giro-nr.
s.f.

Naam en woonplaats
Sociologisch Instituut vd
Rijksuniversiteit Varkensmarkt
2 Utrecht

Opgen. door
tvb

| Klasse | Ktbest | Kantoor van afzending UTRECHT | Nr. 34 1606 | Wdn-tal 22 | Datum en tijd 4/10 1700 | Dbvs |

Dr Jaromir Janousek Institute of Psychology Purkynova ul 2 Praha/1

I have to cancel with regrets participation at the conference

Mauk Mulder +

Figure 9.1 Mulder's telegram to Janoušek

GENERAL INFORMATION

September

The International Conference on Social Psychology will take place at the time and under the terms stated before, that is in Prague at the Hotel International from 7th to 11th October, 1968.

The participants and accompanying persons are expected to arrive in Prague on Sunday, 6th October,1968. Those who would come earlier or later are kindly requested to inform the Secretary of the Organizing Committee (address see below). The travel expenses will be reimbursed according to the individual wishes either 1) in Prague, or 2) the participants submit an expense account after the conference.

If further informations are needed, please contact Professor Henri Tajfel, the Chairman of the International Planning Committee, Department of Psychology, University of Bristol, Berkeley Square 8-10, Bristol, England, or the Secretary of the Organizing Committee.

Looking forward to see you in Prague.

Dr Jaromír Janoušek, Secretary
Organizing Committee
Institute of Psychology
Purkyňova ul. 2
Praha 1 - Czechoslovakia

Figure 9.2   Janoušek's information on the Prague conference

The letter continued by asking his addressees to say that if they still felt that he was 'taking inappropriate action without consulting other members of the Committee', they should let him know their view. If members still felt, despite Tajfel's explanations, that he was acting inappropriately, he wished 'to resign from the Committee of the Association immediately on my return from Prague. The resignation will also include my withdrawal from any participation in the funds provided by the Ford Foundation.' Mulder, the Secretary of the Association, having received a telephone call from Tajfel, had 'a sleepless night' but eventually gave 'complete consent to the Association's sponsorship of the Conference'.[25] However, personally, he felt 'brought into a very unfree situation, and thus really frustrated'. He would not go to Prague.[26,27]

Attendance at the Conference thus became a personal matter. Many delegates from the West continued with their arrangements and took part in the conference. Others did not go. The two members of the Transnational Committee, Moscovici and Koekebakker, did not go. Of the members of the EAESP, in addition to Moscovici, Mulder and Nuttin did not go.

From the USSR, instead of four invitees, there was only one representative, Mansurov. Yadov, who was the Committee's most important contact, did not come. Of the other 12 invitees from Hungary, Yugoslavia, Romania, Bulgaria, Poland and GDR, only four were present. Of these four participants, two (Jezernik and Rot) came from Yugoslavia, one from Poland and one from Romania.[28]

The programme went more or less as anticipated (Janoušek, 1969). It included three plenary sessions and six working group meetings. The three plenary sessions based on invited lectures, were followed by discussion. Campbell gave a lecture on 'Quasi-experimental Designs for the Social Psychological Evaluation of Institutional Ameliorative Experiments' (discussant: Jezernik). Himmelweit spoke on 'Social Psychological Aspects of Education' (discussant: Frijda) and Deutsch spoke on 'Conflicts: Productive and Destructive (discussant: Mansurov).

Six working groups, consisting of approximately six people, each discussed specific topics. These comprised: socialization in childhood and youth, cognitive and behavioural consistency, interpersonal conflict, social psychology of language, intergroup relations; and social perception. The closing plenary session discussed problems of further transnational cooperation in the advancement of social psychology. In particular, discussions centred on advancing opportunities for communication and informal scholarly contacts among younger research workers.

The article about the conference was published in the SSRC *Items*. The authors, Janoušek and Tajfel (1969), emphasized that 'the Czechoslovak hosts stressed the value of holding the conference in their country at a time when it was particularly important for them to maintain international scientific and cultural bonds.' Otherwise, the report is as neutral as possible, as if everything was absolutely normal and there were no other concerns but scientific ones.

A critical review by Zdeněk Helus (1969), published in the Czechoslovakian psychological journal, is more telling. While Helus describes the content of plenary lectures by Campbell and Himmelweit, he totally changes his style when he talks about Deutsch's paper: 'Deutsch, after Festinger perhaps the second leading figure to come out of the Lewin school, is nearly a legendary personality in social psychology. He has become famous through his ground-breaking experiments in game theory' (ibid., p. 381; our translation). Helus describes Deutsch's plenary lecture on conflict in detail, dealing with conflict in a broad sense and giving interpersonal, intrapersonal and international examples. Destructive conflicts are characterized by the tendency to expand and to escalate. They rely on a strategy of power and upon tactics of threat, coercion and deception. They increase pressure for uniformity of opinion and they invest in militant tendencies and combat. The last part of Deutsch's lecture was devoted to strategies available to groups with limited power. These included opting out from situations, separating from groups with high power, mobilizing own resources, activating subgroups, using existing legal procedures to bring pressure for change and using harassment techniques to increase the other's costs of adhering to the status quo.

One can imagine the impact of this lecture on Czechoslovakian scientists whose country was occupied yet who had to pretend that their scientific conference was taking place under normal circumstances. While still 'neutral' science, Deutsch's lecture must have sounded like music to these humiliated social psychologists, investing it probably with more political meaning than the author himself intended.

In his autobiographical chapter, Deutsch (1999, p. 30) recalls his 1968 lecture on conflict in Prague:

> We met in Prague shortly after the USSR had sent its troops into Czechoslovakia to squash an incipient rebellion against Soviet domination. Despite our misgivings, we came at the strong urging of our Czech colleagues who wanted to maintain their contacts with the West. My paper included a section on what strategies and tactics were available to 'low-power' groups when confronting 'high-power' groups. The Czechs loved it and widely circulated a tape recording they made of it.

Czechoslovakian social psychologists expressed gratitude to the Transnational Committee for not modifying its plans; it was the first international group to keep its commitment to meet in the country after military occupation. They pointed out that the conference helped them maintain their contacts with Western psychologists. The Transnational Committee invited Janoušek to attend its next meeting in November 1968 and afterwards to become a member of the Committee.

After the Conference, the EAESP had a difficult time. Tajfel continued to clarify his position, both with respect to his decision about the conference and other issues, such as bad communication, the possibility of his resignation from the Committee and withdrawal from the Ford grant. While admitting that 'it would be easy for me to use post facto arguments . . . no one who has been to Prague can doubt that it was right to hold the conference and to continue the sponsorship by the Association,'[29] he did not do that. He repeated, that under pressure from Prague and from Riecken, 'I came to the firm conclusion that the conference *should* take place, and it would have taken very strong arguments to move me from that position.' Regarding the grant from Ford, despite being dissatisfied with the way Ford wanted to administer it, he decided to accept the situation. And, despite his disappointment with criticism over bad communication, he did not resign from the Committee. The Association soon recovered from the drama of the Prague conference. The grant from Ford to the 'Moscovici's centres' and to the EAESP got it back on the level.

10

A Strange Animal

After the Prague conference, the situation looked bleak. There was a general informal consensus, both in the West and the East, that to re-establish healthy relationships that had been so badly disrupted would take a great deal of time and energy. Moreover, student revolutions in May 1968 resulted in dramatic changes at many West European and American universities. These led to heated disputes and negotiations which had implications for science and higher education. The Transnational Committee tried to reflect on and comprehend the situation. What had made some people take part in the Prague conference while others decided not to go?

Nevertheless, the Committee restarted its work, creating a subcommittee chaired by Koekebakker, members of which included Kelley, Janoušek and Tajfel, to assess the situation. As we shall see, it would take six long years to reach a satisfactory solution and re-establish fertile relationships between East and West. In this infinitely slow process, the two-man team of Deutsch and Tajfel played a crucial role in bringing the task to a most successful conclusion. Deutsch, as Chairman of the Transnational Committee since 1969, coordinated different aspects of the work while Tajfel chaired the task group working in the field.

The Finnish Intermezzo

All East Europeans agreed that, in order to establish fruitful relationships, the first necessity was to involve the Soviets and secure their participation. No effort on the part of the Transnational

Committee would have any lasting effect in communist Europe without Soviet approval. The first and most obvious undertaking was to find a place where the next conference could be held in politically agreeable territory in the West but near enough to the USSR that Russians could attend relatively easily. There was not really much choice in this respect. The country closest to the Soviet border that was relatively 'neutral' was Finland. Thus it was first felt that perhaps Helsinki would be a suitable venue for the next conference. But who knew anything about social psychology in Finland? Who could be a mediator between Finnish social psychologists and the Transnational Committee? It transpired that Robert Abelson from Yale University had some contacts with Finns so he was approached. In late October 1968, Abelson wrote to Kullervo Rainio[1] at the Institute of Social Psychology in Helsinki and enquired about the possibility of organizing an East–West meeting of the EAESP in the summer of 1970. Rainio responded positively, passing Abelson's letter on to the Psychological Society of Finland which was also in favour.

In his letter to Rainio, Koekebakker[2] spoke about searching for suitable topics and finding good social psychologists from Eastern Europe. Most importantly, he emphasized that 'keeping the political sensitivities in mind, we all feel that Finland would be the preferred location, especially if we could attract some colleagues from Russia.' The quest for a central theme for the conference began and suggestions were made for suitable topics in which to train young social psychologists, and for a well-chosen focus which would lend itself to practical application. East European countries preferred topics relating to conflict studies, social influence and aggression.[3] As the Staff Officer of the Transnational Committee, Lehmann had already outlined the basic arrangement for the Helsinki conference at the Executive Committee of the SSRC in March 1969.[4]

In May 1969, Koekebakker visited East European countries to assess the prospects for holding the conference. He found that social psychologists there were very interested in taking part in another joint venture but signs of difficulty were already surfacing. Koekebakker's report stated that 'In seeking opinions and suggestions concerning an international conference, he found that although the proposal received general and enthusiastic acceptance, a number of would-be participants would have some trouble in travelling to such a conference because of restrictions imposed by East European countries'.[5] This suggested that, despite the fact that Finland was considered a suitable country with a sensitively balanced diplomacy and was geographically close to the USSR, it did not provide a suitable solution. While the task group decided to continue with preparations for the proposed conference, individual members made additional efforts to contact East European social psychologists. Irle was invited to join as he had contacts in the German Democratic Republic.

The task group met in Prague in late January 1970 and strongly emphasized that, although 'the time is propitious for such a conference',

> steps should be taken to insure the participation of psychologists from the USSR. It was suggested that contact with high-level officials of the Soviet Academy of Sciences be made by letter as soon as possible and that informal contacts with Eastern European social psychologists be maintained in order to compile a roster of interested and active research scholars in the field, to decide on topics of mutual interest and to determine the most appropriate site for such a conference.[6]

This was the clearest statement that Helsinki was not considered 'the most appropriate site'. Only the agreement of the Soviets could provide a 'legal' kind of approval in the very hot political situation which was Eastern Europe. The Transnational Committee was well aware that it was important not to do anything that could be interpreted as anti-Soviet.

The Awakening of Soviet Sociology

Despite the political ferment in the aftermath of the invasion of Czechoslovakia, social sciences in the USSR had some good years; indeed, Vladimir Shlapentokh (1987) refers to the years 1965–1972 as the 'golden years of Soviet sociology'. Sociological publications started appearing, symposia and seminars were organized and sociology teaching at universities was introduced, for instance in Moscow by Andreeva, in Leningrad by Yadov and in Novosibirsk by Shlapentokh.

In December 1968, the Soviet Academy of Sciences allowed the creation of the Institute for Concrete Social Research with Alexei Rumiantsev as its director. Rumiantsev was the leader of the Party liberals and, moreover, he was in a key academic and political position as Vice-President of the Soviet Academy of Sciences. He was also a member of the Central Committee of the Party and a former editor-in-chief of the most important daily newspaper, *Pravda*. Above all, he enjoyed the support of Brezhnev (ibid., p. 36).

A letter to Rumiantsev

In order to solve its problems, the Transnational Committee requested the President of the SSRC to make overtures at a high level to the Soviet Academy of 'Sciences, hoping that co-sponsorship of the proposed conference could be arranged.[7] The Soviets, as a superpower, were more interested in negotiating with the opposing superpower, USA, than with West Europeans. Hence it fell to Henry Riecken, the President of the SSRC, to write a letter to the academician Rumiantsev. By coincidence, both Riecken and Rumiantsev were among the invited members of the Executive Committee of the ISSC during the period 1970–3. That fact might also open up an avenue for communication.

Writing a letter to a high-level Soviet official required great sensitivity. Careful wording was needed to avoid any points of possible conflict. The letter to Rumiantsev was not to be sent by post. Instead, it was carried personally by Frederick Burkhardt, President of the American Council of Learned Societies, who was about to visit the USSR and 'kindly agreed to explain on our behalf the circumstances of the Committee and its relationship to American academic social psychology.'[8] And of course, this also ensured that the letter reached its addressee. Although the letter was already nearly three pages long, Burkhardt would have preferred to give the Soviets even more detail about the planned conference. While Riecken agreed, he pointed out that

> on the other hand, the general reaction of social scientists who know the Soviets seems to be that at this stage of the game too much detail is likely to drive them away rather than the other way around. The whole thing is just Kremlinology anyway and I'm sure that no matter how we go about it we will have a difficult time.

Riecken of course was right. There were difficult times ahead. Nevertheless, the first move had been made and Riecken announced to the Transnational Committee that the letter had been successfully delivered:

> Rumiantsev apparently favors the meeting and he turned over my letter to G.V. Osipov of the Institute of Concrete Social Research. Osipov told Burkhardt that he would write a favorable answer, giving suggestions on how and by whom the symposium should be prepared, which Fred Burkhardt could take back to the U.S. If so, we may well have our answer by mid-September.[9]

Rumiantsev indeed responded to Riecken and recommended that joint efforts be made by 'the SSRC, the EAESP, the Soviet Sociological Association and other Soviet organisations . . . to organise a scholarly conference on social psychology'[10] within twelve to eighteen months. This was an encouraging start and the next step was to hold a joint meeting in Moscow. Riecken responded to Rumiantsev on 5 October 1970 by telegram and subsequent letter, suggesting a joint meeting in Paris or Moscow.[11] Deutsch had by now replaced Festinger as chairman of the Transnational Committee[12] and he, Riecken and Tajfel were expected to attend on behalf of the SSRC and the EAESP.[13]

While this exchange of correspondence was going on, Janoušek wrote a letter to the SSRC Staff Officer, Lehmann, informing him that he had had a talk with László Garai from Budapest who had expressed the view that perhaps the conference could be held in Hungary. If that was agreeable, a letter should be sent to the academician Mátrai, President of the Commission for Psychology at the Hungarian Academy of Sciences. That looked very promising but it was necessary to wait for Rumiantsev's response.[14] Time went by and there was no response from the Soviets. Riecken left it until the spring of 1971 before writing to Rumiantsev once again.[15] However, no response was forthcoming.

Where to meet?

Nearly a year had passed since 5 October 1970. In late September 1971, Deutsch, Festinger and Tajfel decided to follow up

Garai's earlier suggestion for a conference in Budapest. They jointly wrote to the academician, Mátrai, and enquired about the possibility of an East–West conference in Hungary.[16]

At that time Hungary had the biggest social psychology group in Eastern Europe. Since the Hungarian revolution of 1956, the Kadar regime had allowed citizens a certain degree of internal freedom not available in other communist countries. In a way, the Kadar regime had made an implicit pact with its citizens. As long as they were cautious, did not overstep the limits of that permitted freedom and did not get involved in political matters, they could live relatively normal lives. Of these social psychologists, the most active individuals were Garai and Pataki. From the beginning, they were supportive of an East–West conference in Hungary.

The letter that Deutsch, Festinger and Tajfel sent to the academician László Mátrai was simple. In contrast to the letter to Rumiantsev, no reasons were given for organizing the conference. Mátrai responded positively but cautiously.[17] The conference required serious consideration and that would take time. Therefore, he asked his correspondents for their patience; and said he would inform them of the decision in due course.

No letter followed. Deutsch wrote again to Mátrai, proposing a visit by representatives of the Transnational Committee and the EAESP[18] to discuss the possibility of a conference, probably in 1973 or 1974.

The Strange Animal

Again, there was no response to Deutsch's letter. Nevertheless, despite the silence from behind the 'Iron Curtain', further developments were taking place. At the plenary conference of the EAESP in Louvain in 1972, Tajfel received an 'unofficial' message from Garai who was present at the conference. Thus Tajfel wrote to Deutsch: 'Apparently, the bureaucracy of the Academy of Sciences in Budapest was quite satisfied about organizing a conference together with the EAESP, but started delaying this, not being quite sure what was that strange animal, the "Transnational Committee of the SSRC". Further delays will occur until this is cleared up.'[19] Tajfel urged Deutsch to write to Mátrai again. For the Hungarians, at that time, the Transnational Committee, which did not have any real official status, was indeed a strange animal. And yet this Committee was able to take initiatives in organizing and negotiating conferences and activities involving the Academies of Sciences in Eastern Europe.

Search for an Official Umbrella

Financial support for the conference was another sensitive issue. What kind of support would be acceptable to the Soviets? Some funds for the proposed conference were still available from the 1968 Ford grant. This had been intended for 'partial support of an international conference, with permission to use the unexpended balance for an additional international conference or for travel by East and West European social psychologists to facilitate greater cooperation and collaborative research'.[20]

Moreover, to smooth relations and avoid eventual friction with and criticism by the political establishment, it appeared that everything would be easier if some international institutions working in the region would give their blessing to the project. In other words, it would be useful to have a more official umbrella. One such institution was the Vienna Centre, created to facilitate such relations. Therefore an extensive correspondence passed between Henry Riecken and Allen Kassof, the Executive Director of the International Research and Exchanges Board (IREX).[21] In addition, a great deal of correspóndence passed between Samy Friedman, the General Secretary of the ISSC in Paris, and Deutsch, chairman of the Transnational Committee. It was hoped that the two international institutions, that is, the ISSC and the Vienna Centre, would satisfy Soviet bloc requirements for international mediation at the conference.

Tajfel wrote to László Mátrai, giving him the news[22] that the Vienna Centre and the IREX Board would be mediators. In the summer of 1972, he visited Nijmegen, Vienna and Hungary. It must have been 'one of the more complicated trips I've made in some time,'[23] he wrote, but he made good progress with the project. The purpose of his trip to Nijmegen was to inform and in particular to seek the authorization of the EAESP 'to continue representing them in future negotiations concerning the projected East–West conference'. In Vienna Tajfel met Riccardo Petrella, the Director of the Vienna Centre and they discussed how the Centre might function as a conference mediator. The most important part of Tajfel's trip was his visit to Budapest. It seemed that any progress was dependent on the academician Imre Szabo, the Vice-President of the Academy of Sciences. Tajfel wrote:

> However keen they may be, the Hungarian social psychologists by themselves can do nothing much about promoting the conference. It is entirely within the competence of higher powers. Even Mátrai could do very little. It all depended on the decisions of Szabo, and therefore – I was told – my meeting with him was crucial. I was also told, however, that once he commits himself, he stays committed. This point is important in view of the results . . . of my discussions with him.[24]

Not surprisingly, Tajfel, 'after this series of caveats' went 'to meet Szabo next day with considerable trepidation'. That meeting confirmed that if the conference were to take place in the West, for example, in Vienna, it would have to be financed entirely by international, and not by American, institutions. If it took place in a communist country, in this case in Budapest,

> then it must be sponsored by the Academy of Science and by *international* organisations. Both alternatives leave out the SSRC which is not only not international, but also happens to be American (although I did my best to explain the international composition of the Transnational Committee). As I understand it, the fact that the Committee is American means that anyone outside the USSR would be extraordinarily careful in infringing the Soviet prerogative of dealing officially and directly (on an equal level?) with the Americans.[25]

Tajfel also pointed out that the Hungarians often referred to 'juridical' matters, meaning that the conference had to be funded by proper sources. He commented, however, that these 'juridical' issues were not the real ones. They amounted to a euphemism for the fact that academic freedom in the Soviet bloc was very limited with respect to any initiatives or contacts with the West. And even if freedom had not been so limited, people would not risk initiating something 'unless they are fully and "juridically" covered . . . providing the juridical cover and protection exist, we could find a lot of goodwill and cooperation . . . we can have the conference in Budapest and such a conference would be welcome.'

Nevertheless, it was still necessary to proceed carefully. Szabo still needed the support of other communist countries and of the USSR in order to go ahead. Therefore, he had to write to all Vice-Presidents of Academies of Sciences in communist countries to ask them to participate. He also arranged for Garai to go to Moscow to discuss the matter with the psychologists Lomov and Leontiev and with the new Vice-President of the Academy, Fedossev. The golden years of Soviet sociology had ended and Rumiantsev, the previous Vice-President of the Academy, was no longer in that role. He was too liberal for the Soviet regime and had been sacked in 1971.

Responses from other communist countries were slow. When Flament, then President of the EAESP, visited Szabo and others in Budapest in the autumn of 1972, no replies had been received. But Szabo promised Flament that the moment he received at least *one* reply he would definitely go ahead with organizing the conference in Budapest. In the event, *two* responses finally arrived, from the German Democratic Republic and from Romania. The sequence of events clearly shows that, individually or collectively, and despite their competence, intelligence and hard work, social psychologists could not make the decisions as these were made by bureaucratic and political institutions alone.

The organizing committee of the East–West conference met in Budapest on 15–16 December 1972. Present were Tajfel as Chairman, Deutsch, Chairman of the Transnational Committee, Flament, President of the EAESP, Fraser, secretary of the EAESP, Garai, Janoušek and Pataki.[26]

The official sponsors of the conference were the Hungarian Academy of Sciences, the EAESP and the ISSC. As the Minutes of the Transnational Committee stated: 'The Transnational Committee is an "organizer" of the conference; particularly with respect to American participation; neither the Committee nor the Council will be a sponsor.'[27] So, in the final analysis, the Transnational Committee was given the job of organizing, not participating in, the showpiece – this was how things were done at the time.

The Visegrad Conference

The time and place was 6–10 May 1974, Visegrad, about 30 km from Budapest in a castle courtesy of the University of Budapest. It was one of the best organized, most beautiful and active conferences that anyone could remember. After years of trying to find a place for the meeting, instead of a 'neutral' place, Helsinki in Western Europe, the Transnational Committee had hit upon a 'neutral' place in Eastern Europe. Visegrad was a small, uncrowded city, not far from the Danube. The participants had their own space within the guarded and pleasant natural surroundings. It was spring. There were 42 participants[28] and 16 observers from Hungary and everybody seemed relaxed. As for the members of the Transnational Committee, after such an arduous journey, Visegrad seemed like the Promised Land.

Yet the Transnational Committee remained the 'strange animal'. It was not officially invited to take part in the conference, despite all the work it had put into its preparation during those six long years. It was represented on the conference by the task group but otherwise it had no official status. Similarly, the SSRC did not sponsor the conference. Everything was done indirectly. Funds in support of American participants were officially obtained by the task group from the IREX Board, although in fact the SSRC was one of the governing bodies of IREX.

The West Europeans and the Americans more or less knew one another and they got to know the Hungarians. And of course, as in a Gestalt, the Russians were the Figure, and the rest were the Ground. It was partially so because the Russians were a discrete and mysterious group. At their centre was the figure of Alexei Leontiev. Moscovici remembers that he looked like someone cut out of a photograph from *la belle époque*. He was like an aristocrat from a French or Russian novel, very tall, slim and dressed in a well-cut suit, which had been *à la mode* perhaps in the thirties. Leontiev's beautiful hands played with a long cigarette holder and he was quite reticent. Near him most of the time was a small, plump woman who did not seem to speak any language other than Russian, except perhaps a little English. So, immediately a rumour started among the Western delegates (naturally, everybody was analysing the group) that she was overseeing Leontiev. It was difficult to make any contact with her. Moscovici spoke with Leontiev on several occasions in French but only for very short periods. Moscovici did not know whether anybody else engaged in any scientific discussion with him as most of the time he was with the woman who accompanied him. Possibly, Leontiev was distant because he was not a social psychologist. But nonetheless, he was a notable historical and scientific figure, part of the famous *trojka* of Leontiev, Vygotsky and Luria, and it was significant that the Soviets had sent someone like him to the conference.

There was a rumour at the time that one ought to be careful about speaking in enclosed areas because there might be microphones in the rooms. So the Western participants talked with their East European colleagues outside. As for any such police surveillance, one might have supposed it just a fantasy. Nevertheless, Moscovici went for a walk one evening some distance from the main conference building where a security guard with a dog told him that he was not allowed to go any further. Looking back on these rumours of surveillance, one might say that there were two conferences in Visegrad, an indoor conference and an outdoor one – and these were not one and the same. The outdoor conference did a lot for the success of the indoor one in cementing relationships which after the conference became more dependable.

The overall theme of the conference was 'The Social Psychology of Change'. There were three invited addresses at plenary sessions, each representing a region of international social psychology. The academician Leontiev represented Eastern Europe, Campbell represented North America and Moscovici represented Western Europe.

Leontiev spoke about the possible role of social psychology in the study of social change. According to him, social change could be studied at three levels: the socio-political nature of society, societal institutions and individuals/groups. Change often involved conflict and conflict resolution but many social psychology studies were based on laboratory experiments and were therefore sterile. Such studies attempted to 'psychologize' objective and historical factors.

Donald Campbell, who was President-elect of the American Psychological Association (APA), discussed social experiments and quasi-experiments and policy innovations in the USA and Western Europe. Campbell was critical of the validity and impact of planned social intervention and argued for moving towards an 'experimenting society'.

Moscovici spoke about the two views of social conflict. According to the traditional view, groups form themselves on the basis of shared interests and move towards a common goal. Alternatively, a group maintains a current equilibrium and serves essentially inertial purposes. In this situation, 'it is precisely the subversive action of group members who are divergent or in the minority that serves . . . to move the group away from stasis and toward social change. Social psychologists must study not only conflict resolution, but conflict arousal.'[29]

The report on the conference by Staff Officer Jenness states that there was much critical discussion concerning Moscovici's paper. The paper was mainly criticized by Western colleagues who thought that the more relevant dimension of conflict was between groups rather than within them. But 'one lengthy and sharp criticism of Moscovici's presentation came, finally, from a Soviet participant, who called the study of group dynamics "technological trivia", and was disturbed by what he considered the manipulation or provocation of conflict, in the guise of studying it.'[30] Moscovici had talked about social change in the sense of innovation and about conflict arousal because this is what minorities create.[31] He spoke about it at a time when he was working on groups but he had also just started writing about dissident movements. So it appears that the picture of the dissident movement, as depicted in his paper, had made the Soviets uneasy. Moscovici had intended the analogy in his paper because he thought it important to address intellectuals, especially in Hungary. One could say they were dissidents and social psychologists should speak out.

Of course, science cannot produce merely 'neutral' knowledge of social turbulence. It is expected to fight against obscurantism and for the emancipation of oppressed people. Moscovici thought that social psychologists should not remain insensitive to the preoccupation of intellectuals in Eastern Europe, especially in Hungary. It is also true that he was friendly with some dissidents in Hungary, among them János Kis and Ferenc Mérei, a Lewinian who worked on leadership. Mérei had been in prison for five years but was freed after the Hungarian revolution, by the Kadar regime, becoming something of a hero in his country.

Most of the conference time was spent in working groups. These included:

1 *Assumptions and methods in the social psychological study of change*

   This group was led by Leontiev and Campbell and mainly considered issues raised in Leontiev's plenary address such as the level, origin and agency of individual and social activity in the process of social change.

2 *Social change and socialization*

   Bronfenbrenner and Kon acted as chairmen in this group. The group discussed socialization as a process leading to reciprocal patterns of interaction and motivation in enduring social contexts.

3 *The social psychology of organizational change*

   This group was chaired by Kahn and Mansurov and was concerned with empirical work and social scientific theory of organizational activities, the formation and implementation of decisions.

4 *Social change and cognitive behaviour*

   Andreeva and Flament acted as chairmen and the group discussed ways in which social behaviour in various settings is constructed and conceptualized. The concept of representation was closely related to this topic.

In his report assessing the conference, Jenness[32] pointed out that the topic of social change was an excellent choice for the conference, being provocative and at the same time providing the possibility for discussion in empirical terms. He concluded 'after a cautious beginning, the level of apparent genuine interest and free interchange reached a high plane; and although several areas of sharp disagreement (not necessarily along East–West lines) were encountered, these were treated as exciting opportunities, stimulating a more thoughtful and precise development of viewpoints, rather than a threat to mutual communication.'

The report also states that incidents of dogmatism or simple reiteration of conventional views was very low. Instead, personal courtesy that promised future cooperation dominated interaction at the conference. Enthusiasm, hard work and cordiality were the most significant markers of informal interactions: 'There was a generally expressed hope that another international conference of social psychologists could take place, well before another six years (the period since the Prague conference) elapse, and as the conference ended there was a strong indication that the Polish Academy of Sciences might be willing to sponsor another conference, in perhaps two years' time.' So the six long years of frustrating effort finished in glory. One way in which the Soviets recognized the success of the conference and the hard work of the Transnational Committee was by issuing an invitation to Deutsch, Kelley and Moscovici to visit Moscow for ten days.[33] This invitation was also an acknowledgement of the role of the SSRC and of that 'strange animal', the Transnational Committee, which had not been officially invited to take part. Last but not least, let us quote from the letter that Urie Bronfenbrenner[34] wrote to Eleanor Sheldon, President of the SSRC:

> I have just returned from a remarkably successful international conference of social psychologists held in Hungary that I understand was made possible in part through the support of the SSRC. What was unusual about this one was the remarkable sensitivity of the leadership to the delicate requirements needed to preserve and foster communication between East and West, and, as a result, an extraordinary level of genuinely scientific discussion relatively free from ideological pressure and distortion. The foregoing judgment is based not only on my own direct observations but on the comments made to me by East European colleagues, many of whom, as you know, I have known over a long period of time.

IV

The Latin American Experiment

11

Latin American Odyssey

In attempting to widen the map of social psychology, the Transnational Committee took an interest, at approximately the same time, in two regions of the world. Alongside Eastern Europe, it directed its attention towards Latin America. The Committee raised the subject as early as 1966 at its Paris meeting in April. Staff Officer Singer[1] commented that the matter had been on the agenda previously, but since 'the committee was busily planning for the Vienna conference and was also contemplating future Asian and African involvement, no Latin American action was taken' until after the Vienna conference. It was very ambitious for such a small group of scientific pioneers to take on the exploration of a very large and unknown continent. Vast distances, lack of contact with the field and a very few widely dispersed social psychologists were bound to create major obstacles for the Transnational Committee.

The First Contact with Latin America

In his brief history of the Transnational Committee, Festinger[2] recalled the beginnings of its involvement with Latin America. It was in the mid-1960s that two social psychologists, Jorge García-Bouza from the Instituto Torcuato Di Tella in Buenos Aires, Argentina, and Aroldo Rodrigues from Pontificia Universidade Catolica in Rio de Janeiro, Brazil, approached the Transnational Committee. They 'independently urged the committee to attempt to do the same thing in that area of the world that had been so successfully done in Western Europe'.[3] These two psychologists did not know each other and were only vaguely familiar with other Latin American centres of social psychology.

In late 1966 and early 1967, García-Bouza visited several social psychologists in the USA. He was interested in organizing a conference that would involve both North and Latin Americans and he sought support for this venture and for co-sponsorship. He visited, among others, Festinger, Schachter, Lanzetta and Singer. Singer pointed out in his letter to Riecken[4] that García-Bouza was an enthusiastic traveller and letter writer. After talking to some members of the Transnational Committee, he immediately started planning a conference. Of these visits, perhaps the most significant was García-Bouza's meeting with Festinger in October 1966. He summarized his notes in a long letter.[5] He envisaged linking up with the Transnational Committee, with the Foundation for European Summer Schools and with the EPHE in Paris.

After the successful first East–West meeting in Vienna in April 1967, the idea of extending the map of social psychology into Latin America became a serious item on the Transnational Committee's agenda. Having made a mark in Europe by reaching East European social psychologists, and with the Prague conference in preparation, it seemed feasible to turn the spotlight on Latin America. By the May meeting in 1967 in New York, the Committee was firmly committed to initiating proceedings in unknown territory. It discussed the potential contributions it could make,[6] specifically, as a first move, supporting a small international conference in Buenos Aires proposed by García-Bouza. Generally speaking, it was understood that the Transnational Committee would apply the same strategy it had used in Europe. Of course, it was necessary to explore the terrain, to find and meet social psychologists before starting association building.

The Transnational Committee asked Koekebakker and Lanzetta to investigate where they should start and García-Bouza and Rodrigues were invited to join them. Yet, despite all the enthusiasm, it was clear that the Committee lacked the knowledge about Latin America that would enable it to take useful steps. The Committee was just about to submit a proposal to Ford for a seven-year support of its ambitious programme,[7] so it made provision for two Latin American conferences, two summer training institutes and some scholarly exchanges.

When Koekebakker, Lanzetta, García-Bouza and Rodrigues met in Amsterdam in September 1967, they were able to clarify more concretely the status of Latin American social psychology although they considered it hazardous to rely on the experience of two countries only, Argentina (García-Bouza) and Brazil (Rodrigues).[8] Nevertheless, they thought that similar problems were likely to exist in most countries, such as a lack of text translation, a scarcity of journals and books, a low level of training and lack of competence. A major contributor to poor standards was low student aspirations. This seemed to result from a scarcity of well-trained staff. However, there were also positive signs. Although there were very few Latin American social psychologists with PhDs, they were all highly committed to social psychology and teaching and held positions of responsibility. Some graduate students were being trained in the USA. In addition, research collaborations between the USA and Europe already existed. Another advantage to higher education in Latin America were low tuition fees and dependable governmental support for graduate studies.

Searching for social psychologists

While there were some similarities between the establishment of social psychology in Europe and in Latin America, there were also substantial differences. For example, if the Transnational Committee wanted to approach specific individuals in Europe to establish scientific or professional contacts, it had to do so through their associated institutions. In general, the academic institutional basis in Europe had a long tradition. Some academies and learned societies were two or three centuries old and had developed strict procedures. Universities, too, had firm structures and organizations. In Eastern Europe, the Soviet regime ossified the structural basis of institutions and their hierarchical structure. In dealing with institutions in the Soviet bloc, it was necessary to follow a certain road-map of rules and regulations. This enterprise took a great deal of energy and required much attention because the Cold War had created a tense divide between Eastern communist and Western capitalist countries. The work of the Transnational Committee in these conditions was at first mainly dedicated to maintaining and creating good relationships with colleagues and only later to focusing on scientific matters.

In Latin America, the institutional structure was weak. In fact, as we have seen, García-Bouza was well aware of the necessity to develop an institutional basis there. When the Transnational Committee started working in Latin America, it was only through the efforts of interested individuals that any progress was made. Institutions were not very visible – or at least, the Committee did not encounter them in the first instance.

It was clear that the question of the unfamiliar map skewed the members' way of thinking. Reporting on the work in Latin America, Lanzetta wrote:

> There is certainly much more uncertainty in Latin America than there was in Western Europe about the available number of capable social psychologists (and junior coming men) in the region. There is also the problem posed by the tremendous distances between major centers. This last factor especially could hamper the development of a network. Doubts cannot help arise as to whether a 'Sorrento' type of conference would be the most effective catalyst for such a network.[9]

The problem of distance in particular could hamper the development of a working network. The flight from Europe to Buenos Aires took 14–16 hours; from New York it was 12 hours,[10] not to mention the necessity of finding sufficient funds to bring people together. Due to these problems, the two Latin American members of the subcommittee began to hesitate as to whether a conference would be an effective first step, if there were no means of following it up. Moreover, could one find a suitable location for a conference? Was there indeed an alternative way? For example, would it not be a better idea to start with a summer school? Should the Transnational Committee develop a 'Centre of Excellence' there? There were many unknowns.

A three-man mission to Latin America

It was Lanzetta who suggested a preliminary mission to find social psychologists and social scientists who would be interested in a

Latin American conference and future activities.[11] And so in summer 1968 Festinger, Lanzetta and Hereford (Texas) made an exploratory mission to Venezuela, Brazil, Uruguay, Argentina, Chile and Mexico.[12]

In Caracas, Venezuela,[13] they first visited Professor Chirinos, a neuro-psychiatrist, at the Central University. They also visited Professors Sanchez, Santor, Casalta and Caielo. All expressed interest in applied social psychology and in discussing interdisciplinary research into contemporary social problems. A programme in which students would do cross-disciplinary work in anthropology, sociology and social psychology was underway. Although these scholars did not themselves have a clear model of how they should proceed, they were resistant to outside influences that might detract from their long-term goals. In a nutshell, they entertained suspicions of North Americans.

In Rio de Janeiro, Brazil, the visitors met Rodrigues at the Catholic University. A student of Kelley's, he had received his doctorate in the USA. He was already an experimental social psychologist who had his own laboratory. Brazil was the only Latin American country with licensing legislation after a five-year training. No higher qualification was legally recognized and, consequently, very few students were motivated to obtain any further training. There was a strong tradition in Brazil which favoured psychoanalytic theory and an overriding concern with applied problems. Rodrigues would have preferred to have competent indigenous professors and researchers rather than visiting professors. Unfortunately, competent people, trained at North American universities, were very dissatisfied with the local situation and often left for lucrative positions in the USA so Rodrigues thought that an advanced Latin American centre was highly desirable and would respond to local needs.

The team visited the Federal University of Rio de Janeiro and the universities of São Paolo. They met Professors Schneider, Angelini and Lane, who perhaps were surprised by their mission but sympathetic to its goals. At the University of Gerais, the travellers met Celia Garcia, a quite unknown Brazilian social psychologist. They were impressed by his enthusiasm and broad perspectives. They left encouraged by him and his colleagues, Fernando and Pier Wiel. They were also impressed by an encounter in Montevideo, Uruguay, with Varela, a brilliant applied social psychologist. He explained to them why, despite numerous dissimilarities, all Latin American countries had the same problems and the same need to develop the social sciences and social psychology specifically. He was ready to provide all help he could. In Buenos Aires, Argentina, the Instituto Torcuato Di Tella housed the Centre for Social Science. There were about twenty scientists on the Centre's staff. Of these, only García-Bouza and Catalina Weinerman identified themselves as social psychologists. The others, like Eliseo Verón, Malvina Segre and Peter Heinz, were sociologists. At the Argentina Catholic University, they met sociologists Roberto Marcenaro Boutell, Adolfo Critto, Carlos Sacheri and Susana Frank.

In Santiago, Chile, at the Institute of Psychology, Abel Toro Toro was the director of the industrial psychology department with an interest in 'industrial social' affairs. At the UNESCO's Latin American faculty of social sciences, the primary contact was Ramallo, a young, vigorous Jesuit who had come to Paraguay from Spain at the age of 21 years. Ramallo received his PhD with McClelland at Harvard. He was then acting director of the faculty in Santiago. He described the situation as tenuous due to lack of funds and relationships with the university. A two-year postgraduate programme drew students from all over Latin America. The faculty provided a very useful model for an advanced training centre in social psychology. Lanzetta[14] described Luis Ramallo as impressive, intelligent, vigorous, outspoken and a very useful resource person and the faculty provided a very useful model for an advanced training centre in social psychology.

The beginning of a new association building

The three-man mission performed a similar function in Latin America as the one carried out by Lanzetta in Europe. It was now possible to reunite the nucleus of the active group of social psychologists who would expedite the task further. The next Congress of the Inter-American Society of Psychology was to be held in Montevideo, Uruguay, in April 1969 and this seemed a good opportunity to get started. The organizers of the Montevideo conference agreed to allocate a special day for social psychology. In addition to promoting a social psychology programme, this venture promised to be important for future Latin America collaboration.

On the basis of work carried out by the three-man mission in 1968, the Transnational Committee formed a group of eight Latin Americans and three members of the Transnational Committee. These included Bayley (University of Venezuela), Capello, Díaz-Guerrero, Gozman Jezior and Lara-Tapia, all of the National Autonomous University of Mexico, García-Bouza (Buenos Aires), Ramallo (Santiago) and Rodrigues (Rio de Janeiro). The Transnational Committee was represented by Lanzetta, Moscovici and Lehmann. The conference, in Mexico City in January 1969[15] accomplished a number of things. It not only prepared a plan for the structure and content of the 'Day for Social Psychology' during the Congress in Montevideo but reviewed the whole standing of social psychology on the Latin American continent. Above all, the Mexico conference nominated a general planning committee made up of Ramallo as chairman, García-Bouza, Rodrigues and Lara Tapia.[16] This group would become active at the Montevideo conference and begin to organize the Association.

The 'Day for Social Psychology' took place on 2 April 1969. Festinger, Tajfel and Lehmann represented the Transnational Committee. The morning sessions were devoted to scientific papers while the afternoon sessions were concerned with the status of Latin American social psychology: its needs and resources, training and plans for research seminars. In addition, Varela demonstrated social psychology 'in action' during an evening session (*Items*, 1969, p. 11).

The planning committee nominated in Mexico was formally elected on the day. Clearly, the wide, although vague, interest in social psychology was now being matched by a desire to carry out high level work by a small group of senior social psychologists. Once on this road-map, the new Association could start growing and its future looked bright.

Training Seminar in Valparaíso, Viña del Mar

The new Latin America planning committee started preparing a summer training seminar as a modified version of the European seminar in Louvain. As expected, the major problem was fundraising and the committee submitted a proposal to the SSRC in New York to solicit funds which the Transnational Committee enthusiastically supported. Ramallo, the chairman of the Latin American committee, was in charge of the training seminar. He was a highly competent organizer[17] who solved a variety of problems, yet, despite his efforts, for a number of reasons the process was very slow. Delays were encountered in planning and financing and these were aggravated by the slowness of mail on both continents as well as a lack of qualified students. A broad representation of social psychology from different Latin American countries was not possible to achieve.

The training seminar took place in Chile, at the campus Viña del Mar of the Universidad Federico Santa Maria in Valparaíso on 5–27 January, 1970.[18,19] Viña del Mar, the sister-city of Valparaíso, is known as the 'garden city' where tourists go for its beauty and entertainment. The faculty staff included Ramallo, who was chairman, and Rodrigues, secretary. Teaching professors included Berkowitz, Deutsch, Gerard and Ramallo. There were twenty-one students on the course.

Berkowitz's group took up the social psychological aspects of aggression and altruism; Deutsch's group was concerned with the psychology of conflict and conflict resolution. Gerard's group focused on decision making within the framework of dissonance theory. Ramallo's group had not originally been envisaged but was introduced because some participants did not speak English. His group was concerned with achievement motivation. Research groups of five to six students were structured differently in each case although there were similarities. They all reviewed literature in their subject matter but none engaged in specific discussions of actual research projects. Only Deutsch's group designed experiments and carried out pilot studies.

Evening sessions were devoted to general topics. These included teaching social psychology, its definition and place among the social sciences, the organization of the planning committee and general problems experienced by Latin American academics. One difficulty for Latin American social psychologists was the lack of local textbooks. Textbooks came largely from the USA and students objected to the 'intellectual imperialism' of being handed their substantive contents. A publication committee was set up to develop a programme for the preparation of local textbooks and other scholarly materials.

Both the relationship between North American and Latin American social psychology and the relevance of social psychology were widely discussed. For example, is the science relevant to the study of social problems? How can it be demonstrated convincingly to students that it is not remote from their concerns?

In his evaluation of the training seminar, Deutsch[20] pointed out that its success consisted largely of providing a most valuable experience for all those who had not been trained in the USA. Many participants agreed that the next most urgent problem was to train more Latin American social psychologists. They did not believe that more social psychologists should be trained in the USA: 'if trained here they are inclined to remain here, and it is better for them to acquire their primary training in contact with other Latin Americans'.[21]

There was a general consensus among participants that they could not afford to be interested in theory alone but that they had to be well informed about those aspects of psychology that were directly connected with social problems in Latin American countries. One problem concerned the extremely strong pressures to which students were subject: with little training they were drawn into complicated research on governmental and industrial problems that required much more sophistication than they had acquired in simple laboratory training. Deutsch concluded: 'it is not enough to offer only experimental laboratory training; this is merely the basis for the further training needed.' The planning committee also agreed that for the future training the faculty was to be European rather than North American.[22] Many participants of the first seminar hoped that there would be a follow-up seminar and felt that it was important to provide incentives to carry through these activities.

Following these important events which were a milestone in the work of the Transnational Committee, a new member from the region, Ramallo, was invited to join.[23] Soon after the Valparaíso research training seminar, he put a proposal[24] to the Transnational Committee for financial support to coordinate the interests of the Latin American social psychologists. The planning committee was intended to represent as many social psychologists as possible, drawn from all the Latin American countries, to engage in any pertinent programmes which might generate research.

If we try and understand why the Transnational Committee helped build the Latin American Association in the way it did and how it accomplished this task despite the prevailing arduous conditions, we run into difficulties. It would have been a mistake to leave it to chance or to improvisation. It is quite certain that in its grand orientation, the Transnational Committee followed the model it had created in Europe. This avoided the risks of trial and error and, indeed, it accelerated the process of association building. For example, it is evident from archival documents[25] that the summer school in Valparaíso was organized along the lines of the Louvain summer school. And it is significant that the stages during the formation of the Latin American Association recall, with their grand economy of means, those that were being followed in Europe. Latin Americans themselves were satisfied with this strategy for reasons that are easy to understand. However, it is also clear that the Transnational Committee would have completely failed had it not understood from the very beginning that it was necessary to respect the uniqueness of Latin America. This is not to say that some universities were more developed than others and that the quality of research was better or worse here or there. Rather, the Committee had to be sensitive to working in different historical conditions and with people longing for respect and frankness. This inevitably required that the Committee insist on and recognize that culture's traditions. But how does one achieve that? To what extent can we say that the Transnational Committee was sensitive to the specific circumstances of its Latin American endeavour? And, indeed, did it succeed? Of course, we could simply answer all these questions positively. But instead of a general answer, we would like to give an example of the Committee's sensitivity to the context in which it worked. We find it in a letter from Kelley to Campbell concerning a draft proposal for the Latin American workshop in applied social psychology:

> I'd propose the consistent use . . . of 'social psychological research relating to public policies'. This gets rid of some of the awkward lingo about data collection, analysis and input. And more importantly, it moves the focus away from working for (inputting to,

aiding) the government. I'd not like to see our role limited here to providing information to the government. One might want to influence other organizations and institutions, or work 'in the public interest', 'on behalf of poor people', or even merely to influence certain sectors of public opinion. The broader definition may be particularly important for social psychologists who feel little rapport with their current governments but may still want to work on such things as you've mentioned.[26]

Hence we learn that the practice of association building followed a model that succeeded elsewhere but had to be periodically revised to stay in close touch with the milieu in which it was applied. It could succeed only if the Transnational Committee constantly reassessed its understanding of the problems. The birth of the Latin American Association bears out the validity of combining all these factors.

12

A Second Encounter
with History

The First Association of Latin American Social Psychologists

The Latin American Committee met in January 1970 and extensive minutes[1] enable us to appreciate the envisaged organization of the newly formed Association. As there were so few social psychologists in Latin America, it was necessary to resolve a number of questions related to future membership. These included the nature of this new Association, its functions and who should be accepted as members. Last but not least, what should be the relationships of the Latin American Committee with other organizations like the APA, the Society for Inter-American Psychology and the SSRC? The participants of the meeting unanimously voted that the Latin American Committee should not be a committee of the Society for Inter-American Psychology, although they should be associated with it. They wished to be independent. With respect to criteria of admission to the Committee, members voted that psychologists, sociologists and people interested in social psychology, providing they were connected with universities, should be allowed to become members.

The organization of the Committee was to be undertaken by the General Executive Council. The Council consisted of Ramallo as chairman, Rodrigues as secretary and Cappello (Mexico), García-Bouza (Argentina) and Zúñiga (Chile) as members. Ramallo was also appointed Executive Secretary. The whole of the Latin American continent was divided into three zones, each of them with its own secretary. García-Bouza became coordinator for Argentina, Uruguay, Brazil and Paraguay; Zúñiga was Transnational Committee coordinator for Chile, Peru, Ecuador, Bolivia,

Columbia and Venezuela; and Capello was coordinator for Mexico, Central America and the Caribbean region.

Be that as it may, on the road from failure to success there always comes a moment when what started as an adventure with an uncertain future finally takes shape and is acknowledged. Just as the creation of the EAESP was celebrated in Royaumont in 1966, so the Latin American Association was celebrated in Mexico City on 28–9 December 1970. It was not surprising that the members of both the Latin American Committee and of the Transnational Committee devoted a large part of the conference to a meeting of minds, to a vision of the future and to considering how to cooperate smoothly and efficiently.

Among a range of issues, the primary objective of the Transnational Committee, together with Latin Americans, was to develop cooperative research training programmes. Both committees centred on the question of training advanced students from Latin American universities in social psychology.[2] It was agreed that the Latin American Committee should formally launch a training programme whose sponsorship ideally would be shared by Latin American institutions and the foreign universities attended by students. Whenever possible, the doctoral research would be done in the home country, with the foreign institution providing a period of advanced training under the guidance of interested senior professors. It did not seem likely that more than three institutions in Latin America[3] could provide advanced training at that time or indeed in the near future. These institutions were the Autonomous University of Mexico, the Catholic University in Brazil and a two-year master's course scheduled to run in Chile. These three courses, however, formed a satisfactory basis for the cooperative training programme.

The Transnational Committee, while securing funds for Latin American research training programmes, was encouraging the Executive Council of the Latin American Committee to find minimal funding to enable it to function. It prepared a proposal soliciting funds for these purposes. Some efforts were also being made to find a more permanent institutional base for the Committee.

After the Mexico meeting in December 1970, the Transnational Committee met in Tepoztlan, Mexico, between 31 December and

1 January 1971.[4] The general impression of the Committee was that the way was now clear and that in quite a short time they had succeeded in uniting Latin American social psychologists. An exchange programme had been established, scholars were going to Europe or the USA and the Latin American Committee was functional. Everything seemed fine.

At that time the Committee had to devote a great deal of energy to the European East–West meeting that was taking place in Visegrad. However, the Transnational Committee planned after Visegrad to engage itself more with Latin America where members had found so much enthusiasm.

The Military Coup in Chile

The three-man mission of 1968 that we described in the previous chapter was not the only visit by North Americans to Latin America. Another traveller, Clark Bailey, visited four Latin American countries in January 1968, Peru, Argentina, Chile and Brazil. He went there on behalf of the Foundations' Fund for Research in Psychiatry to oversee the progress of projects that were supported by the Foundations' Fund grants to behavioural science research. This fund also sponsored the Latin American activities of the Transnational Committee. Reporting on his trip, Bailey contrasted his experience of Chile with other countries: 'things always seem to be running smoothly, quietly, and competently in Santiago . . . Chile is one Latin American country that has never had a revolution'.[5] Historians of the pre-1973 era refer to the unique politics of Chile that sustained democracy for many decades (Drake, 1991) and to the flexible system of multiple political parties, non-involvement of the military in politics and, indeed, civil-military concurrence (Nunn, 1976).

However, during the 1960s the country had to deal with persistent and difficult economic and social problems, leading to changes and reforms that were not altogether successful. In 1970, a narrow majority elected the left-wing senator Salvador Allende as President over the conservative-liberal, Jorge Alessandri. He was faced with formidable economic problems, inflation and the growth of political polarization. Moreover, the Chilean economy was largely dependent on the USA and, due to Allende's socialist policies, there was a great deal of interference from America. The rising dissatisfaction made it easier for a military junta to stage a conspiracy against President Allende, led by General Pinochet. With the complicity of other Latin American generals and, as is now known, the CIA, the military junta succeeded in overthrowing the government in a brutal military coup on 11 September 1973, thus ending Chilean democracy and the rule of law (Angell, 1991). Allende was assassinated, thousands of civilians murdered, political suspects imprisoned and tortured. The military junta exerted a pitiless and bloody repression, reminiscent of General Franco in Spain. With the passing days, the situation became more dramatic and waves of arrests swept through the country which was occupied by its own army. The military totally rejected democratic tradition and substituted it with regimentation, hierarchy, discipline and total subjugation to authority and power. As Wittgenstein wrote, foreseeing the worst when contemplating the consequences of Nazi usurpation: 'Just think what it must mean, when the government of a country is taken over by a set of gangsters. The dark ages are coming again.' (cf. Rhees, 1981, p. 152)

Historians wonder what might explain the terrible degree of violence and repression that had seemed inconceivable in a country like Chile (Angell, 1991). The answer to this question is not easy; it was not the first or last time that a peaceful country saw passions unleashed that led to horrendous violence. Yet we are often astonished that we do not learn from historical events, that they do not prompt us to take them into account and envisage the possibility of their future recurrence. It is undoubtedly because we repeat these events and feel that it is too difficult to envisage when they might take place. Each time such events descend upon us, we are outraged; surprised that we were not prepared; that we were not equipped with knowledge; that, basically, there is nothing new under the sun.

Thus the assassination of Allende, in September 1973 was a tremendous shock for the Transnational Committee. The situation radically changed its available options in Latin America. The military conspiracy against Chilean democracy developed quite openly and this was perhaps why barely anybody expected such a tragic outcome. As the historian maintains, 'very little is known about the way the military saw political life or why men who were not psychopaths acquiesced to the government's use of torture. Although many politicians foresaw the coup in 1973, only those of the extreme Right and Left expected such a high level of repression and such a prolonged period of military rule' (Angell, 1991, pp. 360–1).

Although by this time they knew the geography of Latin America and closely associated with their Latin American colleagues, the members of the Transnational Committee were not perhaps sufficiently familiar with the region's social climate and politics before and after 1973. For many it is difficult, even today, to make sense of a letter from Rodrigues[6] to Ramallo, and to know whether what he wrote was a premonition or a warning: 'I wish you luck in the coming years of Allende's government, but I must say that I am quite concerned for the fate of my Chilean friends.'

Misunderstanding and Developments

Unfortunately, the military coup in Chile was not the only difficult task that the Transnational Committee had to face in 1973. Interpersonal problems among Latin American social psychologists surfaced approximately the same time as the Chilean military coup. In August 1973, Rodrigues informed Festinger about the Bogota meeting in Colombia on 9–11 August 1973 at which sixteen Latin American social psychologists were present.[7] This meeting changed the name of the Latin American Committee for Social Psychology into the Latin American Association for Social Psychology ('La Associación Latinoamericana de Psicología Social' (ALAPSO). The meeting elected Rodrigues as chairman, thus replacing Ramallo, who had not been invited to the meeting. Festinger responded to Rodrigues' letter, hoping that at 'some time the various difficulties in Latin America and the problems of interpersonal relations can get straightened out and I assure you I will do whatever I can to help'.[8]

ALAPSO elected a 'technical committee' which, in addition to chairman Rodrigues, included Héctor Cappello (Mexico), Ricardo Zúñiga (Chile), Gerardo Marín (Colombia), José Salazar (Venezuela) and Catalina Weinerman (Argentina).

In the meantime, the Transnational Committee was working on a proposal for a research seminar in early 1973 in order to submit it to the Joint Committee on Latin American Studies. The proposal emphasized a duality of goals. First, there was the goal of improving professional skills through training. Second, there was a longer-range, in some ways competing, goal of developing an autonomous self-sustaining community among Latin American social psychologists, comparable to that which now exists in literature and the humanities. However, independently of all that, Rodrigues wrote to Ford in October 1973, asking for a grant for an Inter-Latin-American training seminar. Rodrigues informed Ford that he had just been elected President of ALAPSO, pointing out that the Association had grown out of the efforts of the Transnational Committee.

When the Transnational Committee realized that the proposal for the Inter-Latin-American seminar had not proceeded through the proper channels, Deutsch[9] wrote to Rodrigues and explained the situation to him. In the event, the proposal for the seminar was turned down which avoided a potentially sticky situation. The Transnational Committee was prepared to collaborate with ALAPSO, despite the problems that this created. If the Transnational Committee continues its activities in Latin America, Deutsch[10] wrote to Campbell, it seemed highly desirable that Rodrigues should be added to its membership. Of course, Ramallo would continue his member-ship of the Committee. Otherwise, it would be difficult for the Transnational Committee to do anything there. It was difficult to obtain general-purpose funds for the Committee enabling further involvement in Latin America, and it was tragic that Ramallo might be in personal danger at the end of the Allende 'experiment'. Deutsch added, 'there are so few societies in the world that seem really worth "experimenting" with, except of course for those with totalitarian motives.'

Ramallo remained a member of the Transnational Committee and moved the Faculty of Social Sciences from Santiago to Buenos Aires in Argentina. Since in the end he had to leave Chile and move to Buenos Aires, the Transnational Committee considered it important that social psychological research and training were developed within the existing structures of social science. Ramallo and Deutsch were asked to communicate this view to their Latin

American colleagues, and specifically to Rodrigues who was chairman of ALAPSO and to Weinerman, the ALAPSO coordinator for Argentina. It was also thought that the training seminar that was designed by Ramallo, Campbell and Kelley might be revised and support sought for it as a project associated with ALAPSO, although 'not necessarily under its governance'.[11]

The new Association took the decision to publish a *Bulletin ALAPSO* starting in December 1974, so that it was ready for late December when the new committee met again during the Fifteenth Congress of Inter-American Congress of Psychology[12] and publicly announced the creation of the Association.

Rodrigues continued trying to find finances for various ALAPSO projects but it was a very difficult time. In the years 1974 and 1975, there were no funds for Latin American and Caribbean programmes. He sent proposals to the NSF but he did not communicate with the Transnational Committee.

On Political Preferences and 'Scientific Behaviour'

The Transnational Committee faced a delicate problem in respect of Latin Americans. For the Committee, the political problem in Chile could not be separated from the scientific problem. The Committee was not sure, however, whether Latin Americans saw things in the same way. It was curious that no letters were exchanged, at that time, between Latin Americans and the Committee about the historic and tragic events in Chile. Neither did the *Bulletin ALAPSO* write about Zúñiga and others[13] – it behaved as if the problem did not exist. It was important for the Transnational Committee but was it for Latin Americans?

Several members of the Transnational Committee had in their past experienced exile, dictatorship or military repression. It was likely that their actions were dictated by what they had lived through and their concern for the future of social psychology was partly determined by that experience. That did not seem to be the case in Latin America. The Transnational Committee tried to maintain relations with ALAPSO. It avoided judging individual members or interfering in the business of its internal organization.

But it was natural to wonder what influence the events in Chile had on relations with ALAPSO.

Indeed it was not apparent. It was difficult for the Transnational Committee to realize what the tensions were in ALAPSO. Moreover, it is significant that Rodrigues did not try to explain the position of ALAPSO with respect to the tragedy in Chile and take into account what social psychologists in the rest of America and Europe knew about it. This would have at least opened up a dialogue that a letter from Rio de Janeiro, in January 1974, seemed to exclude:

> Zúñiga and García-Bouza have chosen to leave Latin America . . . are still welcome in the Association. Actually, Zúñiga has been invited to the Mexico meeting, even though he now lives in the USA. It should be a good time to make clear to you, and to other committee members, who do not know me, that as far as I am concerned, one's political preference and one's scientific behavior are two distinct sets with no intersection between them.[14]

Clearly, Zúñiga and García-Bouza had 'chosen' to leave Latin America for political reasons. Although the adherence of the Brazilian social psychologist to the alleged dogma of separation of science and society still serves as a topic for specialists discussing the political role of scientists, his message came at a bad time. In London, New York and Paris, there were other concerns and not everyone saw things the same way. But one did not give up on rectifying them.

In order to explain more fully what happened, let us remember that the Committee had undertaken the creation of the social psychology map. This necessitated making contact with colleagues, organizing summer schools, building associations, convincing institutions to take part in these events and so on. But there was no external pressure which obliged the Committee to do this. It was its internal urge to develop the young science of social psychology. And it was their freedom and sense of duty that underlay their perseverance and their accomplishments. They were not prepared for and did not expect that in the modest sphere of their activities they would be pushed into the great waves of history and have to face violent and brutal movements. Despite all that, the Committee was prepared to accomplish the task it had assigned to itself rather than seek refuge in calmer waters. As archival documents witness, the concerns that these events provoked did not lead to hesitation or attempts to change direction in the fog of events. The Transnational Committee knew that certain things had to be faced and endured. And when it acted, it was according to that perspective, which brought about its end, as we shall see later.

13

An 'Invisible College'

The Barcelona Meeting

Tossed on the crests of administrative waves and confronted by political questions, it is difficult for researchers to feel at ease. The life to which they are accustomed while carrying out their own work is gone. One can well imagine the danger that threatens the existence of a group of researchers if administrative and political questions start predominating: the loss of any intellectual significance to what they are doing. Under such conditions, the work becomes impersonal and mechanical. Thus we can suppose that it was in an attempt to alleviate this danger as well as to stimulate their scientific field that, once the EAESP was established, the Transnational Committee defined a scientific agenda. This happened at the Barcelona meeting in the winter of 1967.

It is not difficult to understand why, until then, the focus of the Transnational Committee was on 'down-to-earth' matters. On the one hand, it was necessary to clarify the European situation and to ensure the visibility of the Committee in the eyes of the SSRC. And, on the other hand, there was a need to overcome some of the interpersonal barriers which were having an effect on the work of the Committee. With respect to the latter, there seemed to be a certain hesitation, shyness or distance on the part of some Europeans with regard to the Americans. It may not be an exaggeration to say there were feelings of inferiority. The Americans, on the other hand, had an air of prudence or discretion, perhaps indifference, which was revealed whenever the discussion turned towards what other people were doing in terms of research.

But then, once the EAESP was established, the situation began to change. The Transnational Committee was now orientated towards finding out what Europeans could contribute that would benefit the field as a whole. This explains why Festinger started turning his attention to scientific matters. Earlier that year he wrote to Moscovici who had not been able to attend the Committee meeting in New York in 1967, 'Everybody was sorry that you could not come . . . We had a good committee meeting and I think, as you will see when you receive the minutes, much greater proportion of our effort will go into scientific things and substantive conferences. This, I think, is in line with your wishes.'[1] In writing this letter, Festinger was probably referring to the conversation he had had with Moscovici in Rome 1964, when the latter insisted that the main focus of the work of the Committee should be on research rather than training.

At the Barcelona meeting, several invited speakers prepared substantial working papers, which were general in scope yet related to specific ongoing research. For the invitees, the preparation of these papers was challenging because, although the audience was small, it represented the quintessence of social psychology at the time. The speakers were addressing reputable social psychologists who were well known for their severely critical and sharp judgement of work carried out in the discipline. Thus the individuals who had chosen to place Europe on the disciplinary map had to face the consequences of that choice. The challenge was stimulating. It was necessary to present oneself at the height of one's faculties and to earn respect from others at the outset. The participants felt they were attending a strange, yet high-powered seminar. Discussions were tonic, spiced with New-Yorker jokes and seasoned with fruitful suggestions. In retrospect it was a happy beginning. Relating to and getting to know one another as scientists was one of the most exciting aspects of the Committee's life. It soothed everyone's ego. As a result, an implicit decision was taken to create worthwhile and ongoing research seminars that would follow the work in progress on selected topics. The initial list included four topics in the following order: Moscovici's work on minority innovation in society, Schachter's project on developmental social psychology, Rommetveit's study of linguistics and social psychology and Tajfel's ideas on elitist ideologies in intergroup relations.

To this list we must add – or indeed start with – a critical monograph review involving an evaluation of cross-national studies in experimental social psychology. This topic had been at the heart of the Committee's concerns from the very beginning and was inspired by Festinger's interest in transnational matters and his search for an answer to what international social psychology is – or should be.[2] Claude Faucheux, who was charged with the task of writing a monograph review, was invited to attend the Barcelona meeting to discuss questions about its organization, including problems of the definition of the field, breadth of the monograph, comprehensiveness and annotation of the bibliography. The Transnational Committee named Festinger, Koekebakker, Lanzetta and Tajfel to serve as a consultant group for Faucheux.

To an outsider at that time, such an apparently complex meeting organized in Franco's dark Spain and which attempted to alter the course of social psychology might have seemed impractical. The members of the Committee shared memories of the impact of the Spanish Civil War and the dramatic years which followed. It was for this precise reason that some members of the Committee were reluctant to go to Spain. Moreover, we must not forget the very difficult political and intellectual conditions under which the Committee worked. These included enduring the ups and downs of the Cold War and the unforeseen events of the civilian Hot Wars. In addition, the Transnational Committee had to counter a great deal of misunderstanding concerning its vision of social psychology and its role as a social science. It had to feel its way by trial and error in order to further its work. Nevertheless, if it fulfilled its mission, it was accomplished largely informally and, we could add, in isolation. The Committee remained much less visible than the associations that it placed on solid ground, than the training schools it created and the conferences that it organized. This is probably why our own discipline has never appreciated, and, indeed does not appreciate today, the achievements of the Transnational Committee. Its discreet, informal and yet efficient style of working permitted it to advance like a Land Rover in all kinds of terrain.

And so in the end, Barcelona appeared to be the right place to give birth to an 'invisible college'; it seemed to be living in a bygone time yet longed for a new and exciting future. This was largely the result of circumstances. And circumstances were also responsible for the topics in which the Committee became interested, which it addressed and debated. Some of these very important topics then were themselves transformed into concrete scientific projects.

We may perhaps better understand the Committee's work practices and goals if we consider the fact that its members did not represent trends or fashions at the time. On the contrary, most members were bound together by a firm view of what social psychology should become in the future and what its aims should be. The Transnational Committee even risked distancing itself from the tradition that more and more dominated the field. As a result, its existence as a Committee of the SSRC was threatened. This risk, as we shall see later, is clearly apparent in archival documents.

Distancing itself from the mainstream tradition, however, was not a passive move. Instead, at the heart of this 'invisible college' was another tradition, the Lewinian tradition,[3] that most of its members shared, including the first two staff officers of the Committee, Willerman and Singer.

The Comparative Method and its Riddles

The pervading universality of the law of gravity is striking in cases as diverse as a falling stone or the collapse of the Twin Towers in New York. Mechanical properties of such falling bodies are similar all over the world and they vastly transcend any individual case; they are largely independent of the place where the fall is witnessed, be it Baghdad or Tokyo. Galileo Galilei made this revolutionary observation four centuries ago when he claimed that there was no reason why an observation made in the Middle East would yield different results from one made in Italy. Even if we take relatively simple human phenomena like walking or running, it may seem useful to verify whether Mexicans and Frenchmen walk or run in the same manner and, if they do not, what could be the explanation for the differences. However, the presumption of a similar kind of universality should be regarded with a sceptical eye when dealing with mental and social phenomena. In other words, it seems reasonable to assume that mental and social phenomena in one part of the world can be compared, using scientific methods, with those in other places.

The story of a two-year or a ten-year report

The main vision of the Transnational Committee was to create an international social psychology. And the Committee's main concerns pointed to the following problems: How can we make sense of comparative method, which should be self-evident and yet, in many cases, appears to be deceptive? Is there no other way of building and shaping international social psychology apart from making comparisons? If so, one would assume that social psychologists who wished to build international social psychology on the basis of existing research methods would think it necessary to critically review comparative studies and their methods of exploration in order to find solutions to such weighty questions.

Faucheux was entrusted with finding some answers. He was a true follower of Lewin's ideas. Moreover, he had a profound knowledge of social psychology: he was conversant in group psychology and in experimental approaches. In addition, he had experience of working with Lévi-Strauss and he had carried out anthropological fieldwork in Corsica. He was known to most members of the Committee because he visited the USA every year to keep in touch with and learn about current research by Lewin's former students. He was therefore an ideal candidate for a study of this 'sea serpent' which the comparative method in social psychology seemed to have turned into. We can read in the research proposal to the NSF that the Transnational Committee 'envisages a highly competent psychologist bringing together and evaluating the work in this area . . . After due deliberation it unanimously selected Faucheux as best qualified to undertake this review . . . [he was] fluent in several languages . . . highly respected for his critical abilities, well versed in a variety of experimental techniques, and of course has considerable familiarity with the literature.'[4]

It was expected that during the preliminary phase Faucheux would review journals specializing in comparative studies and select those dealing with experimental social psychology and then review journals of experimental social psychology dealing with comparative studies. The Committee would help Faucheux by providing information about unpublished studies which were circulating in draft or mimeograph form. The second stage would involve the organization of the review. It was expected that members of the Committee would be available for consultation, suggestions and bibliographic aid.[5] Singer, the Staff Officer, became the principal investigator charged with obtaining the research contract. It was suggested that the 'Transnational Committee, in addition to holding specific meetings with Mr Faucheux, will discuss and evaluate the review as an agenda item at their regular meetings'.[6]

Clearly, the Transnational Committee took this task very seriously and the project was funded by the NSF. Over the following two years, Faucheux and his assistants assembled and placed on cards 1500 bibliographical items in cross-cultural social psychological research. The bibliography included studies of the 'prisoner's dilemma' game, colour recognition and communication of colour information, studies of attitudes and value and anthropological studies like those of Berry on field dependence and field independence. There were bibliographic references to conformity based on Asch-type situations in very different ecological systems such as the Temne of Sierra Leone and the Eskimos of Baffin Island. This list of topics gives an idea of the diversity of the collected materials. Not only every topic but nearly each study raised different theoretical issues, to which the Committee devoted time during its meetings up to 1970. A number of individuals became interested in the survey, like Triandis who wished to include Faucheux's findings in the Annual Review, or Kelley, who wanted 'to read it'.[7]

References to comparative method were one thing, but quite another issue concerned disagreement about method – and it was the latter that did not pass unanimously because the Committee was preoccupied with puzzles of method. For example, how to select populations for study and how to interpret different observed effects in two different locations. Clearly, one could not identify all factors that were related to significant cultural differences. But perhaps most disconcerting was the obviousness of results obtained, its 'bubba psychology' and the paltry theoretical significance of the studies. In any case, it was out of the question that method could 'inform' theories and established facts.

Several perspectives were looming. One perspective on cross-cultural studies was silently universalistic. This included comparative studies on colour perception and language as well as the assembly of evidence of universal categories and rules across different cultures. The second and the opposing perspective could have been a surprising discovery in empirical social psychology. Unfortunately, this did not happen and no convincing arguments were advanced that would point to such empirical discoveries to which one could attribute 'truth', or at least partial 'truth'. The third perspective was related to the attitude of researchers towards their inquiry. Were they sensitive to or interested in understanding culture? Did they have anthropological skills? Or did they only want to replicate an experiment which would be executed by 'indigenous' social psychologists who would then examine, analyse, compute the results and interpret them in the solitude of their offices? The intercultural experience of social psychologists being what it was, their knowledge of anthropology was limited. They observed phenomena with untrained eyes. What conclusions could be drawn about the conformity of French people by taking percentages of answers in an Asch-type situation and comparing them with percentages taken in America? The cultural significance of such percentages of conformity in France and in the USA has never been defined and understood and therefore no basis for establishing approximation of conformity has ever been created. In a way, the process of comparison itself should have been an object of scientific inquiry. Under any circumstances, however, should it serve as a criterion of scientific truth or universality?

In passing we may note that the social scientific climate was not enthusiastically inclined towards comparative psychological studies. Such findings were seldom exciting, and their common-sense interpretation rarely convincing. Or at least, it seemed so. At the same time, comparative psychology provided an opportunity for an exchange of views about social psychology. Faucheux's review took longer than was anticipated and the NSF became impatient. Finally, in 1970 it resorted to a letter addressed to the grant-holder Singer,[8] saying: 'We are pleased that we could assist you with your research and we are looking forward to reading your report on the findings of the project.'

In fact we have not found a trace of this review monograph and it is not clear that it is in anybody's possession. In 1972, Festinger reported:

> Such a monograph is commissioned. It represents the single out-standing unequivocal failure for the Committee. No coherent monograph was ever produced. The reasons for this are not entirely known but we do not think the failure is primarily due to the person selected for the task. It is possible that the literature is so diverse and so amorphous that integration is impossible. Perhaps the only thing that can be said is that work does not add up. Even so, it would have been valuable to have such a conclusion made and documented. As it is, we can say little or nothing.[9]

Festinger, writing on behalf of the Transnational Committee, admitted in his report that there was a gulf between the promise to deliver the monograph and the disappointing final outcome. Yet even so, Festinger's admission of the undocumented and unexpressed conclusion is impressive.

Yet Faucheux did finish the project in 1969; it had taken him two years.[10] The report was written and Lehmann wrote a summary for which Faucheux[11] thanked him: 'Congratulations for your summary report on my monograph: this was certainly not an easy thing to do.' However, only five years later a long paper by Faucheux (1976) appeared in the *European Journal of Social Psychology*. In this article Faucheux acknowledges that it 'has been written at the request of the Transnational Committee of the SSRC and with the support of the NSF during the years 1968–1969' (ibid., p. 269).

Faucheux on 'playful' and 'earnest' approaches in cross-cultural research

Although Faucheux's paper is highly original and well argued, we can understand that this review did not satisfy the expectations of the Committee, which hoped for some clear direction in cross-cultural research that would help in their efforts to create international social psychology.

Yet it is important to reflect on Faucheux's vision of cross-cultural research and on his struggles in the late 1960s, even more so because the problems over which he agonized have not disappeared. Indeed, today, they are just as real as they were 45 years ago. We only need to recall the use of Euro-Barometers, World Studies of Values and European data-bases, all believing that they can capture, across nations and cultures, any social phenomena ranging from 'happiness' to 'nationalism' or 'identity'.

In a nutshell, inspired by Lewin and perhaps by Lévi-Strauss, Faucheux (1976, p. 269) affirms that the problem in cross-cultural research is not comparative method but 'a malaise characteristic of the social sciences in general and of social psychology in particular'. The malaise is due to the distrust of the *a priori* theoretical reflection that Lewin advocated. Instead, social psychologists endeavour 'to accumulate the "facts" from which "empirical generalizations" could be made and tables of correlation between phenomena or observables could be established' (ibid., p. 269). Moreover, social psychologists no longer believe, as did Lewin, that they can study cultural reality. They have drifted towards general cognitive psychology, ignoring characteristically social phenomena.

Faucheux's arguments are passionate and subtle and they carry the moral that not all comparison is an empirical matter; rather, it is a matter of theory. This 'atheoretical mosaic' in social psychology becomes even more marked when compared with neighbouring disciplines such as linguistics, anthropology, primatology and ethnoscience which all study social phenomena in their richness and diversity without trivializing them. It is a very time-consuming project to carry out cross-cultural research well. You have to master an ethological approach and to understand a culture in order to undertake comparisons. It is not enough to travel from one country to another in search of differences for the sake of research. In other words, the social psychological theory of the studied phenomena, for example dissonance or conformity, must also be a theory of cultural differences or similarities. Researchers must know why they search for differences or similarities and why they can find their evidence in one culture rather than in another.

Faucheux summarizes approaches in cross-cultural research under three headings. First, the most common approach, characterizing the majority of existing studies, is 'playful' research. It contents itself with scoring similarities and differences on questionnaires and scales and with replications of experiments in different countries. Depending where their inclinations lie, researchers either 'reassure themselves that people are all alike or all different' (ibid., p. 314).

The second approach, i.e. the first 'earnest attitude', considers culture as a 'bias', an artefact or a historical accident. It searches for universals and for 'culture-free' theories.

Finally, there is another 'earnest' approach that is rare and that considers culture to be a reality to be studied and understood. The analysis of studies carried out by Berry of two societies, the Temne of Sierra Leone in Africa and the Eskimo of Baffin Islands in Canada, enabled Faucheux to show the relevance of his arguments. In the rare approach, a common code of culture originates from, is acquired through and develops within communication. Faucheux concludes his paper as follows. 'If social psychology is ever to become a specific discipline, if a theory of social relations is ever to be made, then, academic boundaries between social psychology and cultural anthropology and the illusion of a culture-free theory of social behaviour have to be dropped' (ibid., p. 315).

As we have shown, Faucheux's paper was published rather late. It was supposed to eliminate the impression of failure of the first project carried out by the Transnational Committee. There is little reason to suppose that this thoughtful and original article had much success. It has rarely been referred to and has fallen into silence. Much of cross-cultural psychology continues to do what it was doing in the 1960s.

The conflict project

This sounds like a diversion. Already in 1966 Lanzetta had held, with the help of the ONR, a transnational seminar on 'the dynamics of conflict'. It was during an era when many researchers used the game matrices of John von Neumann to study cooperation and competition in mixed-motive conflicts. Complexities of the conflict aside, this topic also had a clear political relevance.

Lanzetta organized the first conference at Dartmouth College in August 1966. He assembled a very impressive group, including several members of the Transnational Committee and of the EAESP (Lanzetta, 1967). Position papers defined a broad theoretical framework and outlined possibilities for collaborative research. The main question of the seminar was: What kind of bargaining experiment could be designed? In order to answer this question, the participants jointly worked on a solution during the conference. Plenary sessions were also devoted to elaborating a general conceptual framework for categorizing and organizing research in the area, identifying significant gaps in approaches and problems currently under investigation. In the end, some concrete suggestions were made and several studies on bargaining were designed.

Faucheux and Flament organized the second conference in Nice, France, in January 1967. In addition to the twelve participants who were at Dartmouth, Moscovici and Rabbie were present. The participants designed a task that was rich and flexible enough to be used by experimenters in different locations and it was supposed to yield results that would be comparable. The idea was to assess the value of replications in several cultures using a simple but a large study. The main questions were the following. What does the replication of a study in one location, for example in New York, mean in another location, for example, in Paris? Do the results indicate a difference or similarity between Americans and French? This kind of inference could not make much sense given the differences and similarities within the countries themselves, for example, those between rural and urban areas and between big and small cities. The problem and a mystery is that comparative studies between countries disregarded the obvious comparisons within the country. Lanzetta's group planned a vast study in several countries to show empirically the similarities in bargaining situations in different countries, e.g. in Paris and London, rather than those within the country, e.g. between Paris and Nice or London and Guildford.

The third meeting, involving the same researchers, was organized at Santa Monica, Los Angeles, in November 1967. The meeting was concerned both with simple as well as with highly sophisticated questions, owing to the discovery of computer technologies unknown to most participants at the time. Not only the results but also the background to game research, like the Vietnam War, was discussed. But the value of the meeting was the first-hand learning of game theory from the major figures in the field, like Deutsch and Kelley. The participants subsequently carried out experiments in different countries helped by Garry Shure, the most prominent computing specialist in the group (Kelley et al., 1970).

There were no other meetings, probably owing to the dynamics of the conflicts on campus in those years, and the stream of game research dwindled. Why bother making explicit what is for the most part obvious? The knowledge had strengthened personal and intellectual relations between those who had hardly known one another two years earlier and who were discovering the pleasure of doing things together. A propos of that group, Deutsch wrote: 'We met about twice a year, alternating locales between Europe and the US. We had many good discussions, excellent wine and food, and formed some lasting friendships. We also did a cross-national experiment on bargaining that has rarely been cited. It was a wonderful period to be a social psychologist' (Deutsch, 1999, p. 31).

Conference on Innovation by Minorities

In some ways Festinger was quite un-American. He was not an adept in positive thinking and rhetorical overstatement. Under the modest heading 'Other activities' in his brief history of the Transnational Committee, he wrote 'From the beginning the Committee felt that it did not want to concentrate exclusively on bringing people together and stimulating contacts. If now and then substantive issues arose that were relevant to its concerns, the Committee wanted to be involved.'[12] At the time of the Barcelona meeting in 1967, Festinger was leaving social psychology to study perception and was in the process of moving from Stanford University in California to the New School of Social Research in New York. What made this move unusual was that he continued to put as much energy as before in fostering international social psychology. His eagerness and talent for efficient work appeared incredible. Undoubtedly, he was tough, sharp and yet patient. And in contrast to what some people used to say, he was affectionate and ready to listen but, of course, he listened critically.

The paper presented by Moscovici[13] on 'Social Influence, Socialization and the Individual: Preliminary Notes' at the Barcelona conference was no exception. Festinger listened as did all those present but responded only later by asking Moscovici to send the draft of the paper to Brehm, Kelley, Katz, Lanzetta, McGuire, Novak, Zajonc and Ziller. Moscovici asked the addressees for their observations and suggestions on the basis of which the text could be rewritten as a definitive version. This version would serve as a basis for convening a conference and possibly for an international research programme.[14]

Let us try to understand what it was that captured the attention of the Transnational Committee and its chairman about minority innovation. The study of conformity was the major phenomenon being studied in both the fields of group dynamics and social psychology of influence. From the point of view of these approaches, the majority appeared to be resistant to change. Different perspectives with respect to majority judgements were considered either as deviance or as a sign of individualism or independence. Since, quite naturally, it was assumed that all processes of influence or social action originated from within the group and its knowledge, this implied, on the one hand, conservatism of the group and, on the other, that individual perspectives tend to move towards conservatism. Excellent researchers like Asch, who set themselves against the 'conformity bias' in social psychology, tried, on various occasions, to point to the independence of the individual in relation to the majority. But by itself, the mere existence of opposition or contrast does not allow us to assert whether the independence of the individual signifies deviance or the rebellion of the individual against the group. These behavioural similarities led social psychology up a blind alley, arising from the difficulty of distinguishing between sociability and conformity. This was the Achilles' heel of social psychology.

This was equally the case in Lewin's group dynamics because his theory was based on assumptions of equilibrium and homeostasis, that is, on a static model. This is best illustrated by Festinger's and Schachter's studies on pressure towards group uniformity that restabilizes equilibrium through conformity of the deviant. Hence, these researchers achieved in social psychology what Merton tried to achieve in sociology.

The problem posed itself in yet another perspective, if considered as a question of the history of its dialectic and actions. Past and contemporary observations show that the concept of a group that changes under its own steam will always be nearer the truth and deserve more attention than the one according to which a group changes due to outside pressure. In other words, the former concept is closer to reality than the latter that ascribes change to blind forces or adaptation to environment. According to the dialectic of history, in order to start change, there must be someone in the group who has 'the cause'. That someone is usually a deviant minority or an independent individual who has the willpower to advance 'the cause' and who wants it to be shared by others. That is the case in politics, religion, economics, even in the history of science. Examination of literature makes us aware of and allows us to understand that history, whether of science or religion, unfolds in particular directions largely due to the effect of major non-conformists:

> Each case of dissidence is brought about by a new group which from time to time emerges on the borders of several sciences as the carrier of know-how and of original concepts. It does not impose itself the very day it emerges or the following day but only after some shorter or longer delay, opposing itself to a scientific community. During that period the scientific community defends its inherited or acquired knowledge, judging it as more compatible with reality than the new knowledge. Supposing that this is an evident process, I posed myself a question which, as I became later aware, Heisenberg (1975) had already explained. Referring to his own experience, he wrote that in order to comprehend scientific revolutions, 'We must ask how a seemingly small group of physicists was able to constrain the others to these changes in the structure of science and thought. It goes without saying that the others at first resisted and were bound to do so.'
>
> What is fascinating in the history of sciences, of religions etc. is that a small cause can have large effects; a handful of innovators decides to overturn deeply rooted beliefs and the ways of living and acting. (Moscovici, 2003)

Hence if we speak about fundamental processes, it is necessary to speak about the predominance of the process of innovation as a singular trait of sociability and modern existence.

The theoretical problem of innovation was to some extent the one that was posed in the eighteenth century by the British historian Gibbon (1910). Gibbon enquired how it was possible for a handful of Christians, a really insignificant group, to obtain 'so remarkable a victory over the established religions of the earth' (Gibbon, 1910, p. 157). For Gibbon, the obvious but satisfactory answer was that it was the convincing evidence of the doctrine as well as 'the inflexible, and, if we may use the expression, the intolerant zeal of the Christians' that, among other factors, led Christianity to victory. The Christian religion became a church that achieved an enormous and seemingly impossible change in Roman history, finally leading to the decline of the Roman Empire.

We do not want to write a history of the research on innovation (Moscovici, 1996). Yet research emerging on this theme (Moscovici and Faucheux, 1972) encountered from the beginning reactions of opposing natures. On the one hand, most Committee members, and among them certainly Festinger and Kelley, were most interested in this topic and attached priority to it. It is useful to quote what Schönbach said about Lewin's group:

> It is the way we were all trained – keep an eye on what is interesting and then when you get an idea about what is happening, test your idea and push it as rigorously as possible as if that is the only factor at work to see what the implications are and how much it overrides. The argument is that if your idea is powerful, it will override other things. (Patnoe, 1988, p. 148)

As one might imagine, this powerful suggestion served as a way of revitalizing the field of influence at the core of social psychology. Above all, it provided grounds for reconsidering group dynamics which had been languishing for some time. 'One of the major accomplishments of social psychology in the USA,' Festinger wrote in his brief history

> was to understand, on a theoretical and empirical level, the ways in which influence was exerted on opinions, attitudes and

behaviour, and how, thereby, conformity to group norms came about. The Committee became very interested when Europeans pointed out that this work had concentrated almost exclusively on how the group affects the individual – on how the majority influences the minority – who knew next to nothing about how a person maintains deviant beliefs and how, sometimes, one such a person can successfully influence a group. A theoretical position paper was prepared by Moscovici on this issue and a long seminar was held with eight persons interested in the problem.[15]

Such an encouragement and such an audience provided important capital for the Europeans. It was decisive in showing the power of their creativity and the ability to make significant contributions to the advancement of the discipline. They could not allow themselves to be considered honorary epigones, any more than to be locked up in cultural and theoretical differences which certainly existed but in which nobody apart from themselves would be interested. It was crucial to show that they could work with the Americans and that the Transnational Committee would profit from that. At the same time, they needed to ensure the possibility of continuing their research in total independence and self-respect, without fear of becoming imitators, passive admirers or simply spectators. The Americans, for their part, attached a great deal of importance to position papers and discussions that took place during meetings. It was here that they attempted to confront, and grab by the horns, the bull of transnational social psychology.

While most Committee members were positive about the study of minority influence and innovation, outside the Committee others opposed the theme on several grounds. The confrontation was sharp, given that social psychologists in the USA were not familiar with this research and were opposed to the ideas on which it was based, as well as being sceptical about the results of Moscovici's experiments. They simply did not accept them. For some colleagues, these findings smacked of Marxism or whatever served the times; for others, minorities were synonymous with race and the issues were considered non-psychological. People dismissed explanatory notions such as 'behavioural style'; the concept of conflict had unpleasant political overtones in an era when social movements were in the ascendant everywhere. One could even hear well-known social psychologists claiming that experiments on minority innovation were nothing but Asch-type experiments on conformity turned inside out, which would have not pleased Asch who had himself invited Moscovici to present these studies at Rutgers University (Moscovici, 1996).

All or most of this could perhaps be ascribed to the fact that, contrary to the classic axiom, in minority/majority influence there was not always a proportional relationship between cause and effect. That is to say, one had to explain how small things and small groups made a big difference in a large group, even in society as a whole. And as Osgood declared at the end of the famous film *Some Like It Hot*, 'Well, nobody's perfect'. Such was the situation, which explains both why the Transnational Committee attached so much importance to the foreseen conference being well attended, and why it was supposed to be held over three weeks.

The decision to launch the action was finally taken in 1969. It was incontestably a wonderful project. It was soon forgotten that it had been nearly impossible to obtain the necessary grants. We read that 'the Committee also wishes to initiate planning for a major experimental study in the field of social influence . . . requests that the Council seek funds for a three-week working conference to develop a theoretical formulation . . . and to design an integrated research project that can be carried on transnation- ally.'[16] The same P&P Minutes also echo the above reservations and arguments, 'that the terminology used in describing the pro- posed project be selected with care, to avoid any impression of American involvement in minority problems in other countries'.[17] It is true to say that this project only concerned Europe and not America; however, it did appear dangerous even if it was only lab- oratory research to isolate social reality. At the same time one recognized that 'research on this subject was considered to be extremely important and timely; university campuses in this country and abroad might provide a most appropriate labora- tory for investigation of related social psychological questions.'[18] Someone deprived of scientific freedom, reading these lines, might ask whether science would not profit from such freedom of explo- ration, criticism and scepticism in the free world. At its next meeting the SSRC Executive Committee[19] voted for the solicita- tion of funds from the NSF. Lanzetta and Moscovici were to organize the conference in 1971 at Dartmouth where Lanzetta was professor. When he took charge of the conference, Lanzetta also stepped out of the Transnational Committee. As to the conference, he remained involved in its planning and organizing. His letter to Riecken[20] reflects Lanzetta's true spirit of friendship and international collaboration at a moment when he distanced himself from what basically was his brainchild.

The conference started on 14 August and lasted until 1 September. Lanzetta saw things grandly. He obtained from the Dartmouth College the Minary Conference Center located on Squam Lake in the middle of New Hampshire. It had previously been the private summer residence of Paley, chairman of the board of Columbia Broadcasting Company, and was a very comfortable and well-appointed place. As the participants of the conference were the sole occupants, they could bring along their families, including their children.

The conference was scheduled every afternoon but in fact meetings and discussions went on all the time. The intention was not to design a transnational research project but, rather, to clarify and cross-examine the problem, explore the theory of innovation by minorities and eventually to contribute to it by experimental study. Each of the participants wanted to assure themselves of the value of their intuitions and approaches. Sessions were devoted largely to the philosophy that formed the background of influence phenomena, the reasons why for accepting minority innovation as a legitimate subject of study and the nature of theoretical concepts and their empirical intuitions.

Without meaning to be so, the conference was an experience in transnational social psychology. All participants brought to it their enduring assumptions from the traditions within which they worked. Discussions permitted everybody to grasp other perspectives with regard to the relevant social phenomena. Importantly, they grasped these phenomena from a point of view never set out in books or published articles. Kelley and Lanzetta, who were more familiarized than other Americans with the problematic of this conference, played the role of intellectual gatekeepers, helping to maintain it at the expected high scientific level. This allowed recognition of emerging new phenomena for social psychology and everybody made suggestions as to what these could be and how they might be studied. One thing was obvious: the import and weight of a new theory is not an improved understanding of old phenomena but the discovery of new ones. In short, a new theory enlarges the phenomenology of science.

Obviously, the participants at the conference were not converted to minority research, each having been involved in his or her own project. Anyway, conversion was not the aim. It was only Moscovici who was converted to experimental research. At last he grasped the meaning of its role and necessity as a method of inventing new phenomena. Doing a satisfying experiment is like painting or composing.

We need to remind ourselves, once again, that the theory of innovation collided with epistemological obstacles with respect to dominant research in the area. Schönbach has summarized it simply in another context:

> If you look at the work of pressures to uniformity, the first Festinger piece in 1950, what you really have is the first layer of foundation beyond Lewin. You might say that it is pure basic research and yet, if you look back at it from a distance of over thirty years, you see that this was a part of a concern with conformity, with cooperation, that was highly salient in American history and it may have had its origins there. It was only later that so much emphasis on conformity attracted the criticism of European social psychologists – you are always concerned about the majority, you forget about the minority. So I think Festinger, as well as Asch and Sherif and all those people, were not clearly independent from their background. (Patnoe, 1988, p. 136)

Discussions at the Dartmouth conference were passionate and enlightening, and the participants decided to continue with more concrete research in this area. They even expressed the desire 'to hold another two-week seminar, perhaps in 1974, when additional research will have been completed'.[21] Henry Riecken, then chairman of the SSRC, wrote to Staff Officer David Jenness.[22] 'John Lanzetta wrote me recently that the Dartmouth Conference on minority influence and groups has been successful. This confirms Hal Kelley's opinion and I must say that I am pleased that we had a good outcome from this one.'

The participants proposed to edit a monograph with the following tentative topics:

Brehm, Kiesler and Lanzetta: Attribution of behavioural style and influence.
Kelley: On metacommunication, power and social influence.
Lamm: The releasing function of the minority.
Moscovici: Two models of social influence and social behaviour.
Ziller: The role of conflict in changing behaviour.
Zúñiga: Relations between majorities and minorities in the process of social change.

However, one year later, only three of these six chapters were available because other participants wished to publish their chapters separately in journals. This was a most embarrassing situation for the Transnational Committee and it insisted 'that it was a matter of some importance to the Committee, the Council and the NSF (the source of funds for the Conference) that a substantial publication result, especially since a prior NSF-supported committee project, a review of cross-national research in social psychology, had come to nothing.'[23]

Despite the fact that two articles actually appeared in journals, the pressure of the Council and of the NSF did not weaken. In order to avoid continuing a dialogue giving the impression that this unique Dartmouth Conference 'had come to nothing', Moscovici had no choice but to write the book himself.

In the first part Moscovici condensed what, in his eyes, formed the background to the Dartmouth discussions. He opposed the *functional* model of the 'old' dominant social psychology and the 'new', emerging *genetic* model. In the introduction he spelled out the problem of active minorities as emerging social actors. He argued for the following case, just as he had in other papers: if the beginning of the twentieth century saw, according to Ortega y Gasset's famous title, the 'revolt of the masses', the end of the century was characterized by the revolt of minorities. The second part of the book was devoted to the theory of innovation by minorities. Moscovici had yet another reason to write this book. Henri Tajfel, the editor of the first social psychology book series, had asked him to contribute a volume, and this was an occasion

for Moscovici to fulfil his promise. Festinger seemed to appreciate the book and was satisfied with the outcome of the initiative
he had formerly taken. The book appeared in English under the
title *Social Influence and Social Change* (1976) and later in French
as *Psychologie des minorités actives* (1979), with an appendix on
Solzhenitsyn and Russian dissidence.

Conference on Making Social Psychology More Useful

During the 1950s and 1960s, mainstream American social
psychology was distancing itself from applied social psychology
and, by the 1970s, the shift away from 'the grey areas of social
problems' was complete. There was no more interest in finding
solutions to applied problems. Instead, in the expectation of better
times, researchers moved to the ivy areas of the campuses and
laboratories occupied themselves with 'pure' problems. This
change was part of a general trend in the social sciences (Riecken,
1969, p. 2).

It appears that the 'redefinition of problems' arose out of the
government's constant suspicion that social scientists were brain
twisters and social sciences were home ground for twisted ideas.
But how could one identify these mysterious 'intrinsic forces'
without identifying 'extrinsic ones'?

At that time the Transnational Committee worked as an association builder in Eastern Europe and in Latin America. For these
parts of the world, applied psychology, orientated to solving
society's problems, was quite essential. In his brief historical
account of the Committee, Festinger wrote:

> Contacts with social psychologists in Eastern Europe and Latin
> America made the Committee realize vividly that, in most parts of
> the world, social psychologists could not afford the luxury of the-
> oretically oriented research but had to make their work directly
> relevant to solving social problems. We also became quite aware
> that there exists a large gap between knowledge in social psycho-
> logy and ability to apply this knowledge. With the conviction that
> the time is ripe for bridging this gap, a conference is planned on
> this topic. The Committee hopes it will be fruitful.[24]

In reality, the organization of this counter-current conference was as much a practical need of the Committee as an intellectual choice by its chairman, Deutsch. As a former student of Lewin, he was very concerned with the disappearance of interest in 'a socially useful psychology'. Being very critical of the state of American social psychology, Deutsch wrote:

> Social psychology has been most deficient in living up to its own distinctive perspective in its failure to consider in detail the specific properties of the individual and the social as they relate to one another . . . Many of us believe we know a good deal about how abstract man will behave in abstract situations, but we know very little about how particular men behave in particular situations. We know little about how different sorts of people behave in the different kinds of situations that populate their everyday lives'. (Deutsch, 1976, p. 5)

Thus while the Committee was involved in external problems of the social and political world, and in establishing the place of social psychology in this world, the discipline in the USA was entirely focused on its internal concerns. Bearing in mind the Transnational Committee's involvement in Eastern Europe and Latin America where finding solutions to social problems was of paramount importance, it is difficult to imagine that any further clarification was needed to highlight the relevant role that social psychology could play. Deutsch was careful to emphasize that the goal was to develop useful knowledge by remaining aware of the unique character of social psychology in the resolution of concrete problems. Specifically, it has a distinctive perspective: 'This perspective arises from the unique focus of social psychology upon the interplay between psychological and social processes' (Deutsch, 1976, p. 4).

Inevitably, perhaps, the motto of the conference had to be: 'We must also develop a social psychology that is useful.' The proposal for the conference was outlined by Harvey Hornstein and Morton Deutsch (Columbia University), with assistance from Barbara Bunker (Buffalo).[25] After describing the state of the art, the proposal suggested holding two kinds of conferences. One conference would be devoted to surveying the range of social intervention practices, articulated on the basis of their underlying social psychological assumptions. The second proposal concerned a network of conferences consisting of regional meetings: Eastern USA, Mid-Western USA, Western USA, Europe and Latin America. The purpose of each regional meeting was 'to examine the plans and ideas . . . about the specific ways of improving graduate training in applied social psychology'.[26] During the autumn of 1971 this project was submitted to the Transnational Committee but encountered some difficulties with the NSF. It took many months before it could reconcile the demands of the NSF, the Council and the involved researchers. In July 1972, an invitation was sent to the expected participants to a seminar aiming 'to stimulate systematic thinking about the application of social psychology', scheduled to take place on 24–7 April 1973 in Mallorca, Spain.

The lectures were circulated to all participants before the seminar. Some of those, who did not present a paper, such as Moscovici and Tajfel, led discussions during the sessions. Their task was to make some opening remarks on pre-selected issues for debate or to summarize discussions, attempting to pull loose threads out of the session.

Deutsch opened the conference. He explained vividly why social psychology had given up its interest in applied science and pointed out that it had paid a heavy price for its choice. It was becoming increasingly an abstraction, losing contact with reality. It is good to be 'a science' but it is even better if it is useful. Deutsch outlined a programme that would permit social psychology to achieve this goal, that is, to prove itself useful. Conference papers concerned specific applied research questions, such as the usefulness of social psychology in the understanding of real life issues, as in the papers by Himmelweit, Zimbardo and Walton. Faucheux and Varela focused on the experience of researchers in consulting practices. Hornstein and Maslach presented their conclusions on social intervention and on the social psychologist as an agent of change. Finally, Kelley and Deutsch shared with participants their perspectives on training students in the applied field.

As the conference was so well planned, it was decided to publish papers in a book entitled *Applying Social Psychology*, edited by Deutsch and Hornstein (1975). It is still today a rich source of information and reflection. Yet, besides thrashing out ideas, the conference legitimized the Transnational Committee's scientific policy in Eastern Europe and in Latin America. And it did more than that: it renewed the unfinished dialogue between 'pure' and 'applied' social psychology.

With these successful enterprises the 'invisible college' became unusually confident. On the back of the conferences that had taken place, it envisaged several others, for example, on implicit theory and on national identity.

Achieving an *Intercultural Habitus*

Over the years, the Transnational Committee unwittingly created an 'invisible college' as a model for reflecting on and progressing towards an international social psychology. This non-designed project has passed through several stages.

The first step consisted of an attempt to export a superordinate theory and, more especially method, all over the world. It was thought necessary, in the first place, to unite social psychologists from different countries and then to proceed in their training and in initiating research. This was a planetary model with a fixed centre and with planets revolving around. Anyhow, this step did not pose any problems for social psychologists save one: do the planets exist?

The second step raised the question: what was to be done if they did exist? And, of course, the answer was to train them to replicate experiments or other studies, and compare the results. However, as we have seen, discussions in Sorrento and in the Faucheux review on comparative method did not offer an unambiguous answer. It involved much work and gained little knowledge. The experiment designed by the Lanzetta group, planned in Nice and discussed at Santa Monica, was an attempt to save the idea of comparison. The outcome was a logical but very deceptive one.

The third step was an obvious one although the most difficult. If there are no hidden or distant planets, the researcher is free to create the centre himself. In reality, no definition of social psychology was absolutely satisfactory and no scientific situation has as yet been clearly defined. It is more reasonable to accept this universal and cultural diversity, and refrain from diminishing it with theories that do not correspond to social experience and practices.

It took some time to perceive, throughout the workings of the Committee, that its principal role had started to turn to the scientific community itself, to the norms it fostered and the practices it diffused among its members. In particular, the Committee realized that it was necessary to handle other people's work with care, to understand their point of view and to show some respect for it. It was momentous for the Committee to realize that communication between scholars in different countries can contribute to emerging theories. The Transnational Committee recognized that what might be called an 'intercultural habitus' was essential in its daily work and in striving towards a transnational social psychology. It demanded that everyone should approach the 'other's' theory, research and so on as if it belonged to one's own culture and field. It is the habitus of recognition instead of comparison, the search for truth and not merely for precision. But this should not come as a surprise. The most simple and the most familiar are not only what we do not see but what we resist seeing. And it is this that the Transnational Committee has succeeded in making visible.

V

Crossing the Atlantic

14

A Crisis Delayed

The Travelling Committee

'The travelling committee' was a highly appropriate metaphor by which Deutsch (1999, p. 31) described the Transnational Committee. As the anecdote goes, when someone asked why Festinger had created this Committee, he supposedly responded, in order to avoid answering, that he wanted to travel. The Committee was certainly guilty of many sins of which the tribunal of history could accuse it and which it could never contest. The first of them was that it did not have a paper with a letterhead and no place that it could claim as its address. It led a nomadic life, holding meetings wherever convenient and wherever its members could work together. For instance, the Committee met in 1966 in Paris after the Royaumont Conference and in 1973 in Formentor, after the conference on applied social psychology. It was as simple as that: the Committee existed and worked on the move.

The reason why the Transnational Committee was not incorporated into something visible and stable was that it was in a class of its own. Its unofficial status was the reason why the Hungarian organizers of the Visegrad conference, who were familiar with most academic institutions throughout the world, called it 'a strange animal', refusing its sponsorship. Possibly it was a strange animal, but nonetheless a discreet one. There were few people who knew about it and the Committee did little to publicize itself. It tried hard to establish relations or to bypass obstacles in the different countries where it operated, and avoided unveiling itself too much in public. Despite numerous contacts and quasi-permanent connections with universities, foundations and individuals all over the world, the Transnational Committee preferred informal and personal relations. This might appear strange but it was nonetheless a realistic strategy: legitimacy and prestige were conferred on the Transnational Committee by the renown of its members and not the other way round, as is usually the case. It can be seen that membership did not contribute much to the individual's status or reputation: no letterhead and no visiting cards.

All this also explained its manner of functioning. The Transnational Committee revolved around two focal points. One was its chairman, whose task was to navigate the projects, stimulate collaboration between members and formulate policy. There were three chairmen: Festinger, Deutsch and Moscovici. The other focal point was the Staff Officer, who ensured mediation between the SSRC and the chairman of the Transnational Committee. He monitored, if possible on a daily basis, the development of the projects in progress, ensuring the flow of correspondence and so on. In a sense, he was the gatekeeper. He was the only person with the power to control the flow of information. He also represented the Committee on the SSRC Council and vice-versa. The quality of relations between these two bodies and between chairman and the members of the Transnational Committee were largely dependent on him. This consequently had an effect on the group as a whole. In a way, the Staff Officer was the only sedentary element in the nomadic life of the Committee.

Willerman was the first Staff Officer appointed on the creation of the Transnational Committee and Jenness was the last one at the time the Committee left the SSRC. The second Staff Officer, Singer, had a provisional role. As for the third one, Lehmann, there was an unstable relationship between him and Festinger who, towards the end, withdrew his confidence in him. It was necessary that Staff Officers had authority which they could justifiably exercise. As Festinger maintains in his brief history,[1] this rather small committee accomplished a number of different things. The projects were conceived by subcommittees but, despite the informal climate, it was the chairman who in the last instance chose the projects, defining the work and composition of the subcommittees. Thanks to him, the Transnational Committee could both enlarge its field of action and attract competences which it needed at any given moment. For example, the subcommittee of the Louvain Summer School included Nuttin, a non-member of the

Committee, and the subcommittee which organized the Visegrad conference assembled colleagues from several countries in Eastern and Western Europe around Deutsch and Tajfel. It was also thanks to subcommittees that the Committee was open towards various scientific communities and their lively intellectual milieu. If it were not for this broad-minded attitude, the Committee would have risked insularity and isolation, a danger for many academic institutions. Anyhow, the Committee had very few members and all activities were voluntary. No rule prescribed either the number of members or their duration in office. When a new country, or a new continent – Latin America, Eastern Europe or Japan – were added to the map, a representative of that part of the world was co-opted to the Committee. Progressively, as social psychology became more international, so the Committee, too, followed an international expansion. Or perhaps we could say that it did so in theory, because in practice, its activities depended on its financial means as well as on the freedom of movement of the new members.

Why are we saying all this? Why do we describe the travelling committee by specifying its personal, informal and above all, its very discreet character? No doubt, we wish to bring out a particular image of a group that accomplished a singular and considerable task in social psychology. Moreover, we want to explain why the Transnational Committee never had time or inclination to address the problem of its organization, and more seriously, of its status. When it tried to do that, it was too late. At the time when the question of its existence was raised in 1972, its members were: Deutsch (Chairman), Campbell, Festinger, Irle, Janoušek, Kelley, Moscovici, Ramallo and Tajfel. And this is what we find very difficult to explain: why did they continue to see their task as something of great importance, despite the fact that their work on the Committee did not influence their career or reputation? They were reasonable beyond reason.

The Crisis Brewing in New York

Although precise dates have only symbolic importance, let us remind ourselves that the Transnational Committee took shape in 1964 in New York. Little is known about negotiations and people involved before it was composed and sponsored by the SSRC. Such preliminary and informal transactions rarely leave written traces.

At first, progress was better than expected. Success of the Committee and efficient cooperation with the SSRC allowed the resolution of problems that occurred en route. In 1972, a year of crisis, the EAESP and the Latin American Committee were already organized and expanding. And although these associations worked towards their autonomy, they did not tend to loosen relations either with the Transnational Committee or with the 'invisible college'. Moreover, as it happened, Festinger moved from Stanford to the New School, and Moscovici to part-time professor, also at the New School,[2] so with Deutsch at Columbia University nearly half of the Committee after 1970 was in New York.

It is tempting to look for some causes of the crisis that hit the Transnational Committee. In the early 1970s, a change took place in the USA, as we learn from a score of books. Optimism that existed in the aftermath of the Second World War had now vanished. It was the epoch of the Vietnam War and protests at universities. Moreover, social sciences were under scrutiny and funds for social research were gradually eroded. Long, prosperous years were succeeded by lean years. The new president of the SSRC, Eleanor Sheldon, proclaimed that the funds for research were levelling off at a time when the demand for money was rapidly increasing (Worcester, 2001, p. 58).

The SSRC in general had few financial assets of its own for support of committees and new committees were expected to generate their own operating means from private foundations or governmental agencies.

The Transnational Committee did not secure any continuous support. There were always financial problems. The support of the NSF and sometimes of Ford or other foundations allowed main projects to be undertaken. But as far as the SSRC was concerned, there was no long-term perspective that would guarantee funds, as for example the Ford grant supporting the European Association. At that time of scarce resources the SSRC preferred to study some specific problems or issues 'rather than supporting the rather vague program of international collaboration that the Transnational Committee proposed' (Riecken, 2004).

And one should not overlook the fact that there was some intellectual discontent that the Transnational Committee did not devote itself to exporting existing American models. Festinger clarified the Committee's orientation:

> When communication between such scholars in different countries is adequate, the attempts to integrate their knowledge on a theoretical level, the emerging theories do represent an 'interculturalisation' of knowledge about social behavior. The immediate purpose of the Committee there is to promote better training of social psychologists, primarily in the experimental field, in various countries, and bring them together in conferences or informal meetings, an initial step in the long-term process of advancing knowledge of social behavior.[3]

But that does not mean that these arguments were convincing. One may find different kinds of reservation regarding the value and future actions of the Committee were held, for instance, by experts such as the sociologist, Neil Smelser.[4] To him, the intellectual substance of both the Mallorca and Hungarian conferences seemed diffuse, and he did not expect much to come out of the Hungarian conference. Social psychology, he thought, was 'not highly regarded in Eastern Europe and the USSR, where interest centres in problem-defined areas and "concrete" work'.[5] Supporting these views, a highly respected social psychologist, M. Brewster Smith, was of the opinion that the Transnational Committee

> represented a tradition in social psychology that was in the process of changing. The original mission of the committee had been to proselytize American methods and theory, and in Europe it had been successful. But now in the US the field was moving toward socially relevant concerns; in some ways the Europeans, with their deeply anti-positivist traditions, had initiated this change.[6]

Equally, Gardner Lindzey agreed that the Committee had done its work well in the past and that the Committee's missionary role had grown obsolete. He suggested that the Committee should be encouraged to consider dissolving itself after its present projects were completed.

The most gracious evaluation of the East–West meeting to which the Committee and so many people had devoted six long years was that it would lead to nothing. But it could be that all such judgements were expressing an opinion about social psychology, which was not highly regarded in Eastern Europe and the USSR. It was in fact forbidden for political reasons; and other social sciences, too, were severely restricted. This political background produced the 'problem-defined areas', as the Soviet sociologist Yadov had explained at the conference in Vienna in 1967. And after the success of the meeting in Visegrad, the situation started to change in most East European countries.

Finally, Lindzey had reason to observe 'that the Committee itself represented a tradition' and that European social psychology started to serve as a model for American social psychology. But is it not this tradition, dare we say the Lewinian tradition, which was inherent in the origin of the Transnational Committee and its leading ideas? Considering the comments of his colleagues, Lindzey decided that the Committee had accomplished its mission and could be discharged at a convenient date.

But the SSRC Council's criticism was not the most shocking thing. What is shocking even today is that its experts did not consider discussing the matter with the Transnational Committee members and respecting their views on the state of the art. Whatever the prestige of these experts, the taste of experience and the colour of reality were familiar to those who invented the Committee and who fulfilled its mission.

The uncertainties concerning the reappointment of the Transnational Committee surfaced in 1972. Little by little one perceived that the subject was raised more and more often, although it did not amount to anything resembling a decision. It was symptomatic, however, at the Executive Committee meeting in June 1972 that David Jenness proposed that the Committee should now appoint a European chairman. The minutes state 'The European members have been most active, and selection of a chairman from among them and the possibility that its European activities may become predominant had been suggested . . .'[7] This suggestion was probably made for two reasons but we can neither prove nor disprove such conjecture.

The first was the departure in 1971 of Riecken, a former student of Festinger, who assumed the presidency of the SSRC in

1969. In many ways, he cared a great deal about the Transnational Committee. He was also a co-author, with Leon Festinger and Stanley Schachter, of the classic *When Prophecy Fails* (1964). Activities of Festinger and Riecken coincided at this crucial moment. Riecken had just resigned from his presidency of the SSRC and Festinger intended to resign from the Transnational Committee. After Riecken's departure it was easier for the SSRC to decide that it could no longer be the main or sole source of financing it. In a letter to Riecken, Festinger[8] alludes to 'affairs' that had already been the subject of discussion. They were so serious, Festinger thought, that it was necessary for past and present chairmen to meet in order to see what could be done in order to envisage a different outcome. Since the issue is rather delicate, it is more appropriate to stick to archive documents rather than rely upon distant memories or testimonies that critics might dismiss as motivated by specific positions. Referring to Festinger's resignation from the Transnational Committee, Riecken responded to Festinger as follows:

> I hope it is unnecessary for me to repeat that I think you have been a valuable and contributing member of the Committee even though your professional interests have moved far away from social psychology. The question of whether you continue on the Committee or resign ought to be taken in consideration with Mort [Deutsch] and in a somewhat broader context than the staffing of the Committee as such. I don't have a firm opinion either way, and I'd be very glad to talk further with you and Mort about it. I have in fact proposed to him that we try to get together to discuss several aspects of the Committee's affairs . . .[9]

One might easily imagine that these 'affairs' were serious if it seemed necessary to have both past and present chairmen meet in order to influence the outcome.

The second reason why the question of the Committee's re-appointment was raised may have been related to its goal. The Transnational Committee was created in a period when the majority of American institutions were interested in Europe as a resource for social science and a place of great ideological confrontation during the Cold War. From this perspective, the Committee has achieved its mission in Western and Eastern Europe.

The Transnational Committee was reappointed in 1972 but the discussion shows the extent to which the question of chairmanship itself became the subject of dispute. Obviously, no one wished to change the chairman who was in charge of negotiations concerning the establishment of more permanent East–West scientific relations. As the proverb says, you can't swap horses in midstream.

But a letter from Sheldon, the new president of the SSRC, to Deutsch, re-appointing him as chairman, warns him about the situation and the longevity of the Transnational Committee:

> Since 1964, the Transnational Committee has been of central importance in stimulating the consolidation outside the US of a significant field of research and theory. The various changes in emphasis and in membership in the committee's history . . . are signs not of a lack of clarity of purpose, but of the ability of the committee members to keep up to date with the evolution of the discipline and changing needs in the field. I am sure that the committee will continue to act flexibly and imaginatively in these regards.

Festinger's Brief History

Most Committee members accepted their reappointment but not Festinger,[10] who repeated his decision to resign. However, he was not a man of anger but of reflection which was why he decided to write a 'defence and illustration' of the Transnational Committee in the hope that it would change the point of view of the SSRC and its president.

In October 1972 he wrote a simple and passionate text.[11] There are two or three versions of this ten-page account that can be viewed today as one of the most significant documents in contemporary social psychology. We quote verbatim two pages of his brief history here, giving a bird's eye view of the origin and purpose of the Transnational Committee.

> In March of 1964, after more than a year of planning and discussion, the SSRC established an international committee to further

communication and cooperation among social psychologists from different countries and different cultures. In an effort to avoid words that had developed connotations in other contexts, the committee, somewhat clumsily, decided on the title of 'transnational social psychology'. The original members of the committee were Ancona (Italy), Koekebakker (Holland), Lanzetta (USA), Moscovici (France), de Sola Pool (USA), Rommetweit (Norway), Schachter (USA) and Festinger (USA), its chairman.

Today, after more than eight years, the committee is still in existence. During its existence the membership of the committee has gradually changed so that now there are only two persons remaining from the original group, namely, Serge Moscovici and Leon Festinger (no longer chairman). The others currently on the committee are Donald T. Campbell, U.S.A.; Martin Irle, Germany; Jaromír Janoušek, Czechoslovakia; Harold H. Kelley, U.S.A.; Luis I. Ramallo, Chile; Henri Tajfel, England; and Morton Deutsch, U.S.A. (chairman).

When a committee that has been established for a specific purpose remains in existence for such a long time, it is legitimate to wonder whether it still has a viable purpose or continues out of inertia. When the membership of a committee changes so drastically, it is legitimate to wonder whether this represents instability or purposeful action. The following brief history of the committee may help to cast light on these issues.

Beginnings and purposes:
The decade following World War II saw a great expansion of research in social psychology in the United States. With this expansion came some very rapid advances in knowledge about social behaviour and attitudes. Since the vast bulk (perhaps about 99%) of this research had been carried out in the United States, it was natural to question whether something was being learned about humans generally or was it all just a reflection of the particular brand of Western culture that existed in this country. There were, of course, numerous attempts to repeat, in other countries, studies that had been originally conducted in the United States. This did not however seem to be a fruitful approach. One cannot simply 'repeat' a procedure in another country with another language and a different culture. One has to 'translate' the procedure. Then how does one know to what extent agreement or lack of agreement in the results of the studies is due to lack of cleverness or too much cleverness in the 'translation'.

Many who were concerned with the problem came to believe that it was necessary to proceed differently. If there could be sufficient training of, interaction among, and opportunities for research for social psychologists in widely diverse places, then indigenous research programs would develop, sparked by the ideas of the local investigator. Given interaction among many such persons, the 'international social psychology' would gradually come about as a result of the formulation of theories that would have to integrate and explain the diversity of data. This was the purpose and the motivation of the committee on transnational social psychology – to help provide the training, the opportunity for interaction, and the opportunity for independent indigenous research in social psychology.

Probably the major influence in precipitating the formation of the committee was provided by John Lanzetta. During the academic year 1962–3 he visited most of the countries in Western Europe, seeking out and establishing contact with social psychologists. He was impressed by the fact that, in almost every country, he would find knowledgeable, competent social psychologists who had some contact with someone in the United States but had no contact or interaction among each other. He became convinced that it was important to bring these people together, establish interaction among them, and provide opportunities for them to collaborate on research. This, then, was the first task assumed by the committee when it came into existence.[12]

Having written this too modest and yet impressive account, Festinger could tell himself as the Romans did *dixi et salvavi animam meam*. Given his eminence in the field, this was the only thing he could do for himself and his colleagues. It framed their experience and their lives.

15

Crossing the Atlantic

Formentor, the Meeting of the Last Chance

Sometimes we may doubt whether Europeans and Americans, who have so much in common, can nevertheless understand one another's institutions. We can discuss at length the reasons for the crisis that brewed in New York, without being able to say 'now we understand'. But despite this, one fact allows us to overcome misgivings.

Be that as it may, it was understood that after the conference of applied social psychology, organized by Hornstein and Deutsch at Formentor in 1973, the members of the Transnational Committee would meet with the President of the SSRC. In his memorandum the Staff Officer wrote:

> I should like to ask now, for agenda items for the Committee meeting . . . Please write not only about specific items of business but also about your thoughts as to what the principal concerns of the Committee ought to be and what tasks it should set for itself. What should be the range of substantive interests? The balance between attention to training and emphasis on the advancement of research . . . the possible appropriateness of an enlarged or altered membership?[1]

There was clearly one problem which everybody was thinking about and which they started to discuss: whether members wanted to continue the Committee and, if so, how to proceed. As David Jenness put it in another memorandum 'The over-riding agenda item is the question of the committee's direction and plans for the future. . . . May I urge all of you who wish to, to write Mort fully and candidly in advance of the meeting'.[2] In a nutshell, people had to make up their minds.

The programme of the meeting was long and diverse. Eleanor Sheldon thus could see the true richness of the Transnational Committee's activities and how it worked. Jenness reported:

> that in the Council, at the directors' level, it had recently been questioned whether the committee should be reappointed; it had become one of the oldest committees; many of its accomplishments (e.g. the EAESP) were now well secured; in a time when the Council committees in general are becoming more international and cross-disciplinary, it could be argued that this committee had, on the one hand, lost its unique transnational character, and on the other hand, now seemed somewhat parochial in disciplinary terms; and finally, the committee has not been able, over the years, to find general-purpose funding for its meetings and routine activities.[3]

The discussion[4] evinced an encouraging but very vulnerable situation in Latin American and East European countries. It would have been more satisfactory to see improvement in the short-term but that would have needed a miracle. When the EAESP was created, thanks to a happy combination of circumstances at that time, the possibilities for research cooperation were much better than in 1973. It was of the highest importance, for East and West alike, that their scientific potential was preserved, and that their stimulated efforts could continue to develop. It was pointed out by several members that the Transnational Committee had never been doctrinaire in its approach, and that in fact it had responded to and encouraged those concerned with sociological or problem-defined areas, as well as those who were involved with experimental social psychology.

It was this point in particular, the definition of social psychology as a broad and autonomous science, that was so daring and so all encompassing that even today one would hesitate to endorse it. 'At a time, when many sociopolitical and intellectual forces conduce to a greater emphasis on cross-disciplinary, problem-focused research, it was in fact crucial for a committee such as this one to cleave to its own identity, as a committee of social psychologists, and not to try to be all things to all men'[5] Gradually but inevitably, discussions reached a point where a definitive answer was expected. And the unanimous answer was that 'the committee, through recognizing the difficulties in its continuation by the SSRC, concluded that it could not responsibly agree to its own termination.' The SSRC Council, the East–West Conference, the Latin American situation, the conferences on theoretical issues, among others 'required the continued existence of a Transnational Committee of influential persons, since by definition the voluntary efforts of individuals along these lines had to be coordinated in order to succeed'.[6] But the Committee needed neither massive funding nor too many 'projects'; it did need a continued existence in which it could operate flexibly. If the SSRC could not offer such permanence, for obvious reasons, the Committee would have to go its own way: 'the group would need to find other auspices.' Without protesting or imposing demands, the Transnational Committee had made its own choice, a choice determined by the responsibilities that it had taken towards others and towards its discipline. As Erasmus wrote, such is 'the conduct of all reasonable people, when they see that resistance would be futile'.

There were moments of tension and moments of calm. The placating gesture was made by Sheldon when she proposed reappointing the Transnational Committee as a Committee of the SSRC for another year and further discussing how it could 'operate autonomously, as long as this method of operation is made clear to all concerned'. And yet, the end of this crucial meeting saw its most intense moment when Festinger handed in his resignation. It was understood that he had set out along the road that the group was going to follow.

Death in Chile

This is not a new phenomenon: things look different according to the perspective from which we view them. We have seen how they appeared to the Transnational Committee in April 1973 at Formentor. In the eyes of the P&P, it was a simple equation: the Committee had no further funds but has asked to be reappointed for 1973–4. If new funds were not obtained, the Committee would not plan any more projects, but would consider the possibility of becoming autonomous or, alternatively, of affiliating with another organization. In either case, it would cease to be the SSRC's committee.[7]

This is why, having returned home, the Committee members were in a position of strange embarrassment. Of course, they had to start seeking funds. But they also had to come up with an alternative, a way of continuing under other auspices. But under what auspices and where? During that time, the train of history rode with utmost speed and carried much correspondence.

By June 1973, Jenness[8] had drafted a letter to the Aquinas, Guggenheim and Kettering Foundations. The likelihood that these foundations would respond positively was minimal. Their resources for international projects could not be compared with the Ford or Rockefeller Foundations and they could not give the Transnational Committee's applications favourable consideration. This was clear by the late autumn of 1973.

One only has to reflect for a moment, to see that, given the denial of the seven-year grant by Ford, the situation was precarious. It was in fact the NSF, supported by its Program Director for social psychology, Roland Radloff, which enabled the Transnational Committee to carry out most of its projects. The Transnational Committee certainly learned how to live precariously, continuously seeking financing. It was, as Valéry said, 'the case of the temporary becoming permanent'. But one should add, only up to a point. If the Committee had obtained these grants, none of these problems with the SSRC would have arisen and it could have continued its work as expected. At the same time, just as Deutsch had done, so Irle in Germany began to look for the necessary resources.

We can never reread these letters and projects without thinking yet again of the event which ruined any hope of recovery or of a new start: the military coup by Pinochet in Chile.

For the Transnational Committee, it was like a fire in the house. Exactly five years earlier, in 1968, the Committee had for the first time been thwarted by historical events; now it faced a similar drama. That was when the Soviet army and its allies had brutally invaded Czechoslovakia which had been trying to transform totalitarian socialism into socialism with a human face. At that time the Transnational Committee was split as to what kind of attitude to take with respect to the Soviet occupation and the suppression of freedom. In those days the Committee had not yet engaged in concrete ways with colleagues in Eastern Europe and therefore did not have to deal with any consequence. But this time, without conferring with one another, their response was spontaneous and unanimous. The alarm was raised in a telegram from the EAESP on 18 September 1973, requiring the Committee to intervene for the safety of Chilean colleagues.

Deutsch, then Chairman of the Transnational Committee wrote to Sheldon.[9] He informed her that he had just received a telegram from the EAESP, which had requested him, as the Chairman of the Committee, to ask the SSRC 'to mobilise pressure to help prevent persecution of academics and intellectuals in Chile'. Deutsch endorsed this request personally and urged the SSRC to take whatever action it thought helpful to preserve and protect the personal and academic freedom of social science colleagues in Chile. This commitment stemmed from the seminar held in Valparaíso and the Committee's close association with Ricardo Zúñiga. Deutsch concluded his letter: 'Thus I feel not only one abstract obligation to our colleagues in Chile but also a personal one'. He wrote also to Kenneth Little,[10] the Executive Secretary of the APA. Not long afterwards, Campbell[11] sent word to Little: 'This is to second Deutsch's letter . . .'.

The military coup in Chile had a tremendous impact on Europe and the USA, where demonstrations and protests were held. As people started leaving Latin America and Chile in particular, refugees were received with much sympathy on other continents. Zúñiga, then at the Catholic University of Chile and one of the founding members of the Latin American Committee, was among the first in danger. He and his wife had participated at the Conference in Dartmouth in 1971 on active minorities and he belonged to the Chilean revolutionary movement. He wrote a letter to Donald Campbell,[12] sent by registered mail from Argentina. Zúñiga explained his situation, pointing out that all schools of sociology in Chile would be forced to close. His Institute would also vanish because it was seen to be controlled by Marxists. The term 'Marxist' was applied to everybody from

terrorists to leftists and including Zúñiga personally. He saw no
option but to leave the country and was prepared to take any job
just to survive. He emphasized in his letter that he was not 'cling-
ing', but seeking advice on what possibilities there were for him
abroad. Campbell was the first to undertake to find an academic
post for him. An inter-office mail says it all:

> To: David Jenness
> From: Donald Campbell
> Subject: Ricardo Zúñiga's letter is also being sent to Deutsch,
> Festinger, Irle, Kelley, Moscovici and Tajfel. I am working on a
> couple of angles for Zúñiga. Don.[13]

Moscovici contacted Mrs Zúñiga by letter. The MSH began
organizing exile for the Chileans. Subsequently, the MSH witnessed the clandestine existence of intellectuals, persecutions and
assassinations carried out over the next several years.

Then there was Luis Ramallo, a member of the Transnational
Committee itself. Jenness wrote to the members of the Committee
informing them that he had spoken by telephone to Ramallo in
Santiago.[14] They had a guarded discussion, not knowing whether
censorship was operating. Ramallo reported that things were
fairly stable at the Latin American Faculty in Social Sciences,
although some non-Chileans had been removed from their positions, among them, the Secretary General, Ricardo Lagos. Ramallo
had taken over his post, at least temporarily, in order to provide as
much protection as possible for members of the Faculty. When
Jenness asked whether anything could be done for the Chilean
intellectuals, Ramallo said that it would be helpful if Chileans could
participate in activities abroad and, therefore, he urged that they
may be sent invitations. Even if they could not travel, it would be
important for them to feel that they were part of the international
community. Jenness at once sent a report of their conversation to
the members of the Transnational Committee, which ended: 'Luis
expressed great pleasure at having evidence of our concern, and
sends all of you his big "abrazo".'

Jenness[15] wrote to a number of people informing them that
Zúñiga was in the US. Initially he was to work with Campbell on
the experimenting society, his main interest, and then he was to

take up an academic post. As Jenness said in his memorandum: 'This was brought about through the good offices of those who know Zúñiga . . . Presumably there will be other cases like this coming to our attention, which perhaps can be handled in the same way.'

As to the future, it seemed even less clear. Jenness[16] wrote to Campbell who on the Transnational Committee best knew the situation in Latin America:

> Thank you for writing about the situation of the Latin American Committee. It confirms from another source the difficulty we all have known about, really, for some time. Earlier this summer we have got a letter from Rodrigues that gives much the same view, though less clearly. There is a Rashomon-like situation here; I doubt that any one view is completely fair.

Although news of this profoundly disturbing situation was difficult to face, it presented everybody with an unexpected decision to be made about the future. There is no doubt that what happened in Chile was one of the main factors that influenced decisions about the future of the Committee.

The Pilgrimage from New York to Paris

During these events, some changes of hearts and minds took place. At first, Deutsch and Jenness tried to solicit general-purpose funds from three American foundations. As the chances of obtaining funds decreased, so did the chances of remaining a Committee of the SSRC. The moment had almost arrived to consider whether and how it would be possible to find an alternative solution.

An alternative had to be found in any case. As the preparation for the East–West conference had shown, the Committee's difficulties were due in part to its being perceived as both an American and a Transnational Committee. So it needed help from UNESCO and the Vienna Centre in order to conclude its task. This is not a bogus problem: in extreme situations one can get lost in the subtle differentiation between science and politics. In Latin America the Transnational Committee started its work under more favourable political conditions than in Eastern Europe. But the anti-American attitudes, sparked off by American support for the military coup in Chile, became a major obstacle threatening everything that had been achieved. Kelley wrote to Sheldon:

> Please excuse my tardiness in replying to your letter . . . since you wrote, much has happened with regard to the Committee's plans . . . I am very uncertain about the activities in Latin America . . . We have had many ups and downs before but the gap between the possibilities and the activities in Latin America is most frustrating.[17]

These preoccupations of American members had even greater significance because it was they who were in charge of the building of ALAPSO. This is why the Transnational Committee started to entertain the hypothesis that it would be much easier, even logical, for the Transnational Committee to continue under the auspices of an international organization. Deutsch and Tajfel already worked with UNESCO and it is likely that they made such a suggestion. Whatever the case, it was Tajfel who led negotiations with Samy Friedman, General Secretary of the International Social Science of UNESCO, who informed him that the UNESCO Council 'should be happy to sponsor the activities' of the Transnational Committee.[18] Sheldon was informed about these developments by Jenness. 'Morton Deutsch,' he wrote, 'called me today to say that Samy Friedman has written to Tajfel that the ISSC will be prepared to provide official international auspices, receive funds, etc. I said that it would no doubt be possible for the SSRC to discharge the committee before next September, if it seemed desirable.'[19]

So at the end of 1973 everything still seemed open, as one may divine from a letter from Deutsch[20] to Sheldon saying that he was happy to continue as chairman of the Transnational Committee during 1973–4.

Left open also was the possibility that the Committee would be forced to cross the Atlantic. One does not separate one's heart lightly from what represents a great part of one's history. But the hour of the departure had not yet quite arrived because the SSRC Council reappointed the Transnational Committee for another year.

16

Pilgrims' Progress

A Historic Meeting in Bad Homburg

Who are these people? What are they doing and how did they get here? These questions raised by the ISSC were quite easily answered and the answers given were accepted. This was so perhaps because the UNESCO Council and the EPHE belonged to the same 'small world' and their connections were historical. We may remember that Lévi-Strauss was the first Secretary-General of the ISSC and that Heller served as Deputy Secretary-General (1963–9) (Platt, 2002). As we mentioned earlier, Deutsch and Tajfel had first contacted the UNESCO Council before the Visegrad conference and these overtures were successful. But the most pressing task was to provide information in the form of brief notes for the UNESCO's Council Secretary, who was preparing the agenda for the next executive meeting. This was an opportunity to find out whether the Transnational Committee would enjoy a sufficient degree of freedom to achieve its objectives. It also became obvious that becoming part of the UNESCO's Council represented recognition of social psychology by the human science international community. That meant that the Committee meeting that took place immediately after the Visegrad Conference at the Werner-Reimers-Stiftung in Bad Homburg, Germany, on 13–14 May 1974,[1] was of historic importance.

The beautiful setting of the Werner-Reimers-Stiftung contributed to the aura of the event. Quite paradoxically, the meeting followed the usual agenda and even Staff-Officer Jenness was invited to fulfil his normal function. The report on the Visegrad conference was the first item on the agenda. The ensuing discussion of this six-year joint endeavour with the EAESP took up a great deal of time.

The reports about the Latin American activities were most eagerly awaited. Ramallo gave an account of the situation on his continent, then Campbell and Kelley described the training seminar that they intended to hold there. It appeared that although ALAPSO had undergone difficult internal tensions, the seeds of growth had germinated and the association continued to develop. Tajfel reported on his cross-national training programme to be carried out with the financial support of UNESCO and British grants.

The last point on the agenda was the reorganization and future of the Transnational Committee. It was anticipated and approved 'that the committee will cease to be sponsored' by the SSRC as from September 1974. 'Prior to that action, the ISSC'[2] was expected to invite the Transnational Committee to affiliate with the ISSC as one of its committees. The change of sponsorship was accompanied by a change in chairmanship. Moscovici would succeed Deutsch as chairman of the Transnational Committee and Irle would become vice-chairman. Financial problems did not dominate the meeting. The new chairman knew that he could rely upon the Maison des Sciences de l'Homme in Paris for assistance. More significant was the decision to set the next Committee meeting in Lisbon in May 1975. One reads in the minutes[3] that the purpose of the meeting would be not only to conduct business but to stimulate the development of social psychology in Portugal under its new government.

The End of an Era . . .

The journey from Rome 1964 to Paris 1974 had been arduous and long. But the separation from the SSRC took far less time. In his letter, Jenness[4] informed Moscovici that he was to send, from New York to Paris, his 'package of basic documents concerning the Transnational Committee from about 1970 to date'.[5] Taking possession of that heritage, Moscovici responded to Jenness, thanking him for the letter and the documents and announcing the decision of the ISSC 'to take on our Committee and they have even congratulated us on our programme. This marks the end of an era and another one is coming to life and I hope that our relationships will continue as in the past.'[6]

In discussing these issues, the Council made it clear that it was necessary to adopt the proposed changes. More generally, the situation suggested that progress towards a transnational social psychology did not require, at least for the time being, American leadership. Moreover, the Transnational Committee's Annual Report 1973–4 stated:

> At the same time, research funds in the US for the development of social psychology are less easily obtainable than in the previous decade, reflecting both a general financial stringency and the widespread opinion that the discipline is going through a period of transition and a re-ordering of concerns whose outcome is as yet unclear.
>
> For these reasons, among others, it has recently been agreed that the committee should cease to be a committee of the Council. However, the group's long range goal, to continue to encourage social psychological research and to facilitate communication and cooperation in various parts of the world, is still an important one. In response to inquiries on behalf of the committee, the ISSC had indicated willingness to assume sponsorship.[7]

And of course that had already happened by the end of June of that same year, 1974.

And a New Beginning

One of the most terrible jokes in Beckett's *Endgame* reads:

> *Clov*: Do you believe in life to come?
> *Hamm*: Mine was always that.

The punch line is that a life of waiting for life to come is all that such a life ever is. The long and precarious existence, institutional hesitations and uncertain status of the Transnational Committee

all illustrate this joke. For a long time its members teased themselves that if only they could achieve it all, obtain all-purpose
funding, then the SSRC would fully recognize their achievements
and goals and they would have a better view of the life to
come.

The collegial and even enthusiastic reception by the ISSC, and
especially by its secretary, Friedman, promised the Transnational
Committee a future home. The ISSC appreciated the goals of the
Committee, liked its members and felt that it was UNESCO's
mission to help such internationally orientated activities. At the
meeting of the Executive Committee, 24–7 June 1974, the Secretary General recalled that its sponsorship had already been discussed in January of the same year. He added that the Committee
had been in existence for over ten years and that it assembled distinguished scholars whose work was internationally renowned.[8]
The Committee's request had no financial implications for the
Council but it would widen its scope and prestige, while at the
same time it would help the Committee in its operations. It was
at the General Assembly which took place 27–8 June 1974 that
the Committee's proposed programme was presented. Among the
main points one reads:

> If there could be sufficient training of, interaction among, and
> opportunities for research for, social psychologists in widely diverse
> places, then indigenous research programmes would develop,
> sparked by the ideas of the local investigator. Given the interaction
> among many such persons, an 'international social psychology'
> would gradually come about as a result of the formulation of
> theories that would have to integrate and explain the diversity of
> data. This was the purpose and the motivation of the Transnational
> Committee: to help provide the training, the opportunity of inter-
> action, and the opportunity for independent indigenous research
> in social psychology.[9]

This was a necessary reaffirmation of the original goal of the Committee that had been misconstrued as justification for exporting a
model and method to underdeveloped countries. And now, having
been presented to an international forum, this goal became an
official statement, defining the mission of the Transnational
Committee in Paris.

In a welcome letter to Moscovici, the Secretary-General Samy Friedman announced that the ISSC 1974 General Assembly had conferred its sponsorship and added:

> I would appreciate if in the near future we can make contact in order to focus on the modalities of that decision and it goes without saying that Mr Tajfel will be equally welcome to take part in our discussions. I already congratulate myself that this decision was taken. It will enable both establishing links of trustful collaboration between our two organizations and I hope that it will help you to develop your very interesting programme to which the General Assembly has already paid homage.[10]

The world of the happy man is different from the world of the unhappy man, says Wittgenstein in his *Tractatus*. And the world where a group of scientists is welcomed and recognized is probably happier than the one in which a group is subject to continuous evaluation and does not have much hope of being recognized. Still, it came as a surprise that despite the brewing crisis, the arguments since 1972 and Festinger's brief history, the ideas and the work of the Transnational Committee was now appearing in a new light and was re-evaluated accordingly. The decision of the Committee to leave was of course a relief for the SSRC. But it also showed that the Transnational Committee was more than a handful of grant-hunters and that its commitment to certain ideas and goals had meaning 'out there' on the international scene. The SSRC President Sheldon, in a letter to Deutsch, communicated this re-evaluation:

> Very few SSRC committees have been truly transnational, and few have managed to achieve as much in the face of the inevitable difficulties caused by the need to coordinate work among a widely dispersed membership and a relatively low level of financial support . . . I am sure that, not only will the committee continue to work effectively under its new auspices, but that the SSRC will continue to be involved, though indirectly, with its work, through its other committees and programs and through personal contact.[11]

It was natural to express distance and, at the same time, to acknowledge the strength of the bond with the new pilgrims at their point of departure. Obviously, the bond of common history can slacken indefinitely without ever breaking completely. In the event, Tajfel wrote to her, saying that he was 'very glad to learn that our work has been recognised. As you know we hope to continue under the auspices of the ISSC and I take this opportunity for thanking you for your wishes for success for our future activities.'[12] It was a breath of fresh air from across the Atlantic.

17

Rays and Shadows
above the
Transnational Committee

Must We Mean What We Do?

It is fundamental to this historical account that we emphasize
that the crossing of the Atlantic was not voluntary, even though
it was obviously not involuntary either. Can we explain this more
plainly?

It may help to remind readers that the epoch of wars of national
independence, revolutions and dictatorships across the world was
accompanied by a wave of anti-Americanism. And this was
the most sensitive index of bitterness and misunderstanding for
the Transnational Committee after the military coup in Chile. The
members became aware that some parts of the Latin American
academic world had grown suspicious of what they perceived as
a North American committee. In addition, tension could be attributed to political differences in attitude to military dictatorships
associated with the USA. These political issues might not have
been the only grounds for misgivings but they certainly indicated
that the international character of the Transnational Committee,
and of social psychology, had to be made visible once again.

Quite naturally, the Transnational Committee had expected
that once it was recognized as being sponsored by UNESCO, it
would enjoy the credibility and confidence necessary for its work
in Latin America, Eastern Europe and, when the time was ripe,
also in Asia. Moreover, there seemed now to be more open and
informal relations among sociologists, historians and anthropolo-

gists and it was important to develop similar relations among social psychologists if they were to become part of the international community of human sciences. In this association the Committee would be its own master, as Friedman reassured Tajfel: 'Mr Moscovici and I have examined in very general terms the situation which results in the sponsorship of the Council and I have assured him that this will function most efficiently without having the slightest effect on the autonomy of the Transnational Committee.'[1] Hence it was not a question of regretting the choice that had been made but, rather, of finding out what to anticipate in the new reality. Put simply, it was necessary to restart the work that had been interrupted.

A study of the documents sent by Jenness to Paris shows how much work the Transnational Committee had accomplished. In 1974, social psychology was on the map of human science all over Europe, Latin America, and taking its first steps in Asia. Moscovici, however, felt, that the Transnational Committee had extended its links too quickly and too far, and that it should first strengthen its existing contacts. Proposals for improving existing links were made at the meeting of the Transnational Committee in Paris in May 1975. It was the first meeting under the auspices of UNESCO. There were no minutes kept of that meeting, as no Staff Officer was present. Yet we know from a letter from Jenness to Tajfel that 'he was very pleased to hear . . . that the Committee meeting in Paris was successful and that the morale of the group is high.'[2] Tajfel answered that 'Indeed the committee meeting in Paris was fairly successful although I am not over-optimistic about the future. This lack of optimism has nothing to do with the committee but is based on the general climate and objective situation which we shall be meeting increasingly in the years to come.'[3] Thanks to Jenness, the contact with the SSRC was kept alive.[4] Jenness indicated what convergence the Transnational Committee could find with SSRC programmes, and how they fitted with the research interests of the Committee. The old bonds were not broken, while new bonds with UNESCO were being woven.

Following suggestions made at the May meeting of the Transnational Committee in Paris, Irle contacted researchers from Eastern Germany and especially those from Berlin, encouraging them to intensify exchanges with social psychologists in other European countries. A note attests that Kelley and Moscovici travelled to Germany to meet Irle in his laboratory.

Be that as it may, it was necessary to clarify the Committee's actions in Latin America. It was thought better to acknowledge the existing divide and to work on two fronts. The first of these, an institutional one, was represented by the Latin American Faculty of Social Sciences which had moved after the military coup in Chile in 1974 from Santiago, Chile, to Buenos Aires, Argentina. The Faculty was part of a network of international institutions in Latin America linked with UNESCO within which Ramallo, a member of the Transnational Committee, had worked for many years. The second front, let us say, the university front, represented ALAPSO. During that time, Moscovici received some information from Rodrigues, about the ALAPSO newsletter, which was first published in the autumn of 1974. But it was very difficult to maintain this front or even to envisage any exchanges or help because, as Jenness wrote to Campbell, 'The Latin American group now seems too "autonomous" but non-corporeal.'[5] Contact with Latin America was interrupted but never broken and its 'non-corporeal' image was due, largely, to tensions within ALAPSO.

During that time Moscovici met Marín probably twice. Marín, who gave an account of the situation and wished to clarify the relation with the Committee, had learned from the SSRC about the change of sponsorship but could not understand why there were difficulties in accessing financial help for Latin Americans. The Committee clearly could not provide any such help unless justified by proposals on Marín's part. Marín realized that Europeans and Americans followed, as closely as possible, the development of ALAPSO, but they also had to face the important political Latin American changes during that time. Marín seemed to be happy about UNESCO sponsorship and the renewed contact with the Transnational Committee. Last but not least, Marín had come to discuss a collective textbook of social psychology, which was to be published in Mexico. This appeared to be a sign of increasing intellectual cooperation which, above all, was encouraging. The Committee had already decided to co-opt a second member from ALAPSO. In a letter to the SSRC, Kelley asked Sheldon whether it would be possible to obtain financial

help from the USA for '. . . the possibility of support for a Japan-
ese and a Latin American member of the Transnational Committee and/or part of the committee's activities in those areas through
the appropriate Foreign AREA Committee of the Council . . . I
realize we'd be in competition for the shrinking funds, but is there
a reasonable way for us at least to try?'[6] Such a demand was not
outrageous since Sheldon had expressed interest in keeping
contact with the Transnational Committee alive. But the co-
optation of Marín or Rodrigues did not take place not only
because of financial problems but also for reasons that were more
difficult to spell out at the time. What was really needed was a
new mission in Latin America.

The 1975 Committee meeting did not take place in Lisbon, as
had been expected. But during the following two years the chairman made the first initiative towards Portugal and Spain. Due to
long years of dictatorship, universities were no longer at the height
of the fame that they had enjoyed historically. A few contacts
were made through the MSH and Moscovici made a number of
discreet trips there to familiarize himself with the terrain. In
Portugal the situation appeared hopeless. In Spain, fruits were to
come later. Spanish social psychologists themselves suggested that
the development of social psychology in their country could start
with a meeting organized in Barcelona in September 1980.

Regarding the life of the Transnational Committee, we know
that a second meeting took place in 1976, although there is no
written evidence. It continued developing its initiatives with
respect to Japan and Asia. It was Kelley's mission. 'Japan', he wrote
'is a country with a vastly different culture than that shared by
Western nations. But it also has a large number of sophisticated
and active researchers in social psychology. They know and use
much the same procedures that we do, and the communication
between the two groups is easy.'[7] Here we can see more clearly
what constituted differences in various parts of the world with
respect to the Transnational Committee. Relations with Eastern
Europe and Latin America were culturally close but scientifically
distant. In contrast, relations with Japan were culturally distant
but scientifically close. This presented an ideal scene for comparative research. Kelley suggested Jyuji Misumi as the person to be
invited to join the Committee.

The meeting of the Committee in the spring of 1977 took place near New York in Deutsch's summer residence. Misumi, the new member from Kyushi University was a cultivated and open-minded person and one of the leaders in applied social psychology in Japan. He was much inspired by Lewin and had replicated some of Lewin's classic experiments. Consequently, he invited Deutsch, Kelley and Moscovici to Japan in order to take the first steps towards the future collaborative research.

But, as ancient philosophers pointed out, there are things that do not depend on us and there are things that do.

About Things that Do Not Depend on Us

The work of the Transnational Committee progressed normally. At the beginning of 1976, it received a copy of a report on the first ALAPSO seminar. But the feeling of normality only lasted until the day when Tajfel's pessimism was justified by news of the military coup in Argentina in 1976. What Festinger, in his brief history, called 'The Latin American Experience', started on the initiative of an Argentinean colleague. After the military coup in Chile, the Latin American Faculty of Social Sciences took refuge in Argentina where Ramallo reassembled the body of teachers and students who had participated in the experiment from the beginning. Now they were again in danger. We shall not try to convey the feelings of disorientation and indignation in the face of what, in Guiseppe Verdi's opera was called 'La Forza Del Destino'. The founding of ALAPSO, just like that of the EAESP, was one of the main achievements of the Transnational Committee. The Committee hoped that it would accompany ALAPSO until it could operate autonomously in the way that the EAESP had managed to do. But if our social representation of the university in one context is 'adequate', using the same social representation in another context may be 'inadequate'. Social representations of the university as a sheltering institution that is relatively autonomous, protected and respected as a common good in a country may work well in peacetime in parts of Europe, but not at that time in Latin America. And the Transnational Committee should have allowed for the eventuality of another civil war so that it could act accordingly. For instance, it should have prepared some alternative ways of maintaining contacts and receiving or helping colleagues who suffered oppression. It should have known what kinds of strategy could be used to continue social psychological work under some military regimes, as, for example, the one that reigned in Brazil. Of course, at first the Committee tried to maintain relations with Argentinian social psychologists through UNESCO and, particularly, through the MSH which in a sense was always prepared for this kind of emergency. It succeeded in helping in two or three cases. Ramallo was forced to leave Argentina for Spain. No documents testify whether there was an immediate Transnational Committee meeting. But the members of the Committee felt that it was necessary to pause and reflect on the general situation.

This historical account does not address only readers who are familiar with the people and events in question or with our field. It aims also at a larger audience eager to learn about these issues. Of course, the Committee communicated and maintained contact with Latin Americans during the years of military dictatorship and repression. One can see that neither in Eastern Europe nor in Latin America was association building a *sine ira et studio* endeavour. It involved facing the larger historical context of political and military repression that prevented the evolution of learning communities. Why, nevertheless, did it seem to the Committee that it was important to continue? Perhaps it was not a question for that epoch and that post-war generation. But for a historian and for readers interested in the history of their science, it remains a challenging one.

About Things that Do Depend on Us

At the meeting of the Transnational Committee in Rome in 1964, a subcommittee was created to explore the possibility of establishing an international organization. The task was announced as follows:

> The question whether the difficulty of developing experimental social psychology in various countries is related to the lack of clear identity of social psychology as a field, and whether creating an

international organization and having international congresses of social psychology would promote such identity and help the development of the field, were discussed. Moscovici and Lanzetta were appointed to a subcommittee to investigate and think through the pros and cons of such actions. This subject will be on the agenda of the committee's next meeting.[8]

The subject appeared sporadically on the agenda, but was never discussed. That was because the Committee became more involved in association building, stimulating an 'invisible college' and designing an international map of social psychology. It can even be claimed that it had a clear and autonomous identity in the fields of human sciences.

Without wanting to unroll history, we can recall that the Germans had their *Völkerpsychologie* and the French their *psychologie de masse* and *psychologie collective*, in which Halbwachs occupied the first chair at the Collège de France. The Italians and British also had their folk psychology or group psychology. Everyone knew and respected classic scholars like Tarde, McDougall, Wundt, Halbwachs, Bartlett, Le Bon or Lévy-Brühl. A place was reserved for our subject in the course of the reconstruction of universities and research institutions after the Second World War.

When, at the beginning of the 1950s, Lévi-Strauss proposed a new system of classification of social sciences for UNESCO, he assigned a very honourable place to social psychology. Social psychology should have been able to establish its identity and find its place among the human sciences in the simplest possible manner: by calling on its historical tradition. The fact that social psychology did not reclaim its virtual place and its ancestors at a time when the social sciences had regained their vigour was a significant historical mistake from the point of view of *identity and clarity* of the discipline. It blurred the identity and clarity of our discipline. This unexpected oversight was discovered too late and therefore its full power was not recognized.

It was also one of the imperspicuous choices that European 'mavericks', attracted by the American example and the charisma of group dynamics, made in defining their field by *method*, and even more so, by *experimental method*. And so the scientific community got the impression that the new *experimental social psy-*

chology was a branch of psychology which did not concern itself with either questions or phenomena from the former social psychology. Briefly, it became something different and at the same time opposed to what that 'bridge science' was or should have been. It will be recalled that the majority of psychologists opposed the expression 'experimental social psychology' from the beginning (Tajfel, 1972). This expression was imposed on the assumption that it would make social psychology *modern*, even scientific. And sharing Lewin's enthusiasm the European 'mavericks' thought that following this trend, anthropology and sociology, too, would become experimental.

An identity crisis

It was assumed that, however complex phenomena were, social psychologists would be able to prove or disprove them by appropriate laboratory experiments. Moreover, that was seen to be of crucial importance for the advancement of the field. It was presumed that one had to begin from what seemed to be facts or observation, employ hypotheses and make predictions about relations between causes and effects. The theories would have to be deductive and capable of making predictions about the relationship between cause and effect, thus improving their scientific status. Although the experimental method seemed to work and the arguments in its favour were impeccable, it stood at variance with shared epistemology of most social scientists and even psychologists. That is, they *did not accept* the view that one could study complex social phenomena in the laboratory. We may have trouble in seeing plainly that experimental method, instead of bringing social psychology closer to psychology on the one hand and to social science on the other, in fact alienated and even isolated it from both.

On the one hand, it cannot be said that psychologists have been impressed by the experimental study of social phenomena and by the 'two-sentence theories' which make simple predictions about the properties of such phenomena. It was such loss of reality that contributed to psychology remaining indifferent to social psychology, whether experimental or not. It is not that psychologists are against the 'social' per se or do not use 'social claims' in their discourse. But that much is true even today: social psychology is rarely appreciated and much less quoted compared to child or clinical psychology. The latter two largely conform to the familiar principle of epistemology mentioned above, that is, that complex social phenomena cannot be broken down mechanically into elements.

If we turn to other social sciences, we find that they speak about social psychological experiments in a similar way as do psychologists, and treat them with caution. And so even if social psychology had not intended to break the bridge with other social sciences, it happened because the experimental method made our subject 'abstract' and 'illegible'. Above all, it isolated social psychology from *common reality* and *common sense*. It seems to have done what the painter Klee says that one of his friends decided to do: 'I shall now stay at home. I have closed the window and pulled the curtains. I have switched on the lamp and said to myself: "Here is the sun".' Under such circumstances, carrying out experiments and tracing how their procedures work is *to confirm* the already received views and *not to discover* new empirical facts about the world or illuminating facts within it.

What was decisive in the 1950s was the novelty and enthusiasm coming out of the war. However the end of the 1960s and the beginning of the 1970s were years of unrest at universities. They were also years of the *routinization of charisma*. This means that particular ways of training were set up to perform research and to find specific ways of answering questions, which above all belonged to the 'mainstream' that confers the label 'scientific' on a theory and the way it is understood by those belonging to that milieu.

So what in the 1950s had been a choice later became a constraint; *what was a method of invention became a method of proof.* Any kind of result was accessible only to a handful of experts. And the outcome in general was the fragmentation of the field. This method, the method of proof, started by blurring the identity of our science, then plunged it into confusion.

We shall not try to explain how and why this routinization of charisma happened. We shall only mention its consequences, as described by Cartwright, for social psychology:

It is true that the general level of excitement that characterized social psychology immediately after the war has all but disappeared. But since this decline in enthusiasm actually began in the mid-1950s . . . it should not be taken as evidence of deficiencies in the work of recent years but, instead, as a by-product of moving from a programmatic stage of a development to one described by Kuhn as 'normal science' in which the field is engaged in the less glamorous task of collecting detailed data and testing rather limited theoretical hypothesis . . . For social psychology, as we know it today, does have deficiencies and does face some very difficult problems. (Cartwright 1979, p. 87)

The conclusions at which Cartwright arrived are perhaps inevitably full of a great sadness. It was the awareness that the prophetic energy, which had imposed the experimental method, had either been replaced by clerical ritual or melted into thin air. As the prophetic energy was no longer there, the experimental method became the scapegoat or *la bête noire* of everything that was supposed to be wrong with social psychology. And the Transnational Committee was forced to acknowledge what is called an *identity crisis in social psychology*.

The victory of method over science

The second consequence of defining social psychology by its method is of course related to the first one. What one finds most remarkable about the situation of the field is that it continues to take for granted what Nietzsche said about the nineteenth century: 'It is not the victory of science that distinguishes our nineteenth century, but the victory of scientific method over science' (Nietzsche, 1967, p. 283). Physics appears to be the symbol of this triumph, but that is precisely the point: that was the physics of the nineteenth century. Once we arrive at the twentieth century, the growth of science is no longer characterized by the triumph of method. Instead, it is characterized by the triumph of problems and paradoxes (Moscovici, 1992), and these are being solved with the help of new concepts and the invention of new phenomena. A creative scientist looks not only for a solution that could provide an answer but, above all, what it is that he or she wants to know and, therefore, to ask. But it is as if insidiously the social psychologist's obsession with method was breeding fantasies of the nineteenth century and carrying them into the middle of the twentieth century. Our excuse for butting into this controversial point is that the search for new problems seems to have been abandoned.

Diligent source-hunters will presumably discover the consequences of this victory in the gap that revealed itself in the 1970s between the studied reality and the reality to be studied in the name of relevance. This victory had become the flag of a generation that disliked 'problemlessness' and the kind of social psychology it breeds.

But we do not intend to embark here on a discussion of pluses or minuses of our methods and science. This would be, if you like, a negative purpose. The positive purpose was the subject on the agenda in Rome in December 1964, asking 'whether the difficulty of developing experimental social psychology in various countries is related to the lack of a clear identity of social psychology as a field'.[9] The comparison between the beginning of the 1960s and the mid-1970s leads us to an obvious conclusion. The critical spirit of the time, discontents in and outside social psychology, had disestablished its traditional convention and blurred its identity.

Yet the Transnational Committee, despite this malaise, had reason to be optimistic. It was the first time that in the course of the history of the new discipline there were social psychologists, historians and philosophers trying to understand it from diverse points of view, opposing established perspectives rather than condoning their similarities. They expressed their criticism with vigour and found an attentive public. If they did not contribute to the science itself, they contributed to its vitality in that troubled time of self-reflection about the theoretical and cultural splintering of their field. Several members of the Committee participated in this introspection (e.g., Israel and Tajfel, 1972). They took for granted that the intensity of that criticism expressed 'the pressures generated by the student rebellions of the 1960s and, in part, the widespread social malaise and unrest that has been produced by the accelerating pace of sociotechnological change, the War in Vietnam, and the ecological and resource crises' (Deutsch, 1976, p. 1). And what followed was a new assessment of scientific responsibilities and of scientific knowledge for generations to come.

A Matter of Then and Now

The Transnational Committee had now been established in Paris for two or three years with UNESCO. It was reasonable to ask whether it should continue the strategy that enabled the Committee to build continental associations successfully. Despite the dramatic events in Eastern Europe and Latin America, relationships existed and could, no doubt, be cultivated for a long time to come. And there was a good chance of building bridges in Asia. Financial resources for pursuing these activities were not a problem in the 1970s, neither was there a lack of social psychologists willing to take part in these new endeavours. So why change?

The strategy of the past had seemed adequate for diffusion of social psychology, for building one scientific community after another, in this way creating international social psychology. It was assumed that one stage would follow another. But this presumed a sort of work without end and one from which the present community would never benefit because of the exhausting experience of diminishing returns.

Even if the Transnational Committee did have autonomy, it could not continue the same strategy under the auspices of the ISSC. Under the SSRC, the Committee was one of many that fulfilled tasks in specialized fields. It had to justify its existence more to the institution than to the outside world. It may help to reformulate this. The vision of the SSRC was to support activities of direct interest to American social scientists. And it was not very sympathetic to 'international social science associations which are badly organised and funded and not essentially committed to research . . . The national councils were considered to provide a better basis than the international disciplinary associations' (Platt, 2002, p. 33). The exception was, Platt writes, in 'the 1960s the Transnational Committee' (ibid., p. 33) which had crossed the Atlantic and become a part of UNESCO. In 1972, the UNESCO Council became a federation of disciplinary international associations with a very different vision from that held by the SSRC in New York. According to Platt, 'It suggested that a federation would fit the situation in the Third World, where the disciplines were not all well developed or differentiated "better" and this would follow the pattern now existing in the parallel bodies for other disciplinary areas' (Platt, ibid. p. 31). It was possible, perhaps desirable, that this change of strategy expected that the national vision would translate into an international vision. And hence the slogan should be, in the language of the age, 'international social psychology now'.

The Unfinished Task

The fact is that despite all the possibilities now open to the Transnational Committee, in some sense it risked becoming isolated by pursuing past strategies. As a supra-ordinate group, the Transnational Committee played two roles. First, it acted as *mediator* in relationships between other associations so long as their representatives were members of the Committee. Second, by belonging to well-known institutions and by having members of remarkable reputation, the Committee played the role of *a substitute* for the whole scientific community, including the Americans. The role of the Transnational Committee as mediator between associations was often real enough. But that of substitute was not. And that was the Achilles' heel of the Committee. For example, at the 1976 Psychology Congress in Paris, when Moscovici was interviewed by a journalist from the APA or when he was speaking to social psychologists from various committees, including those in USA, it was apparent that they were scarcely aware of the existence of the Committee and its work.

At that time, the Transnational Committee started to enhance its visibility by participating in or inspiring new research initiatives in various scientific communities, and creating new 'invisible colleges', so to speak. One example was the study group on 'Historical Change in Social Psychology' that, in the late 1970s, included Graumann, Moscovici, Festinger and Farr, and attracted social psychologists from many countries. It was sponsored by the Werner-Reimers-Stiftung in Bad Homburg, Germany. Another example was the establishment, in 1976, of the European Laboratory of Social Psychology (LEPS) in the MSH in Paris. The initial group, which included Cranach, Doise, Moscovici, Scherer and Tajfel, brought into focus the study of new fields of research like intergroup conflict, language, social representations, ethology and emotions, among others. The main principle of the laboratory was to reunite researchers from Europe and America who came from various human sciences. Each research topic enabled the building of bridges between human science and social psychology. The LEPS has become a thriving laboratory without walls. It continues its work today, in particular developing *intercultural habitus* with researchers from all over Europe and Latin America. But despite these initiatives, it was apparent that a new strategy was required. If we return to the above quotation from Rome 1964, it seemed a new organization was urgently needed which not only reunited continental associations, but which also involved the scientific community *as such*. Is 'transnational social psychology' an accurate phrase by which to express the relation between community and science, which apparently does not take into consideration the changing new map of social psychology and the widening net of international research? If it had expressed these changing realities, the problem of its internal organization would be less serious than it was.

So it seemed that a new strategy was required in order to form more stable and enduring relations in social psychology, as we find later in Cartwright:

> Social psychology, more than any other branch of science, with the possible exception of anthropology, requires a breadth of perspective that can only be achieved by a truly international community of scholars. Social psychologists are not merely students of society, they are also participants in it, and despite their best efforts to attain a detached objectivity in their research, their thinking is affected by the particular culture in which they live. (Cartwright, 1979, p. 85)

But how does one undertake such a task? In 1980 the International Congress of Psychology took place in Leipzig. Towards the end of the Congress, with the help of their German friends, Kelley, Moscovici and some other colleagues brought together approximately 150–200 social psychologists from different countries. It was rather difficult to explain the purpose of this meeting. Kelley, Moscovici and others tried to explain how and why it was important to create international social psychology and the speakers seemed to receive the general approbation of those present. In particular, it was agreed that in four years' time, immediately after the next International Congress of Psychology, a day would be devoted to international social psychology and its organization. We find a reference to this reunion in the presidential address to the EAESP. Doise says:

> At our meeting during the Leipzig congress Moscovici argued very strongly for establishing . . . links by creating a world federation of national and regional associations of social psychology. An international conference of social psychologists would be a first step in reaching more autonomy at the international level. Let us not forget that at the International Congresses of Psychology, for instance, the programme on social psychology is not necessarily determined by representatives of social psychology associations. (Doise, 1981, p. 109)

That was the ultimate action of the Transnational Committee, as far as we are aware, and it can be described as an unfinished task.

But it remains true that before social psychology can complete that task, it has numerous difficulties to overcome. We do not speak about the desire, specific to a particular kind of social psychology, to bloom as a science of one country and as a science identified by one culture. It is so sure about itself that its image seems to be good for other cultures as well. And, all the same, it is one science that extends itself to a great part of the world.

It should, instead find a form that addresses itself more easily and naturally to people all over the planet. We speak here about the experience, ideas and achievements that were not completed by the Transnational Committee and which await to be rediscovered and adopted by a younger generation with passion and vitality. It is possible that another generation will pursue the vast problems that social psychology must try to solve: our destiny in society and sense of life in community.

But a historical account is about past futures and not about future pasts.

Appendix

Membership of the Committee on Transnational Social Psychology (Transnational Committee):

1964–1965: Leon Festinger (chairman), Leonardo Ancona, Jaap Koekebakker, John Lanzetta, Serge Moscovici, Ragnar Rommetveit, Stanley Schachter, Ithiel de Sola Pool
Staff Officer: Ben Willerman (died 21 June 1965), Jerome Singer

1965–1966: Leon Festinger (chairman), Harold Kelley, Jaap Koekebakker, John Lanzetta, Serge Moscovici, Ragnar Rommetveit, Stanley Schachter, Henri Tajfel
Staff Officer: Jerome Singer

1966–1968: Leon Festinger (chairman), Harold Kelley, Jaap Koekebakker, John Lanzetta, Serge Moscovici, Ragnar Rommetveit, Stanley Schachter, Henri Tajfel
Staff Officer: Jerome Singer

1968–1969: Leon Festinger (chairman), Morton Deutsch, Jaromír Janoušek, Harold Kelley, Jaap Koekebakker, John Lanzetta, Serge Moscovici, Ragnar Rommetveit, Stanley Schachter, Henri Tajfel
Staff Officer: Jerome Singer

1969–1970: Morton Deutsch (chairman), Leon Festinger, Martin Irle, Jaromír Janoušek, Harold Kelley, John Lanzetta, Serge Moscovici, Henri Tajfel
Staff Officer: Stanley Lehmann

1970–1973: Morton Deutsch (chairman), Donald Campbell, Leon Festinger, Martin Irle, Jaromír Janoušek, Harold Kelley, Serge Moscovici, Luis Ramallo, Henri Tajfel
Staff Officer: Stanley Lehmann, David Jenness (from July 2003)

1973–1974: Morton Deutsch (chairman), Donald Campbell, Martin Irle, Jaromír Janoušek, Harold Kelley, Serge Moscovici, Luis Ramallo, Henri Tajfel
Staff Officer: David Jenness

1974–•• Serge Moscovici (chairman), Morton Deutsch, Martin Irle, Jaromír Janoušek, Harold Kelley, Jyuji Misumi, Luis Ramallo, Henri Tajfel
Staff Officer: David Jenness

Notes

Chapter 1 The Birth of a New Science

1 P&P, 8–9.9.1962, Social Science Research Council Archives, Accession 1, Series 1, Committee Projects, Subseries 34, Transnational Social Psychology, box 305, folder 1759, Rockefeller Archive Center, Sleepy Hollow, New York.

2 P&P, 21.3.1963, SSRC Archives, Acc. 1, Series 1, Subseries 34, box 305, folder 1759, RAC.

3 Council, 8–11.9.1963, SSRC Archives, Acc. 1, Series 1, Subseries 34, box 305, folder 1759, RAC.

4 P&P, 25.11.1963, SSRC Archives, Acc. 1, Series 1, Subseries 34, box 305, folder 1759, RAC.

5 Ibid.

6 Ibid.

7 Ibid.

8 P&P, 8–9.9.1962, SSRC Archives, Acc.1, Series 1, Subseries 34, box 305, folder 1759, RAC.

9 P&P, 7.6.1963, SSRC Archives, Acc.1, Series 1, Subseries 34, box 305, folder 1759, RAC.

10 Ibid.

11 Festinger, Transnational Committee: a brief history. Festinger papers 1939–1988, box 3, The Michigan Historical Collections, Bentley Historical Library, University of Michigan.

12 Ibid.

13 Proposal for a Research Training Institute, 6.10.1964, SSRC Archives, Acc. 1, Series 1, Subseries 34, box 304, folder 1753, RAC.

14 Festinger, a brief history (1964–1972), Festinger papers 1939–1988, box 3, MHC.

15 P&P, 7.6.1963, SSRC Archives, Acc. 1, Series 1, Subseries 34, box 305, folder 1759, RAC.

16 Ibid.
17 Ibid.
18 P&P, 7–8.9.1963, SSRC Archives, Acc. 1, Series 1, Subseries 34, box 305, folder 1759, RAC.
19 P&P, 25.11.1963, SSRC Archives, Acc. 1, Series 1, Subseries 34, box 305, folder 1759, RAC.
20 Executive Committee, 13.12.1963, SSRC Archives, Acc. 1, Series 1, Subseries 34, box 305, folder 1759, RAC.
21 P&P, 25.11.1963, SSRC Archives, Acc. 1, Series 1, Subseries 34, box 305, folder 1759, RAC.
22 P&P, 27.1.1964, SSRC Archives, Acc. 1, Series 1, Subseries 34, box 305, folder 1759, RAC.
23 Ibid.
24 P&P, 3.3.1964, SSRC Archives, Acc. 1, Series 1, Subseries 34, box 305, folder 1759, RAC.
25 P&P, 12–13.9.1964, SSRC Archives, Acc. 1, Series 1, Subseries 34, box 305, folder 1759, RAC.

Chapter 2 Two Sources of Modern Social Psychology

1 The term 'tradition' used in the sense that Searle adopts (1993).
2 Page references to Allport are to the second edition (1968).
3 In 1967 Festinger expressed his wish to be relieved of the chairmanship of the Committee. On 13.1.1968 the P&P was 'prepared not only to respond to Leon Festinger's wish . . . but also to broaden its representation of both American approaches and European developments in social psychology.' The P&P voted '[t]hat Robett P. Abelson of Yale University, be appointed to the Transnational Committee with the understanding that he would be willing to serve as its chairman'. SSRC Archives, Acc. 1, Series 1, Subseries 34, box 305, folder 1759, RAC. This did not happen and it was Deutsch who, in 1969, became the chairman of the Transnational Committee.
4 When Heider refers to 'stable', he normally qualifies this by 'relatively stable'.
5 Allport (1924), p. 6: 'Collective consciousness and behavior are simply the aggregation of those states and reactions of individuals which, owing to similarities of constitution, training and common stimulation, are possessed of a similar character.'
6 See chapter 13.

Chapter 3   Americans and Europeans

1   Leavitt, H. Organizational and administrative research in Western Europe, 4.10.1965, *Personal Archives, S. Moscovici.*
2   Participants: *Germany:* Anger; *Belgium:* Nuttin, Jr.; *France:* de Montmollin, Faucheux, Flament, Lambert, Moscovici, Pagès; *Holland:* Hutte, Koekebakker, Mulder, Rabbie; *Italy:* Iacono, Meschieri; *Israel:* Foa, Herman; *Norway:* Rommetveit; *Sweden:* Israel; *UK:* Argyle, Himmelveit, Jahoda, Oppenheim, Tajfel; *USA:* Fiedler, Horowitz, Lanzetta, Pepitone, Petrullo, Thibaut, Willerman.
3   P&P, 27.1.1964. SSRC Archives, Acc. 1, Series 1, Subseries 34, box 305, folder 1759, RAC.
4   Ibid.
5   Ibid.
6   P&P, 27.1.1964, SSRC Archives, Acc. 1, Series 1, Subseries 34, box 305, folder 1759, RAC.
7   Ibid.
8   Tajfel, Report on Frascati, EAESP, Box 1, University Archives, Catholic University of Louvain, Belgium.
9   P&P, 14.7.1964, SSRC Archives, Acc. 1, Series 1, Subseries 34, box 304, folder 1753, RAC.
10   Ibid.
11   Participants: *Germany:* Irle, Schönbach; *Belgium:* Nuttin, Jr.; *France:* de Montmollin, Duflos, Faucheux, Flament, Lambert, Moscovici, Pagès; *Holland:* Cohen, Frijda, Koekebakker, Mulder, Rabbie; *Italy:* Ancona, Iacono, Spaltro; *Israel:* Foa, Herman, Schild; *Lebanon:* Diab; *Sweden:* Israel; *UK:* Argyle, Himmelweit, Jahoda, Laurie, Tajfel; *USA:* Berkowitz, Festinger, Lanzetta, Petrullo, Schachter, Willerman.
12   Tajfel, Report on Frascati, EAESP, Box 1, University Archives, UAL.
13   Ibid.
14   Ibid.

Chapter 4   The Transnational Committee: from New York to Rome

1   P&P, 27.1.1964, SSRC Archives, Acc. 1, Series 1, Subseries 34, box 305, folder 1759, RAC.
2   Ibid.
3   Rommetveit, *personal communication.*
4   Transnational Committee, 9–10 and 16.12.1964, SSRC Archives, Acc. 1, Series 1, Subseries 34, box 304, folder 1753, RAC.

5 Ibid.
6 Council, 13–16.9.1964, SSRC Archives, Acc. 1, Series 1, Subseries 34, box 305, folder 1759, RAC.
7 Transnational Committee, 9–10 and 16.12.1964, SSRC Archives, Acc. 1, Series 1, Subseries 34, box 304, folder 1753, RAC.
8 Ibid.
9 Ibid.
10 P&P, 30.1.1965, SSRC Archives, Acc. 1, Series 1, Subseries 34, box 305, folder 1759, RAC.
11 Tajfel to Festinger, 26.5.1964. Festinger papers 1939–1988, Box 3, MHC.
12 Transnational Committee, 9–10 and 16.12.1964, SSRC Archives, Acc. 1, Series 1, Subseries 34, box 304, folder 1753, RAC.
13 Ibid.

Chapter 5   The European Map of Social Psychology in the Mid-1960s

1 Leavitt, H., Organizational and administrative research in Western Europe, 4.10.1965, *Personal Archives, S. Moscovici.*
2 Leavitt, H. Notes on Western Europe, October 1965, *Personal Archives, S. Moscovici.*

Chapter 6   The Second Milestone for European Social Psychology

1 Tajfel, Report Frascati, EAESP, box 1, UAL.
2 Planning Committee, 6–7.2.1965, EAESP, box 4, UAL.
3 Chapter 5.
4 Planning Committee, 6–7.2.1965, EAESP, box 4, UAL.
5 Planning Committee, 1–3.5.1965, EAESP, box 4, UAL.
6 Chapter 8.
7 Transnational Committee, 8–10.7.1965, SSRC Archives, Acc. 1, Series 1, Subseries 34, box 304, folder 1753, RAC.
8 Participants: *Belgium:* Nuttin, Jr.; *France*: Apfelbaum, Bouillut, Faucheux, Flament, Herzlich, de Montmollin, Moscovici, Pagès, Zavalloni; *Germany*: Irle, Schönbach; *Holland*: Brinkman, Cohen, Frijda, Jaspars, Mulder, Naus, Rabbie; *Italy*: Iacono; *Lebanon*: Diab; *Norway*: Rommetveit; *UK*: Himmelweit, Jahoda, Kendon, Lemon, Tajfel, Venness; *USA*: Festinger, Rasmussen.

9   Festinger to Moscovici, 3.1.1966. Festinger papers 1939–1988, box 2, MHC.

10 EAESP, box 4, UAL.

11 EAESP, box 4, UAL.

12 Executive Committee, 14.3.1966, SSRC Archives, Acc. 1, Series 1, Subseries 34, box 305, folder 1759, RAC.

Chapter 7   The Louvain Summer School

1   Proposal for Research Training Institute, 6.10.1964, SSRC Archives, Acc. 1, Series 1, Subseries 34, box 304, folder 1753, RAC.

2   Council, 12–15.9.1965, SSRC Archives, Acc. 1, Series 1, Subseries 34, box 305, folder 1759, RAC.

3   Ibid.

4   Chapter 4.

5   Council, 12–15.9.1965, SSRC Archives, Acc. 1, Series 1, Subseries 34, box 305, folder 1759, RAC.

6   Planning Committee, 1–3.5.1965, EAESP, Box 4, UAL.

7   Ibid.

8   Van Gils to Moscovici, 16.6.1965, EAESP, Box 4, UAL.

9   Transnational Committee, 8–10.7.1965, SSRC Archives, Acc. 1, Series 1, Subseries 34, box 304, folder 1753, RAC.

10 Council, 12–15.9.1965, SSRC Archives, Acc. 1, Series 1, Subseries 34, box 305, folder 1759, RAC.

11 P&P, 13.11.1965, SSRC Archives, Acc. 1, Series 1, Subseries 34, box 305, folder 1759, RAC.

12 Moscovici to Festinger, 25.9.1965, Festinger papers 1939–1988, box 2, MHC.

13 Festinger to Moscovici, 4.10.1965, Festinger papers 1939–1988, box 2, MHC.

14 Webbink to Festinger, 8.10.1965, Festinger papers 1939–1988, box 3, MHC.

15 Council, 12–15.9.1965, SSRC Archives, Acc. 1, Series 1, Subseries 34, box 305, folder 1759, RAC.

16 Proposal for Research Training Institute, 6.10.1964, SSRC Archives, Acc. 1, Series 1, Subseries 34, box 304, folder 1753, RAC.

17 Ibid.

18 Meeting in Santa Monica, 15–16.11.1966, SSRC Archives, Acc. 1, Series 1, Subseries 34, box 304, folder 1753, RAC.

19 Ibid.

20 Ibid.

21 Nuttin to candidate-participants, EAESP, box 3, UAL.

Chapter 8   The Ford Foundation and Fundraising for Europe

1   Robinson to Moscovici, 19.12.1999. Personal Archives, Moscovici.
2   Moscovici to Robinson, 21.10.1966, file #69–87 Ford Archives, New York.
3   Robinson to Moscovici, 7.11.1966, file #69–87, FA.
4   Moscovici to Nuttin, 18.2.1967, EAESP, box 4, UAL.
5   Moscovici to Robinson, 28.4.1967, file #69–87, FA.
6   SSRC Archives, Acc.1, Series 1, Subseries 34, box 304, folder 1754, RAC.
7   Chapter 9.
8   Moscovici to Robinson, 28.4.1967, file #69–87, FA.
9   SSRC Archives, Acc. 1. Series 1, Subseries 34, box 305, folder 1759, RAC.
10 Ibid.
11 SSRC Archives, Acc.1, Series1, Subseries 34, box 304, folder 1754, RAC.
12 Ibid.
13 Ibid.
14 Ibid.
15 Ibid.
16 Planning Committee, 15.12.1967, EAESP, box 4, UAL.
17 Schmid to Moscovici, 2.5.1967, file #69–87, FA.
18 Schmid, Inter-Office memorandum, 2.6.1967, file #69–87, FA.
19 Ibid.
20 Ibid.
21 Schmid, Inter-Office memorandum to Robinson, 30.6.1967, file #69–87, FA.
22 Ibid.
23 Memorandum between Schmid and Robinson, 5.9.1967, file #69–87, FA.
24 Enseignement Préparatoire à la Recherche Approfondie en Sciences Sociales.
25 Memorandum between Schmid and Robinson, 9.10.1967, file #69–87, FA.
26 Robinson to Moscovici, 12.10.1967, file #69–87, FA.
27 Moscovici to Robinson, 25.10.1967, file #69–87, FA.
28 Moscovici to Robinson, 25.3.1968, file #69–87, FA.
29 Schmid to Moscovici, 27.3.1968, file #69–87, FA.
30 Moscovici to Schmid, 5.4.1968, file #69–87, FA.
31 Schmid, Inter-Office Memorandum, 7.5.1968, file #69–87, FA.
32 Ibid.

33 Schmid, Inter-Office memorandum, 8.5.1968, file #69–87, FA.
34 Ibid.
35 Robinson to Moscovici, 27.12.1999, Personal Archives, Moscovici.
36 de Janosi to Schmid, 20.5.1968, file #69–87, FA.
37 Chamberlain, Inter-Office Memorandum, 3.6.1968, file #69–87, FA.
38 Schmid, Inter-Office Memorandum, 22.5.1967, file #69–87, FA.
39 Schmid to Moscovici, 14.6.1968, file #69–87, FA.
40 Moscovici to Schmid, 26.6.1968, file #69–87, FA.
41 Schmid to Moscovici, 8.5.1969, file #69–87, FA.
42 Schmid to Moscovici, 19.8.1968, file #69–87, FA.
43 Tajfel to Schmid, 26.8.1968, file #69–87, FA.
44 Dressner to Braudel, 27.11.1968, file #69–87, FA.
45 Moscovici to Schmid, 12.12.1968, file #69–87, FA.
46 Moscovici to Dressner, 12.12.1968, file #69–87, FA.
47 de Janosi, Inter-Office Memorandum, 26.5.1977, file #69–87, FA.
48 Document accompanying the awards to the EAESP, 1968, file #69–87, FA.
49 Ibid.
50 Ibid.

Chapter 9   The First Encounter of a Small Science with Big History

1 P&P, 13.11.1965, SSRC Archives, Acc. 1, Series 1, Subseries 34, box 305, folder 1759, RAC.
2 P&P, 2.6.1967, SSRC Archives, Acc. 1, Series 1, Subseries 34, box 305, folder 1759, RAC.
3 Council, 10–13.9.1967, SSRC Archives, Acc. 1, Series 1, Subseries 34, box 304, folder 1754, RAC.
4 P&P, 2.6.1967, SSRC Archives, Acc. 1, Series 1, Subseries 34, box 305, folder 1759, RAC.
5 Ibid.
6 Chapters 1 and 2.
7 Ibid.
8 Council, 10–13.9.1967, SSRC Archives, Acc. 1, Series 1, Subseries 34, box 304, folder 1754, RAC.
9 P&P, 2.6.1967, SSRC Archives, Acc. 1, Series 1, Subseries 34, box 305, folder 1759, RAC.
10 Transnational Committee, 22–23.1.1968, Aix-en-Provence, SSRC Archives, Acc. 1, Series 1, Subseries 34, box 304, folder 1754, RAC.
11 Ibid.

12 Tajfel to EAESP Committee, 30.9.1968, EAESP, box 2, UAL.
13 Ibid.
14 Ibid.
15 Tajfel to Mulder, 12.9.1968, EAESP, box 2, UAL.
16 Tajfel to EAESP Committee, 30.9.1968, EAESP, box 2, UAL.
17 Tajfel to EAESP Committee, 30.9.1968, EAESP, box 2, UAL.
18 Ibid.
19 Tajfel to Mulder, 12.9.1968, EAESP, box 2, UAL.
20 Nuttin to Moscovici, 27.9.1968, EAESP, box 2, UAL.
21 Nuttin to Tajfel, 16.9.1968, EAESP, box 2, UAL.
22 Mulder to Committee members, 26.9.1968, EAESP, box 2, UAL.
23 Mulder to Tajfel, 13.10.1968, EAESP, box 2, UAL.
24 Tajfel to EAESP Committee, 30.9.1968, EAESP, box 2, UAL.
25 Mulder to Tajfel, 6.10.1968, EAESP, box 2, UAL.
26 Mulder's telegram to Janoušek, 4.10.1968, EAESP, box 2, UAL.
27 Janoušek's information on the Prague conference, EAESP, box 2, UAL.
28 Participants: *Canada:* Lambert; *Czechoslovakia:* Bokorová, Hellus, Janoušek, Jurovsky, Kováliková, Křivohlavý, Kubička, Linhart, Odehnal, Papica, Průcha, Říčan, Tardy, Vančurová; *France:* Apfelbaum, Flament, Pecheux; *Germany:* Von Cranach, Irle, Schönbach; *Holland:* Frijda, Jaspars; *Italy:* Barbiero, Galdo, Iacono; *Norway:* Rommetveit; *Poland:* Mika; *Romania:* Slama-Cazacu; *UK:* Himmelweit, Jahoda, Tajfel; *USA:* Abelson, Campbell, Deutsch, Jones, Festinger, Katz, Kelley, Seeman, Singer, Zajonc; *USSR:* Mansurov; *Yugoslavia:* Jezernik, Rot.
29 Tajfel, letter to Moscovici, 16.10.1968, EAESP, box 2, UAL.

Chapter 10   A Strange Animal

1 Abelson to Rainio, 31.10.1968, Social Science Research Council Archives, Acc. 2, Series 1, Committee Projects, Subseries 101, Committee on Transnational Social Psychology, box 619, folder 7557, Rockefeller Archive Center, Sleepy Hollow, New York.
2 Koekebakker to Rainio, 17.2.1969, SSRC Archives, Acc. 2, Series 1, Subseries 101, box 619, folder 7557, RAC.
3 Koekebakker to Kelley and Janoušek, 17.2.1969, SSRC Archives, Acc. 2, Series 1, Subseries 101, box 619, folder 7557, RAC.
4 Executive Committee, 1.3.1969, SSRC Archives, Acc. 1, Series 1, Subseries 34, box 305, folder 1759, RAC.
5 Council 7–10.9.1969, SSRC Archives, Acc. 1, Series 1, Subseries 34, box 305, folder 1756, RAC.

6 Council 13–15.9.1970, SSRC Archives, Acc. 1, Series 1, Subseries 34, box 305, folder 1757, RAC.

7 Ibid.

8 SSRC Archives, Accession 2, Series 1, Committee Projects, Subseries 101, Committee on Transnational Social Psychology, box 619, Folder 7557. Correspondence 1967–1972. Memorandum of H. W. Riecken to the members of Transnational Committee, 14 July 1970, RAC.

9 Riecken to Transnational Committee, 1.9.1970, SSRC Archives, Acc. 2, Series 1, Subseries 101, box 619, folder 7557, RAC.

10 Rumiantsev to Riecken, 11.9.1970, SSRC Archives, Acc. 2, Series 1, Subseries 101, box 619, folder 7557, RAC.

11 Riecken to Rumiantsev, 5.10.1970, SSRC Archives, Acc. 2, Series 1, Subseries 101, box 619, folder 7557, RAC.

12 P&P, 6–7.9.1969, SSRC Archives, Acc. 1, Series 1, Subseries 101, box 305, folder 1759, RAC.

13 P&P, 12–13.9.1970, SSRC Archives, Acc. 1, Series 1, Subseries 34, box 305, folder 1759, RAC.

14 Riecken to Tajfel, 14.7.1970, SSRC Archives, Acc. 2, Series 1, Subseries 101, box 619, folder 7557, RAC.

15 Riecken to Rumiantsev, 31.3.1971, SSRC Archives, Acc. 2, Series 1, Subseries 101, box 619, folder 7557, RAC.

16 Deutsch, Festinger and Tajfel to Mátrai, 30.9. 1971, SSRC Archives, Acc. 2, Series 1, Subseries 101, box 619, folder 7557, RAC.

17 Mátrai to Deutsch, Festinger and Tajfel, 23.11.1971, SSRC Archives, Acc. 2, Series 1, Subseries 101, box 619, folder 7557, RAC.

18 Deutsch to Mátrai, 3.2.1972, SSRC Archives, Acc. 2, Series 1, Subseries 101, box 619, folder 7557, RAC.

19 Tajfel to Deutsch, 11.4.1972, SSRC Archives, Acc. 2, Series 1, Subseries 101, box 619, folder 7557, RAC. 'Strange' may also mean 'suspicious'. It would not be astonishing given the 'spirit' of the time, if the Transnational Committee was judged by academic bureaucracy as politically suspect.

20 Executive Committee, 1.3.1969, SSRC Archives, Acc. 1, Series 1, Subseries 34, box 305, folder 1759, RAC.

21 Letters of 28.7,11.8. and 20.10.1970; Riecken to Friedman, 21.10.1970, SSRC Archives, Acc. 2, Series 1, Subseries 101, box 619, folder 7557, RAC.

22 Tajfel to Mátrai, 15.5.1972, SSRC Archives, Acc. 2, Series 1, Subseries 101, box 619, folder 7557, RAC.

23 Tajfel to Jenness, 10.7.1972, SSRC Archives, Acc. 2, Series 1, Subseries 101, box 619, folder 7557, RAC.

24 Tajfel, Report on visits to Nijmegen, Vienna and Budapest, 10.7.1972, SSRC Archives, Acc. 2, Series 1, Subseries 101, box 619, folder 7556, RAC.

25 Ibid.

26 Tajfel, Report of the organizing committee 15–16.12.1972, SSRC Archives, Acc. 2, Series 1, Subseries 101, box 619, folder 7556, RAC.

27 Transnational Committee, 28–29.4.1973, SSRC Archives, Acc.1, Series 1, Subseries 34, box 305, folder 1758, RAC.

28 Participants: *From Eastern Europe:* Andreeva, Kon, Leontjev, Mansurov, Shorokhova (USSR), Béla, Hunyady, László, Mérei, Pataki (Hungary), Dan (Romania), Draganov (Bulgaria), Fraczek, Matuszewicz, Reykowski (Poland), Hiebsch, Vorweg (GDR), Janoušek, Linhart (Czechoslovakia), Rot (Yugoslavia). *From Americas:* Aronson, Bronfenbrenner, Campbell, Deutsch, Janis, Jenness, Kahn, Kelley, Ramallo, Walster, Zajonc, Zimbardo. *From Western Europe:* Faucheux, Flament, Moscovici (France), Fraser, Himmelweit, Tajfel (UK), Irle, Schönbach, (Germany), Jaspars, Mulder (The Netherlands). *Observers from Hungary:* Barczy, Czepeli, Englender, Erös, Faragó, Gelléri, Habermann, Halész, Helmich, Járó, Keleti, Köcski, Komlossy, Kovács, László, Vajda.

29 Jenness's report on Visegrad, SSRC Archives, Acc. 2, Series 1, Subseries 101, box 619, folder 7556, RAC.

30 Ibid.

31 Chapter 13.

32 Jenness's report on Visegrad, SSRC Archives, Acc. 2, Series 1, Subseries 101, box 619, folder 7556, RAC.

33 Only Deutsch and Kelley accepted the invitation.

34 Bronfenbrenner to Sheldon, 6.6.1974, SSRC Archives, Acc. 2, Series 1, Subseries 101, box 619, folder 7556, RAC.

Chapter 11 Latin American Odyssey

1 Singer to Riecken, 3.4.1968, SSRC Archives, Acc. 2, Series 1, Subseries 101, box 620, folder 7569, RAC.

2 Festinger, Transnational Committee: a brief history (1964–1972), Festinger papers 1939–1988, box 3, MHC.

3 Ibid.

4 Singer to Riecken, 3.4.1968, SSRC Archives, Acc. 2, Series 1, Subseries 101, box 620, folder 7569, RAC.

5 García-Bouza to Festinger, November 1966 (no exact date). Festinger papers 1939–1988, box 3, MHC.

6 Transnational Committee, 15–17.5.1967, SSRC Archives, Acc. 1, Series 1, Subseries 34, box 304, folder 1754, RAC.
7 Chapter 8.
8 Lanzetta, Report on Latin America. Festinger papers 1939–1988, box 3, MHC.
9 Ibid.
10 Ibid.
11 Lanzetta to Festinger, 15.12.1967, Festinger papers 1939–1988, box 3, MHC.
12 P&P, 7–8.9.1968, SSRC Archives, Acc. 1, Series 1, Subseries 34, box 305, folder 1759, RAC.
13 Lanzetta: Notes on Latin American trip, SSRC Archives, Acc. 2, Series 1, Subseries 101, box 620, folder 7569, RAC.
14 Ibid.
15 Council, 7–10.9.1969, SSRC Archives, Acc. 1, Series 1, Subseries 34, box 305, folder 1756, RAC.
16 Ibid.
17 Council, 20–21.3.1970, SSRC Archives, Acc. 1, Series 1, Subseries 34, box 305, folder 1756, RAC.
18 Ibid.
19 Latin-American Committee 20.1.1970, SSRC Archives, Acc. 2, Series 1, Subseries 101, box 620, folder 7569, RAC.
20 Council, 20–21.3.1970, SSRC Archives, Acc. 1, Series 1, Subseries 34, box 305, folder 1756, RAC.
21 Ibid.
22 Ibid.
23 P&P, 12–13.9.1970, SSRC Archives, Acc. 1, Series 1, Subseries 34, box 305, folder 1759, RAC.
24 Ramallo, Proposal to the Transnational Committee, 15.7.1970, Festinger papers 1939–1988, box 3, MHC.
25 Koekebakker and Lanzetta to Festinger, 3.7.1967, Festinger papers, 1939–1988, box 3, MHC; P&P, 7–8.9.1968, SSRC Archives, Acc.1, Series 1, Subseries 34, box 305, folder 1759, RAC.
26 Kelley to Campbell, 30.5.1973, SSRC Archives, Acc. 2, Series 1, Subseries 101, box 619, folder 7559, RAC.

Chapter 12 A Second Encounter with History

1 Latin-American Committee, 20.1.1970, SSRC Archives, Acc. 2, Series 1, Subseries 101, box 620, folder 7569, RAC.

2 Council, 12–14.9.1971, SSRC Archives, Acc. 1, Series 1, Subseries 34, box 305, folder 1757, RAC.
3 Report on Latin-American meeting, 28–29.12.1970, SSRC Archives, Acc. 1, Series 1, Subseries 34, box 305, folder 1757, RAC.
4 Council, 12–14.9.1971, SSRC Archives, Acc. 1, Subseries 34, box 305, folder 1757, RAC.
5 Bailey, Latin-American Trip Report, 14.2.1968, SSRC Archives, Acc. 2, Series 1, Subseries 101, box 620, folder 7569, RAC.
6 Rodrigues to Ramallo, 20.10.1972, SSRC Archives, Acc. 2, Series 1, Subseries 101, box 620, folder 7569, RAC.
7 Rodrigues to Festinger, 14.8.1973. Festinger papers 1939–1988, box 3, MHC.
8 Festinger to Rodrigues, 21.8.1973. Festinger papers 1939–1988, box 3, MHC.
9 Deutsch to Rodrigues, 14.8.1973, SSRC Archives, Acc. 2, Series 1, Subseries 101, box 619, folder 7560, RAC.
10 Deutsch to Campbell, 14.9.1973, SSRC Archives, Acc. 2, Series 1, Subseries 101, box 619, folder 7560, RAC.
11 Transnational Committee, 13–14.5.1974, SSRC Archives, Acc. 1, Series 1, Subseries 34, box 305, folder 1758, RAC.
12 Acta de la reunion de la junta directive . . . durante el XV Congreso Interamericano de Psicología. Festinger papers 1939–1988, box 3, MHC.
13 Chapter 14.
14 Rodrigues to Jenness, 15.1.1974, SSRC Archives, Acc. 2, Series 1, Subseries 101, box 619, folder 7560, RAC.

Chapter 13   An 'Invisible College'

1 Festinger to Moscovici, 16.5.1967, Festinger papers 1939–1988, box 2, MHC.
2 Council, 10–13.9.1967, SSRC Archives, Acc. 1, Series 1, Subseries 34, box 305, folder 1759, RAC.
3 Chapter 2.
4 Proposal to the NSF, SSRC Archives, Acc. 2, Series 1, Subseries 101, box 518, folder 7553, RAC.
5 Ibid.
6 Ibid.
7 Kelley to Lehmann, 13.3.1970; Lehmann to Triandis, 3.11.1971, SSRC Archives, Acc. 2, Series 1, Subseries 101, box 518, folder 7553, RAC.

8 Scott NSF to Singer, 30.11.1970, SSRC Archives, Acc. 2, Series 1, Subseries 101, box 518, folder 7553, RAC.
9 Festinger, Transnational Committee: a brief history (1964–1972). Festinger papers 1939–1988, box 3, MHC.
10 Lehmann to Faucheux, 21.4.1969, SSRC Archives, Acc. 2, Series 1, Subseries 101, box 518, folder 7553, RAC.
11 Faucheux to Lehmann, 5.7.1971, SSRC Archives, Acc. 2, Series 1, Subseries 101, box 518, folder 7553, RAC.
12 Festinger, Transnational Committee: a brief history (1964–1972). Festinger papers 1939–1988, box 3, MHC.
13 Transnational Committee, 5.12.1967, SSRC Archives, Acc. 1, Series 1, Subseries 34, box 304, folder 1754, RAC.
14 Moscovici to Festinger, 7.5.1968. Festinger papers 1939–1988, box 2, MHC.
15 Festinger, Transnational Committee: a brief history (1964–1972). Festinger papers 1939–1988, box 3, MHC.
16 P&P, 15.3.1969, SSRC Archives, Acc.1, Series 1, Subseries 34, box 305, folder 1759, RAC.
17 Ibid.
18 Ibid.
19 Executive Committee, 16.6.1969, SSRC Archives, Acc.1, Series 1, Subseries 34, box 304, folder 1755, RAC.
20 Lanzetta to Riecken, 8.10.1970, SSRC Archives, Acc. 2, Series 1, Subseries 101, box 619, folder 7555, RAC.
21 Transnational Committee, 23–24.6.1972, SSRC Archives, Acc. 1, Series 1, Subseries 34, box 305, folder 1758, RAC.
22 Riecken to Jenness, 13.10.1971, SSRC Archives, Acc. 2, Series 1, Subseries 101, box 619, folder 7555, RAC.
23 Transnational Committee, 28–29.4.1973, SSRC Archives, Acc.1, Series 1, Subseries 34, box 305, folder 1758, RAC.
24 Festinger, Transnational Committee: a brief history (1964–1972). Festinger papers 1939–1988, box 3, MHC.
25 Hornstein, Deutsch, Bunker, 1971, SSRC Archives, Acc. 2, Series 1, Subseries 101, box 620, folder 7571, RAC.
26 Ibid.

Chapter 14 A Crisis Delayed

1 Festinger, Transnational Committee: a brief history (1964–1972). Festinger papers 1939–1988, box 3, MHC.
2 Moscovici to Greenbaum, 28.7.1969, Festinger papers 1939–1988, box 2, MHC.

3 Council, 12–15.9.1965, SSRC Archives, Acc. 1, Series 1, Subseries 34, box 305, folder 1759, RAC.
4 P&P, 22.3.1973, SSRC Archives, Acc. 1, Series 1, Subseries 34, box 305, folder 1759, RAC.
5 Ibid.
6 Ibid.
7 Executive Committee, 6.6.1972, SSRC Archives, Acc. 1, Series 1, Subseries 34, box 305, folder 1759, RAC.
8 Festinger to Riecken, June 1971, Festinger papers 1939–1988, box 3, MHC.
9 Riecken to Festinger, 16.6.1971, SSRC Archives, Acc. 2, Series 1, Subseries 101, box 305, folder 1759, RAC.
10 Festinger to Sheldon, 2.11.1972, SSRC Archives, Acc. 2, Series 1, Subseries 101, box 305, folder 1759, RAC.
11 Festinger to Jenness, 25.10.1972, Festinger papers 1939–1988, box 3, MHC.
12 Festinger, Transnational Committee: a brief history (1964–1972), Festinger papers 1939–1988, box 3, MHC.

Chapter 15   Crossing the Atlantic

1 Jenness to Transnational Committee, 8.1.1973, SSRC Archives, Acc. 2, Series 1, Subseries 101, box 619, folder 7559, RAC.
2 Jenness to Transnational Committee, 13.3.1973, SSRC Archives, Acc. 2, Series 1, Subseries 101, box 619, folder 7559, RAC.
3 Transnational Committee, 28–29.4.1973, SSRC Archives, Acc. 1, Series 1, Subseries 34, box 305, folder 1758, RAC.
4 Ibid.
5 Ibid.
6 Ibid.
7 P&P, 19.6.1972, SSRC Archives, Acc. 1, Series 1, Subseries 34, box 305, folder 1759, RAC.
8 Jenness to Deutsch, 20.6.1973, SSRC Archives, Acc. 2, Series 1, Subseries 101, box 619, folder 7559, RAC.
9 Deutsch to Sheldon, 19.9.1973, SSRC Archives, Acc. 2, Series 1, Subseries 101, box 618, folder 7552, RAC.
10 Deutsch to Little 19.9.1973, SSRC Archives, Acc. 2, Series 1, Subseries 101, box 618, folder 7552, RAC.
11 Campbell to Little, 2.10.1973, SSRC Archives, Acc. 2, Series 1, Subseries 101, box 618, folder 7552, RAC.

12 Zúñiga to Campbell, 25.9.1973, SSRC Archives, Acc. 2, Series 1, Subseries 101, box 618, folder 7552, RAC.
13 Campbell, inter-office memorandum, 8.10.1973, SSRC Archives, Acc. 2, Series 1, Subseries 101, box 618, folder 7552, RAC.
14 Jenness to Transnational Committee, 3.10.1973, SSRC Archives, Acc. 2, Series 1, Subseries 101, box 618, folder 7552, RAC.
15 Jenness to Transnational Committee, 8.11.1973, SSRC Archives, Acc. 2, Series 1, Subseries 101, box 618, folder 7552, RAC.
16 Jenness to Campbell, 14.9.1973, SSRC Archives, Acc. 2, Series 1, Subseries 101, box 618, folder 7552, RAC.
17 Kelley to Sheldon, 2.11.1973, SSRC Archives, Acc. 2, Series 1, Subseries 101, box 618, folder 7552, RAC.
18 Friedman to Tajfel, 16.11.1973, SSRC Archives, Acc. 2, Series 1, Subseries 101, box 619, folder 7559, RAC.
19 Jenness to Sheldon, 6.12.1973, SSRC Archives, Acc. 2, Series 1, Subseries 101, box 619, folder 7559, RAC.
20 Deutsch to Sheldon, 1.10.1973, SSRC Archives, Acc. 2, Series 1, Subseries 101, box 19, folder 7559, RAC.

Chapter 16   Pilgrims' Progress

1   Transnational Committee, 13–14.5.1974, SSRC Archives, Acc. 1, Series 1, Subseries 34, box 305, folder 1758, RAC.
2   Transnational Committee, 13–14.5.1974, SSRC Archives, Acc.1, Series 1, Subseries 34, box 305, folder 1758, RAC.
3   Ibid.
4   Jenness to Moscovici, 18.6.1974, SSRC Archives, Acc. 1, Series 1, Subseries 101, box 619, folder 7559, RAC.
5   Ibid.
6   Moscovici to Jenness, 8.7.1974, SSRC Archives, Acc. 1, Series 1, Subseries 101, box 619, folder 7550, RAC.
7   Ibid.
8   Minutes of the Executive Committee of the ISSC, 24–7.6.1974, Archives ISSC, UNESCO, Paris.
9   Minutes of the General Assembly of the ISSC, 27–8.6.1974, Archives ISSC, UNESCO, Paris.
10 Friedman to Moscovici, 1.7.1974, Archives ISSC, UNESCO, Paris.
11 Sheldon to Deutsch, 1.10.1974, SSRC Archives, Acc. 1, Series 1, Subseries.101, box 619, folder 7559, RAC.
12 Tajfel to Sheldon, 14.10.1974, SSRC Archives, Acc. 1, Series 1, Subseries 101, box 619, folder 7550, RAC.

Chapter 17   Rays and Shadows above the Transnational Committee

1   Friedman to Tajfel, 22.7.1974, Archives ISSC, UNESCO, Paris.
2   Jenness to Tajfel, 9.6.1975, SSRC Archives, Acc. 1, Series 1, Sub-series 101, box 619, folder 7560, RAC.
3   Tajfel to Jenness, 12.6.1975, SSRC Archives, Acc. 1, Series 1, Sub-series 101, box 619, folder 7560, RAC.
4   Jenness to Transnational Committee, 20.10.1975, SSRC Archives, Acc. 1, Series 1, Subseries 101, box 619, folder 7560, RAC.
5   Jenness to Campbell, 19.5.1972, SSRC Archives, Acc. 1, Series 1, Subseries 101, box 619, folder 7558, RAC.
6   Kelley to Jenness, 1.4.1975, SSRC Archives, Acc. 1, Series 1, Sub-series 101, box 619, folder 7560, RAC.
7   Kelley to Jenness, 21.4.1975, SSRC Archives, Acc. 1, Series 1, Sub-series 101, box 619, folder 7560, RAC.
8   Transnational Committee, 9–10 and 16.12.1964, SSRC Archives, Acc. 1, Series 1, Subseries 34, box 304, folder 1753, RAC.
9   Ibid.

References

Allport, F. H. (1924). *Social Psychology.* Boston: Houghton Mifflin.

Allport, G. W. (1954/1968). The historical background of modern social psychology. In G. Lindzey and E. Aronson (eds), *Handbook of Social Psychology*, 2nd ed. Vol 1, 1–80. Reading, Mass.: Addison-Wesley.

Angell, A. (1991). Chile since 1958. Chile, 1930–58. In L. Bethell (ed.), *The Cambridge History of Latin America*, Vol. VIII, pp. 311–82. Cambridge: Cambridge University Press.

Annual Report SSRC 1947/48. New York: SSRC.

Bartlett, F. (1923). *Psychology and Primitive Culture.* Cambridge: Cambridge University Press.

Berkowitz, L. (1999). The change in US social psychology. In A. Rodrigues and R. V. Levine (eds), *Reflections on 100 Years of Experimental Social Psychology*, pp. 158–79. New York: Basic Books.

de Bie, P. (1954). L'enseignement de la sociologie, de la psychologie sociale et de l'anthropologie sociale. In P. de Bie, C. Lévi-Strauss, J. Nuttin and E. Jacobson (1954). *Les Sciences sociales dans l'enseignement supérieur; sociologie, psychologie sociale et anthropologie culturelle,* pp. 11–101. Paris: UNESCO.

de Bie, P., Lévi-Strauss, C., Nuttin, J. and Jacobson, E. (1954). *Les Sciences sociales dans l'enseignement supérieur; sociologie, psychologie sociale et anthropologie culturelle.* Paris: UNESCO.

Cartwright, D. (1948). Social psychology in the US during the Second World War. *Human Relations,* 1, 333–52.

Cartwright, D. (1979). Contemporary social psychology in historical perspective. *Social Psychology Quarterly,* 42, 82–93.

Chomsky, N. (1995). *Language and Thought.* London: Moyer Bell.

Danziger, K. (2000). Making social psychology experimental: a conceptual history, 1920–1970. *Journal of the History of the Behavioral Sciences,* 36, 329–47.

Deutsch, M. (1976). On making social psychology more useful. *Items,* 30, 1, 1–6, SSRC.

Deutsch, M. (1999). A personal perspective on the development of social psychology in the twentieth century. In A. Rodrigues and R. V. Levine (eds), *Reflections on 100 Years of Experimental Social Psychology*, pp. 1–34. New York: Basic Books.

Deutsch, M. and Hornstein, H. A. (1975). *Applying Social Psychology.* Hillsdale: Lawrence Erlbaum.

Doise, W. (1982). Report on the EAESP. *European Journal of Social Psychology*, 12, 105–11.

Drake, P. (1991). Chile 1930–58. In L. Bethell, (ed.), *The Cambridge History of Latin America*, Vol. VIII, pp. 269–310. Cambridge: Cambridge University Press.

Drury, M. O'Connor. (1981). Conversations with Wittgenstein. In R. Rhees (ed.), *Ludwig Wittgenstein: Personal Recollections*, pp. 112–89. Oxford: Blackwell.

Einstein, A. (1949). *Albert Einstein: Philosopher-Scientist.* Vol. 7, II., P. A. Schilpp (ed.) London: Cambridge University Press.

Farr, R. (1993). Common sense, science and social representations. *Public Understanding of Science*, 2, 111–27.

Farr, R. (1996). *The Roots of Modern Social Psychology.* Oxford: Blackwell.

Faucheux, C. (1976). Cross-cultural research in experimental social psychology. *European Journal of Social Psychology*, 6, 269–322.

Festinger, L. (1980). Looking backward. In L. Festinger (ed.), *Retrospections on Social Psychology*, pp. 236–54. New York: Oxford University Press.

Festinger, L., Riecken, H. W. and Schachter, S. (1964). *When Prophecy Fails.* New York: Harper and Row.

Fleck, L. (1935). *Zustehung und Entwicklung einer Wissenschaften Tatsache.* Suhrkamp: Frankfurt-am-Main.

Friedman, S. and Rokkan, S. (1979). The ISSC: 1952–1977. In S. Rokkan (ed.), *A Quarter Century of International Social Science 1952–1977*, pp. 9–15. Paris: ISSC. New Delhi: Concept Publishing.

Gemelli, G. (1995). *Fernand Braudel*, trs. B. Pasquet and B. Marzi. Paris: Editions Odile Jacob.

Gemelli, G. and MacLeod, R. M. (2003) (eds). *American Foundations in Europe.* Brussels: P. I. E. Peter Lang.

Gibbon, E. (1910). *Gibbon's Decline and Fall of the Roman Empire. Volumes 1–6.* London: Everyman's Library.

van Gils, M. R. and Koekebakker, J. (1965). The first European summer school on social psychology, *Items*, 19 (4), 50–4.

Graumann, C. F. (1986). The individualization of the social and the desocialization of the individual. In C. F. Graumann and S. Moscovici (eds). *Changing Conceptions of Crowd Mind and Behavior*, pp. 97–116. New York: Springer.

Greenwood, J. D. (2004). What happened to the 'social' in social psychology? *Journal for the Theory of Social Behaviour*, 34, 19–34.

Heider, F. (1958). *The Psychology of Interpersonal Relations* (1958). Hillsdale: Lawrence Erlbaum.

Heider, F. (1976). A conversation with Fritz Heider. In J. H. Harvey, W. J. Ickes and R. E. Kidd (eds). *New Directions in Attribution Research*, Volume 1, pp. 3–18. Hillsdale: Lawrence Erlbaum.

Heisenberg, W. (1975). *Across the Frontiers*. New York: Harper.

Heisenberg, W. (2003). *Le Manuscrit de 1942*. Paris: Allia.

Helus, Z. (1969). Mezinárodní konference sociálních psychologů v Praze. *Československá Psychologie*, 13, 378–82.

Herring, P. (1964). The SSRC of the US of America, *Social Science Information*, 3, 1, 107–17.

Hobsbawn, E. (2000). *Interesting Times*. Abacus: London.

Israel, J. and Tajfel, H. (1972). *The Context of Social Psychology*. London: Academic Press.

Items, SSRC (1963). *Personnel*, 17, 3.

Items, SSRC (1964). Committee briefs. *Transnational Social Psychology*, 18, 4.

Items, SSRC (1965). Ben Willerman 1917–1965, 19, 3, 43.

Items, SSRC (1969). Committee briefs. *Transnational Social Psychology*, 23, 2, 11.

Jahoda, G. and Moscovici, S. (1967). EAESP. *Social Science Information*, 6, 297–305.

Janoušek, J. (1967). Mezinárodní konference sociálních psychologů ve Vídni. *Československá Psychologie*, 11, 476–7.

Janoušek, J. (1969) (ed). *Experimental Social Psychology*. Prague, October 7–11, 1968. Prague: Institute of Psychology.

Janoušek, J. and Tajfel, H. (1969). The International Conference on Social Psychology in Prague, October 7–11. *Items*, 23, 2, 26–9.

Jones, E. E. (1998). Major developments in five decades of social psychology. In D. T. Gilbert, S. T. Fiske and G. Lindzey (eds). *The Handbook of Social Psychology*, pp. 3–57. Boston: McGraw-Hill.

Jurovsky, A. (1967). Malá medzinárodná konferencia sociálnych psychológov. *Psychológia a Patopsychológia Diet'at'a*, 3, 105–8.

Kelley, H. H. (1967). Attribution theory in social psychology. In D. Levine (ed.). *Nebraska Symposium in Motivation*, pp. 192–240. Lincoln: University of Nebraska.

Kelley, H. (1992). Common sense psychology and scientific psychology. *Annual Review of Psychology*, 43, 1–23.

Kelley, H. H., Shure, G. H., Deutsch, M., Faucheux, C., Lanzetta, J. T., Moscovici, S., Nuttin, J. M. Jr., Rabbie, J. M. and Thibaut, J. W. (1970). A comparative experimental study of negotiation behavior. *Journal of Personality and Social Psychology*, 16, 411–38.

Lacan, J. (1947). La psychiatrie anglaise et la guerre, *L'evolution psychiatrique*, 1, 293–331.

Lanzetta, J. (1963). *European Conference on Experimental Social Psychology, Sorrento, Italy, December 12–16, 1963*. ONR, Project N. R. 177–276. Springfield: NTIS.

Lanzetta, J. (1967). Transnational working group on dynamics of conflict. ONR, Contract #NONR 3987. Springfield: NTIS.

Lanzetta, J., Tajfel, H. and Festinger, L. (1967). Transnational social psychology. *Items*, 21, 3, 30–2.

Leavitt, H. J. (1957). On the export of American management education. *The Journal of Business of the University of Chicago*, 30, 153–61.

Lewin, K. (1939). Field theory and experiment in social psychology. In D. Cartwright (1952), *Field Theory in Social Science*, pp. 130–54. London: Tavistock.

Lewin, K. (1945). The Research Center for Group Dynamics. *Sociometry*, 8, 126–36.

Lewin, K. (1947). Frontiers in group dynamics. In D. Cartwright (1952). *Field Theory in Social Science*, pp. 188–237. London: Tavistock.

Lewin, K. (1973). *Resolving Social Conflicts*. London: Souvenir Press.

Lewin, K. (1981a). Cassirers Wissenschaftsphilosophie und die Sozialwissenschaften. In Kurt-Lewin-Werkausgabe, (hrsg) Carl-Friedrich Graumann. *Wissenschaftstheorie I*, (hrsg) Alexandre Métraux, pp. 347–65. Bern: Hans Huber.

Lewin, K. (1981b). Über Idee und Aufgabe der vergleichenden Wissenschaftslehre. In Kurt-Lewin-Werkausgabe, (hrsg) Carl-Friedrich Graumann. *Wissenschaftstheorie I*, (hrsg) Alexandre Métraux, pp. 49–79. Bern: Hans Huber.

Lindzey, G. and Aronson, E. (1954/1968) (eds), *Handbook of Social Psychology*. Vol. 1, Reading: Addison-Wesley.

Mazon, B. (1988). *Aux Origines de l'Ecole des Hautes Etudes en Sciences Sociales*. Paris: Le Cerf.

Moscovici, S. (1967). Communication processes and the properties of language. In L. Berkowitz (ed.), *Advances in Experimental Social Psychology*, 3, 225–70. New York: Academic Press.

Moscovici, S. (1976). *Social Influence and Social Change*, trs. C. Sherrard and G. Heinz. Cambridge: Cambridge University Press.

Moscovici, S. (1979). *Psychologie des minorités actives*. Paris: Presses Universitaires de France.

Moscovici, S. (1992). The discovery of group polarization. In D. Granberg and G. Sarup (eds). *Social Judgement and Intergroup Relations*, pp. 107–27. New York: Springer.

Moscovici, S. (1996). Just remembering. *The British Journal of Social Psychology*, 35, 5–14.

Moscovici, S. (1997). *Chronique des années egarées: récit autobiographique.* Paris: Stock.

Moscovici, S. (1999). Honoris Causa. In *Laurea Honoris Causa 1999*, pp. 43–61. Università degli Roma *La Sapienza*.

Moscovici, S. (2003). Questions de Psychologie Sociale. *Prix Balzan 2003*.

Moscovici, S. and Faucheux, C. (1972). Social influence, conformity bias and the study of active minorities. In L. Berkowitz (ed.), *Advances in Experimental Social Psychology*, 6, 149–202. London: Academic Press.

Nagel, E. (1961). *The Structure of Science*. New York: Harcourt, Brace and World.

Nietzsche, F. (1967). *The Will to Power*, trs. W. Kaufmann. New York: Random House.

Nunn, F. K. (1976). *The Military in Chilean History*. Albuquerque: University of New Mexico.

Nuttin. J. (1954). Rapport spécial sur l'enseignement de la psychologie sociale dans les sciences sociales. In P. de Bie, C. Lévi-Strauss, J. Nuttin and E. Jacobson (1954). *Les Sciences Sociales dans l'enseignement supérieur; Sociologie, Psychologie Sociale et Anthropologie Culturelle*, pp. 134–59. Paris: UNESCO.

Nuttin, J. M., Jr. (1990). In memoriam: John T. Lanzetta. *European Journal of Experimental Social Psychology*, 20, 363–7.

Nuttin, J. M., Jr. and Jaspers, J. M. F. (1967). The European research training seminar in experimental social psychology, *Items*, 21, 4, 41–5.

Patnoe, S. (1988). *A Narrative History of Experimental Social Psychology*. New York: Springer.

Platt, J. (2002). *50 Years of the ISSC.* Brighton: ISSC.

Rasmussen, J. E. (1966). *European Conference on Experimental Social Psychology.* ONR, technical report ONRL-C-10–66. Springfield: NTIS.

Raven, B. H. (1999). Reflections on interpersonal influence and social power in experimental social psychology. In A. Rodrigues and R. V. Levine (eds), *Reflections on 100 Years of Experimental Social Psychology*, pp. 114–34. New York: Basic Books.

Riecken, H. W. (1969). Social science and contemporary social problems, *Items*, 1, 1–6.

Riecken, H. W. (2004). Personal communication.

Schachter, S., Nuttin, J. M., Jr., de Monchaux, C., Maucorps, P. H., Osmer, D., Duijker, H., Rommetveit, R. and Israel, J. (1954). Cross-cultural experiments on threat and rejection, *Human Relations*, 7, 403–40.

Searle, J. (1993). Rationality and Realism: what is at stake? *Daedalus*, 122, 55–85.

Sherif, M. and Sherif, C. W. (1956). *Social Psychology*. New York: Harper and Row.

Sherif, M. and Sherif, C. W. (1969). Preface. In M. S. and C. W. Sherif (eds), *Interdisciplinary Relationships in the Social Sciences*, pp. vii–xiv. Chicago: Aldine.

Shlapentokh, V. (1987). *The Politics of Sociology in the USSR*. Boulder: Westview.

Sofer, C. (1972). *Organizations in Theory and Practice*. London: Heinemann.

de Sola Pool, I. (1973). Communication in totalitarian societies. In I. de S. Pool and W. Schramm (eds). *Handbook of Communication*, pp. 462–511. Chicago: Rand McNally.

Stouffer, S. A., Lumsdaine, A. A., Lumsdaine, M. H. Williams, R. M., Smith, M. B., Janis, I. L., Star, S. A. and Cottrell, I. S. (eds) (1949). *The American Soldier: Combat and its Aftermath*. Princeton: Princeton University.

Tajfel, H. (1965). Report of the Conference in Frascati. *Social Science Information*, 4, 190–2.

Tajfel, H. (1972). Some developments in European social psychology. *European Journal of Social Psychology*, 2, 307–22.

Triplett, N. (1898). The dynamogenic factors in pacemaking and competition. *American Journal of Psychology*, 9, 507–33.

Trist, E. L., Higgin, G. W., Murray, H. and Pollock, A. B. (1963). *Organizational Choice*. London: Tavistock.

Wolpert, L. (1992). *The Unnatural Nature of Science*. London: Faber and Faber.

Worcester, K. W. (2001). *SSRC 1923–1998*. New York: SSRC.

Young, D. (1952). First steps toward an ISSC. *Items*, 6, 1, 1–3.

Zajonc, R. B. (1966). *Social Psychology*. Belmont: Wadsworth.

Index